exhibition design

Introduction

1. The brief

2. The visitor

3. The site

4. Exhibition strategy

5. 3-D design skills

6. Graphic design skills

First published in 2010, reprinted in 2013
Second edition published in 2015 by
Laurence King Publishing Ltd
361–373 City Road
London EC1V 1LR
United Kingdom
Tel: +44 (0)20 7841 6900
Fax: +44 (0)20 7841 6910
e-mail: enquiries@laurenceking.com
www.laurenceking.com

This book was designed and produced by
Laurence King Publishing Ltd, London

A catalogue record for this book is available
from the British Library.

ISBN: 978-178067-606-7

Designed by Draught Associates

Printed in China

Frontispiece: "The Interpretation Project."
Exhibition design by Ralph Appelbaum Associates.
Crypt exhibit in St Paul's Cathedral, London, UK.
Photograph © Peter Mauss/Esto

Cover photograph © doublespace / VIEW
Eli and Edythe Broad Museum, East Lansing, U.S.
by Zaha Hadid Architects, 2012.

LAURENCE KING

This introduction explains the purpose of the book and how to use it. It describes the significance of exhibitions and their design, and how new museums and galleries are being established throughout the world. It traces the evolution of exhibition design from the eighteenth century to the present day and also highlights the range of skills required by modern designers.

Who this book is for

The respected Dutch designer (and former director of Opera Design) Frans Bevers once remarked that a book on exhibition design should cover not only what is exciting to do, but also what the designer should not forget to do. There are now a large number of books devoted to the former, illustrated with dramatic, bold schemes that photograph well. However, there is little literature devoted to the process of achieving the stunning results that appear regularly in the design press.

Exhibition Design, aimed at students of design, aspiring designers, exhibition professionals and anyone with an interest in the topic, hopes to convey some of the skills necessary to thrill, educate and entertain new generations of exhibition visitors. At the same time, this book also conveys the necessary information about the practical aspects of responsible exhibition practice, such as moving visitors safely through exhibition spaces, designing digestible and legible text, creating appropriate, accessible interaction, the integration of film, and exhibition construction.

Exhibition designers are drawn from a variety of backgrounds, among them interior design, product design, architecture, graphic design, multimedia and construction. This book is structured to help a varied readership to access information in a number of ways. Some may try to examine all the information contained within it systematically, others will browse and selectively concentrate on particular areas, while yet others will skim, stopping occasionally to look at a particularly interesting image or caption. In other words, they will treat this book in the same way that different visitors react to an exhibition. As far as possible, the principles described are accompanied by inspiring examples that demonstrate how these principles are derived from contemporary exhibition practice.

The modern exhibition

The Guggenheim Museum in Bilbao, designed by the Canadian-American architect Frank Gehry, achieved almost instant fame when it opened in 1997. It drew almost a million tourists a year to a pleasant yet declining port, and delivered immediate economic and social benefits to the people of Bilbao. It was successful in a way that could hardly have been envisaged by its administrators or the mayor. This success also polished the already considerable reputation of its architect and sparked a decade-long fascination with the iconic museum designed by a "starchitect", intended to invigorate and bring high-culture cachet to a neglected town.

Achieved with a mixture of private and public funds, the Guggenheim offered a formula sought by governments, planners and museum administrators around the world—a global audience, economic regeneration and high prestige at a relatively low cost. The success of the Guggenheim and a small number of other similar projects sent out a message to national and local governments. With an iconic building designed by one of a small coterie of signature architects, and the collaboration of a "branded" national institution (Tate, National History Museum, Smithsonian, Louvre, etc.), your town could become the next Bilbao. It also heralded a new equation where culture, previously understood to be a drag on successful economies, created wealth and a new sense of purpose and identity.

In the commercial world, continued economic growth in the early years of the twenty-first century buoyed the building of vast exhibition halls, such as the huge and much-extended trade fair halls in Hanover, Milan, Barcelona and Munich, and provided unique opportunities for exhibition designers.

Danish National Maritime Museum, Kossmann.dejong, Helsingør, Denmark, 2013. A signature building designed by Bjarke Ingels Group and an immersive exhibition design by Kossman.dejong brings new audiences to the remarkable story of Danish seafaring.

However, the financial crisis of 2007–8, and the economic slowdown that followed it, seemed to lead to a reduction in exhibition design commissions.

There are signs of recovery today, though, and even during a recession there will always be strands of exhibition practice that will survive, and even thrive. Not surprisingly, many of the exhibition opportunities emerging today are in the countries that were least affected by the global slowdown. The BRIC countries (Brazil, Russia, India and China), in particular, are embracing museums as a tool for educating new generations to take on the future demands of knowledge and technology, and are building vast new centres for culture. The Museum of the Portuguese Language in Brazil's São Paulo, the Jewish Museum and Tolerance Centre in Moscow, the vast science "cities" in India, and the National Museum and Shanghai Science and Technology Museum in China are all examples of this trend. In the mineral-rich Gulf states, such as Abu Dhabi, Qatar, Saudi Arabia and Oman, a succession of new museums are being developed in a rush to engender a sustainable, knowledge-based economy before carbon resources finally run out.

The development of hands-on interactive science centres to communicate the principles of science and engineering through play has continued at a remarkable pace, too. In North America, where this movement was born, and in Europe, science centres are now a key element in the education of a science-literate workforce able to take on the challenges of the modern economy. National programmes of science education supported by science centres, often linked with teacher training programmes, have yielded

Hanover exhibition ground, Hanover, Germany. This complex houses the giant CeBIT Telecoms trade exhibition every year and hosted the World Expo in 2000.

remarkable initiatives in China, Turkey, Saudi Arabia, Bulgaria, Norway, Malta, the Czech Republic and Poland, among others.

In a parallel development, the gathering pace of digitization has begun to affect exhibition practice deeply, and a new breed of digital design agencies has emerged. Exhibitions are now advertised and bookable online, augmented by digital interactives during a visit, frequently accompanied by study packs and opportunities for further understanding. Forums also create opportunities for visitors to open a dialogue with curators and experts long after their visit. The online "Bug Forum" hosted by the UK Natural History Museum is one such example.

However, digitization looks set to have even more far-reaching consequences for the interpretation of collections, as the vast stores of the world's museums are slowly brought into view through incremental scanning and recording. As a result, exhibition designers must be able to manage and work creatively with the digital information that surrounds an exhibition. Increasingly, the assets of a museum will include an electronic database that can be accessed through websites, apps and creative interactive devices within the environs of a gallery interior, in addition to traditional object displays. In a remarkable new development, Google has used its understanding of Internet-based learning to pioneer exhibitions that can be experienced both physically, in an exhibition room, and virtually, through a tablet or computer.

As the channels for distributing content increase, so does the need

Museum of London App, London UK, Smartphone can bring history to life by overlaying archive images over modern photographs as shown in the "Streetmuseum" app commissioned by the Museum of London. This image shows the Royal Exchange in London.

for meaningful organization, prioritization and interpretation. Specialist exhibition content and interpretation developers, with research and writing skills, are now an established and vital part of exhibition design practice. These individuals work in a team environment with three-dimensional designers, architects, graphic or media designers. Clients increasingly also require the work of practised and experienced content developers, capable of sifting, prioritizing and managing raw content to help produce creative design work—truly inspiring interpretive design has come to depend on their skills.

Finally, as exhibition planners and designers develop masterplans for a new generation of exhibition facilities, clients and designers are being made increasingly aware of the social context of public learning. For cultural attractions to continue to be successful, they must employ a mixture of activities—festivals, events, lectures, performances, cafés and restaurants, alongside exhibitions. This blend creates an environment that encourages enthusiasm for public learning as an integrated part of the life of a community. In major cities in particular, museums and interpretive visitor attractions are a hub for a promenading (and increasingly international) public who enjoy a range of activities, complemented by the contemplation, restoration and stimulation that exhibitions provide. The work of imaginative, thoughtful and memorable exhibitions underpins these hubs, and this book explores the tools used by some of the world's most successful designers to achieve this.

The history of exhibition design

Display is an innate element of human behaviour, constantly practised in our daily lives. Most homes have casual arrangements of treasured possessions and images, organized by personal preference and intended to reflect, and be reflected upon by, their owners and others. Shopkeepers and market traders, likewise, develop a sense of the best way to display their wares; how and where to place goods to attract custom and create a sympathetic environment. Above all, religious buildings such as churches, mosques and temples are powerful examples of how techniques of display can be most skilfully employed. Many of them use their architecture to elevate iconic objects, to communicate the need for reverence, to frame views that concentrate attention on a single sacred object or place ("the altar") and to stimulate the senses (scents, music, visual stimulation, tactility), promoting spiritual contemplation in much the same way that other states of heightened apprehension are promoted by modern exhibition designers. Indeed, many museums and exhibition spaces often have something of the atmosphere of a temple, which they often resemble physically. (Noteworthy, in this context, is the degree to which large buildings of the nineteenth century were designed in a temple-like style that drew inspiration from Greek or Roman precedents.)

Museum and art gallery displays mainly evolved out of the collections of rich patrons, whose curiosities and artefacts were normally shown only to other wealthy families. At the end of the eighteenth century, a number of such collections were combined and organized for public display. In many places—

Florence is an example—great works of art commissioned by patrons such as the Medici family merely had to be consolidated in palaces that were extended or adapted for the purpose of exhibiting them. In New York and Washington, collections were largely imported and were sought after not just for their perceived artistic merit, but also for the insight they gave into all things foreign. Quite often, museum or art gallery displays were set up with a dual purpose: to house an existing collection of artefacts and to provide educational opportunities for an increasingly literate and self-educating population. The promise of self-improvement was a central part of their attraction and, much as they do today, they enabled large numbers of visitors to gain a broader and more complex understanding of the world.

The United Kingdom's first dedicated public art gallery was the Dulwich Picture Gallery in south-east London, the building for which was commissioned by Frenchman Noël Desenfans, and his Swiss friend Sir Francis Bourgeois. The two art dealers had originally acquired the Dulwich paintings for the king of Poland, Stanislaus Augustus. Upon abdication in 1795, the king left them with a substantial collection they did not wish to entirely dispose of. They struck upon the idea of opening a public gallery with the support of an elderly widow. The gallery proved to be an important precedent for architects and designers of gallery spaces, demonstrating as it did how a building dedicated to art might look. It famously showed how daylight could be introduced from above at a time when, in most buildings, the walls on which paintings were hung were pierced by windows.

Above left
Sir John Soane Museum, London, UK. Like many museums, this grew out of the private collection of a single patron, Sir John Soane. On his death in 1837, a trust was set up that administers the museum to this day. The building is remarkable for its clever use of daylight from skylights and clerestory windows and for its ingenious use of space, such as the hinged painting racks built into the walls shown in this image.

Above
The Uffizi Gallery, Florence, Italy, 1581. The gallery was built at the request of Granduca Francesco de' Medici, son of Cosimo I. The original design was by Giorgio Vasari, one of the leading painters and architects of the sixteenth century. The museum houses many of the great masterpieces commissioned and collected by the Medici family.

Many institutions began to acquire artefacts at an unprecedented rate to satisfy the appetite of the public. It is hard to imagine the impact that displays of art and science would have had on these visitors, whose opportunities to travel and explore were limited and for whom these displays provided a fascinating insight into a huge range of subjects. Transportation issues aside, there were few restrictions on the movement of artefacts between countries, and many irreplaceable works of art were removed from historic sites, most notoriously, perhaps, the frieze from the Parthenon in Athens which is now in the British Museum in London. Contemporary museum-makers might content themselves with filming or recording a country's cultural products, but in the nineteenth century exotic animals, cultural antiquities, art and other items of interest were simply removed from their original and natural locations.

Although the imported "curiosities" elicited wonder, they were frequently mislabelled and poorly understood. Gallery staff often had only the haziest notion of the function, importance and attribution of their displays. The emphasis was firmly on the creation of "spectacles" intended to provoke and amaze. Many artefacts acquired narratives that, though thrilling, had little or no basis in truth. The introduction of more scrupulous practices was influenced by distinguished scientists such as Charles Darwin and Linnaeus, the Swedish taxonomist, who were concerned with the careful classification and ordering of natural phenomena. Their approach became that of museum curators, whose zeal for careful labelling and scrupulous classification contributed significantly to emerging scientific disciplines.

At the same time as the Western nations were acquiring these vast collections from abroad, public displays began to be used to promote and celebrate these societies' growing industrial and technical accomplishments. The Great Exhibition of 1851 in London, housed in the revolutionary Crystal Palace, was a substantial milestone in the history of exhibitions and, for that matter, in the intellectual history of Europe. (The Great Exhibition represented the beginning of the World Expo movement, currently overseen by the International Exhibitions Bureau in Paris.)

The Crystal Palace building, designed by Joseph Paxton, was itself an engineering marvel, built in just six months using repeated modular components of glass and steel, that profoundly influenced architecture.

The South Kensington Museum in London (later the Victoria & Albert Museum) was set up with the money generated by the Great Exhibition, with the express intention of improving the standards of manufacture and the applied arts. Like many museums and galleries of that period, the South Kensington Museum was not intended for recreation but was established to provide a source of valuable information for designers, craftspeople and manufacturers seeking to improve their products.

Museum and gallery pioneers met the challenges of publicly displaying objects in a number of ways. In an era before electricity or reliable gaslights designers relied on the clever infiltration of natural light into the galleries usually from above so that as much wall area as possible could be used for display. Balconies were often located below a skylight to maximize the use of daylight, leaving a central atrium void that allowed light to flood into the lower tiers of the building.

Display cases with thick wooden frames were the staple of most museum collections, providing security and protection from theft and damage. In conjunction with poor lighting, the glass of these cases meant that many exhibits were difficult to see and also created an important psychological distance between the viewer and the object. Many curators saw themselves as trustees of important collections; meeting the needs of the public was often regarded as a chore rather than a duty, an attitude that was reflected in a hushed atmosphere and the barriers put between the viewer and the artefacts. Displays tended to be very crowded by modern standards, with pictures hung four or five high on the walls, and the highest paintings tilted away from the wall to meet the gaze of the viewer. Many museums felt bound to show as many of their artefacts as they could physically cram into display cases; often the exhibits were impressively comprehensive, but very difficult for the ordinary observer to take in. Conservation features that are considered so important today, such as control of temperature, relative humidity and air pollution were not prevalent.

This is not to suggest that modern display practices are in every respect improvements. A great many paintings and sculptures are nowadays seen in surroundings very different to those in which they were intended to be displayed. In art galleries the picture-hanging device was the picture rail with hooks and chains attached to the framed pictures. Out of step with modern design, this has disappeared from many galleries. Historically, in the homes of art patrons paintings with deep frames were a constituent part of a decorative design scheme that often included intricate plasterwork, patterned wallpaper, dado rails and ornate furniture. Many of the paintings of religious subjects

found in Western museums were originally on view in churches. The format of some of these paintings, for example triptychs, often look awkward in a modern gallery because they are literally out of place.

Pitt Rivers Museum, Oxford, UK, 1884. This remarkable collection of archaeological and anthropological artefacts was bequeathed by Lieutenant-General Augustus Pitt Rivers to Oxford University in 1884. The collection has multiplied many times over since the museum's inception, with little increase in the size of the museum itself.

The evolution of modern display techniques

Modern display techniques are largely influenced by the art and design movements of the early twentieth century, principally the development of abstract art and the principles espoused by avant-garde artists and designers, many of whom studied and taught at the Bauhaus in Germany between 1919 and 1937. These principles caused designers to radically rethink the elements of design, so that walls and floors came to be regarded as "planes", as if they were elements in an abstract sculpture. Modern Movement architects and designers reinterpreted the rooms of buildings in new ways, using the language of "spatial relationships" and "volumes" to influence display environments. Exhibition environments were reconceived in many different forms by Surrealists, Futurists and Constructivists. Simultaneously, artists like Duchamp pioneered installation art in which the envelope of the gallery, formerly treated as an empty shell into which the display was placed, was itself transformed into an element of the artwork.

New approaches to design emphasized a new dedication to combining functionality and aesthetics. In 1924 Frederick Kiesler, influenced by the Bauhaus, designed a free-standing, demountable display system, the L&T system, in the distinctive geometric style of the Modern Movement, which

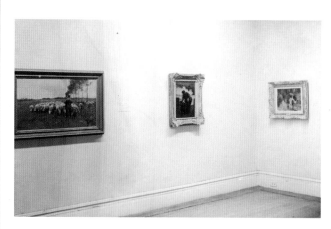

he used for pictures at the Konzerthaus in Vienna. This system, a forerunner of modern collapsible displays, was modular and allowed the combined display of objects and images; it was also adaptable and the viewer could adjust the images and objects to his or her eye level.

Of the strands of display practice that grew out of the Modern Movement, easily the most influential is the spare, minimal environment with white walls developed at the Museum of Modern Art (MoMA) in New York. Inspired by Bauhaus principles, this clinical style, now so pervasive, was developed through a series of experimental exhibitions from the mid-1930s to the early 1940s when the reaction to modern art was still very mixed. The exhibitions introduced smooth-surfaced walls and carefully but sparsely arranged displays to the American public, and were seen as provocative. Philip Johnson's "Machine Art" (1934) showed industrial goods as though they were art pieces. Contrary to some expectations, the exhibition proved to be very popular and the contentious idea that displays of industrial products could be given the reverence normally devoted to art was on the whole accepted as a reasonable premise by the visiting public. The spare style, inspired by the smooth lines of modern ships and the functional leanness of aircraft, suited the display and endeared the new Museum of Modern Art to contemporary patrons.

Other exhibitions at MoMA, such as Herbert Bayer's "Road to Victory", drew on another strand of Bauhaus design practice: the "environment", an all-encompassing experience that overwhelmed the senses of participants, and involved many creative disciplines to achieve a total effect. The exhibition, which took place during the World War II, was conceived literally as a single path, a road to victory on which visitors walked alongside inspirational images of life-size patriotic Americans contributing to the war effort. The story told by the images was intended to have maximum psychological and emotional impact. Symbolically, the path rose several feet over its length and ended with the moment of victory, portrayed by a mural of soldiers on which were superimposed photographs of mothers and fathers at home. Mary Anne Staniszewski, author of *The Power of Display*, which chronicles the MoMA exhibitions, remarked: "The message was one of a fated victory and a certain

Above left
Van Gogh exhibition, MoMA, New York, USA, 1935. Alfred Barr, the founding director of the Museum of Modern Art, devised this Van Gogh exhibition. The show was remarkable for the width of empty wall space allowed between the paintings. This hanging method has become almost ubiquitous for modern painting shows.

Above
"Machine Art" exhibition, MoMA, New York, USA, 1934. Designed by the architect Philip Johnson, the exhibition featured everyday industrial goods. This groundbreaking show, which asserted that functional goods and machinery could be perceived as art, brought widespread public interest. The display was typically spare and unadorned in the Bauhaus tradition.

future; in other words, an idealist and determinist covenant with what had been and what will be was manifest in every nail, piece of wood, caption, and photograph in this installation design." The success of "Road to Victory" also demonstrated how skilful photography, increasingly being used in advertising, could become a powerful emotional tool. Bayer, who would have been familiar with the exhibitions designed by the Constructivists in support of Soviet Communism and the Italian Futurist displays in support of Fascism, employed many of the techniques used for these, though for very different ends.

Perhaps the most defining element of MoMA's display legacy was also its simplest. Alfred Barr, the museum's founding director, pioneered exhibitions of paintings hung at wide intervals, with a sizeable border of empty space around each exhibit. The common practice of "skying" paintings high on the walls, one above the other, was eliminated and a neutral wall colour was chosen, first a beige monk's cloth and later white paint. Barr treated all displays the same, so a 1935 exhibition of Van Gogh's paintings was given a roughly similar treatment to "Italian Masters" in 1940. His method precluded the use of period detail, colour or wall-hanging to communicate the context or period in which an artwork was produced. Visitors were encouraged to ignore the artist's historical and social context and to consider the art separately as an autonomous object. This style, now evident everywhere, was innovative and encouraged viewers to look at art in a new way.

Centre Georges Pompidou, Rogers and Piano, Paris, France, 1972–6. The Centre Georges Pompidou is a landmark in the display of modern art. The organization—vast uninterrupted floors with no internal columns or structural walls—has had a great impact on the type of displays that could be housed. The informal ground-floor exhibition space has more the atmosphere of a city square than a conventional museum.

Interactive exhibitions

In the 1960s a new revolution in exhibition display was brought about by the growth of the "hands-on" exhibition, developed and adopted by institutions such as the Exploratorium in San Francisco. Dissatisfied with traditional methods of teaching science, these institutions introduced a fresh conception of learning, whereby children would actively engage with real science. They developed interactive exhibits that allowed visitors to learn directly from experience and have fun at the same time. The displays sought to engage a type of visitor now known to museum and educational specialists as

"kinaesthetic learners". These visitors, traditionally poorly served by museums, enjoy getting involved with something—"doing" rather than observing. Today, we have come to expect this type of exhibit in our museums, indicating the enormous impact interactive exhibits have had on the way display professionals think about museums and visitor experiences. "Doing" is now the standard approach to the teaching of science, and interactive exhibits continue to populate other areas of exhibition practice, enriched by other types of interactive experience—such as environmental and "find out more" interactives. Contemporary exhibitions, such as the Winston Churchill exhibition in London (see pages 94–95 and 114–15), owe much to these precedents.

Other experiments have sought to dispel the elitist nature of much exhibition practice. The glorious Centre Pompidou in Paris, designed by Italian architect Renzo Piano and British architect Richard Rogers, has, since its inception, attempted to create a less reverential atmosphere, more marketplace than art temple. The hi-tech building with its massive, tubular air ducts, exposed structure and bright colours is in many ways an antidote to the palatial, traditional galleries of the Louvre across town, and is in this sense

Above left
Exploratorium, San Francisco, California, USA, 1983. A heliostat on the roof tracks the sun's movement and reflects the sunlight off a mirror down into the exhibit area. Bouncing off other mirrors, the light reaches a wall of prisms, which break into a spectrum of colours. The scribbles of colour shift with moving air currents.

Above
Exploratorium, San Francisco, California, USA, 1983. Artist Ned Kahn creates warm updrafts and circular air flows. This exhibit combines art and a powerful educational message for children learning about science.

an ideal venue for provocative, experimental installations that might appeal to younger audiences. Additionally, the Centre Pompidou's huge, undivided floor planes and lack of columns or internal load-bearing walls gives the exhibition designer greater freedom to divide spaces according to the dictates of the display, rather than having to respond to the structure of the building.

Recent developments

Recent developments have brought about a realignment in the modes of delivering exhibitions in both the public and private sectors. Younger visitors have begun to pay less attention to traditional advertising and marketing, and increasingly inhabit a parallel digital community. To maintain their relevance to a new generation of potential customers, corporations and institutions are forced to seek out the virtual habitat in which these consumers reside. In turn, exhibitions have become more interactive and increasingly have a dialogue with this virtual world. The visitor will often browse a website before seeing an exhibition and will often consult that website afterwards. More importantly for corporations, the exhibition has become an opportunity to stage a live event that is announced online and portrayed online after it has taken place, allowing the corporation to stake out territory in the digital environment. This "take home" aspect of modern exhibitions has parallels with the traditional "giveaways" handed out to visitors and the themed trinkets from the museum shop. The important difference is that data capture at exhibitions allows institutions to draw the Internet traffic of their target audiences into their digital space, delivering the kind of marketing benefits that mere branded trinkets can no longer provide.

Interestingly, the live, physical experience of holding an event has not been replaced by virtual exhibitions, as was predicted when the Internet was born. The digital experience often leads to a physical visit and seems to encourage rather than discourage visitors. The advent of digital communities such as

Capture the Museum, National Museum of Scotland, Thought Den Ltd, 2013 This app encourages children to virtually "capture" museum objects as part of a team game organized by the museum.

"Second Life" may change this situation in the future, but the evidence so far seems to suggest that the "real" exhibition is a robust feature of modern life and unlikely to be replaced very soon.

For designers and exhibition managers, the developments described above have had a significant impact on the practice of staging exhibitions. Web, multimedia, graphics, sound and lighting designers are expected to work side by side, to deliver a single linked experience that operates with consistency from the first contact on the website to the after-show email. Curators are expected to blog continuously from the moment their exhibition ideas are conceived through the duration of the show. Visitors are expected to interact with the display, give feedback on its value and have their say on its every aspect. The "like it or leave it" attitude of past generations of designers and exhibition managers has been superseded by a less defensive and more flexible attitude towards feedback and comment.

Exhibitions continue to be an extremely efficient medium of communication and, in the words of one commentator, Tony Bennett, "speak to the eyes". Anyone who wishes to gain a substantial understanding of a subject in a manageable time frame would be well advised to visit a well-curated exhibition, where the information they seek is mapped out as a comprehensible three-dimensional journey. Within most major national museums and art galleries, what the visitor takes for granted is an enormous amount of care in the choice of the exhibits and, often, brilliant interpretations of a subject. Many exhibitions will also provide a fascinating sublayer of information for those who wish to delve below the surface. For tourists, visits to museums and galleries are a substantial element of their enjoyment of their stay, and a vital representation of the culture of the country they have travelled to explore. Beautifully lit and presented displays are a minimum requirement for international cultural consumers whose spending fuels the vibrant international tourist economy. The theoretical underpinning and exhibits for these are provided by an army of exhibition professionals, but it is the job of the exhibition designer to orchestrate an environment that connects with the visitor, and transform a collection of exhibits into an inspiring experience. Designers have developed great sophistication in their understanding of their audiences, and must think carefully about how to engage a segmented marketplace.

To an even greater extent, trade fairs afford an opportunity for visitors to gain an overview of an entire subject. Though car shows, for example, have largely become opportunities for branded entertainment, a single event can bring together all the most important players in the car market and allow visitors the luxury of watching the great brands jostle for their attention. For business customers, trade fairs provide a rare opportunity to rub shoulders with their most important contacts in a time-efficient manner, to forge business relationships and to take a snapshot of the most advanced developments in their field. For exhibitors, these fairs are essential to creating a conversation with their customers through the medium of a designed experience. Small wonder that they often spend large sums on the design and construction of their trade stands, with each exhibitor vying to outperform their neighbours. The skill of the exhibition designer may, in the past, have been overlooked by the world of design as well as by many clients. Major contemporary exhibitors, however, need no persuading of the value of exhibition design and designers, and invest heavily in the design of their "customer experiences".

The role of the exhibition designer

Although there are a number of university-level specialist courses in exhibition design, they produce only a fraction of the professionals who are currently practising. There is plenty of evidence to suggest that graduates trained in other design disciplines or art can transfer their skills to exhibition design, though some grounding in its basic principles is always recommended. In many instances, practitioners may work across a range of contexts; for example, in retail or office design or, in the case of graphic designers, in print or digitally based media. In larger exhibition design practices, working across disciplines is more rare as these companies tend to create specialist exhibition teams.

The range of design specialists working on a single project will often depend on the budget. For a small exhibition, the designer will be called upon to be responsible for the three-dimensional design of the structure as well as simple text panels and project management. Larger exhibitions may have a budget large enough to employ specialists from a variety of disciplines. In most cases, there will be a design director who assumes overall responsibility for the outcome and coordinates the work of collaborators. That said, many exhibitions are staged with no design involvement at all—artists who mount their own shows, for example, and exhibitors at trade fairs who put together their own stands. Some of the fundamental rules explained in this book may help such exhibitors to avoid the worst disasters and increase the effectiveness of their displays. Complex shows, however, require the input of experienced exhibition designers.

Exhibition designers often specialize in one of two areas: museum displays for publicly funded institutions or commercial displays for corporate clients. Increasingly, the boundary between these sectors is being broken and designers work in both areas. Some operate externally as consultants called in on contract to address particular design tasks, others may work in-house as part of a team designing a programme of exhibitions. Exhibitions are usually constructed with a time frame in mind, thus temporary installations need to be less durable than permanent ones, and sometimes employ different construction techniques or materials. Typically, exhibition design encompasses areas such as "customer experiences", "brand environments", trade fair stands, launch events, consumer pavilions (including World Expos), museums, art galleries, and science and "discovery" centres.

Further opportunities exist for design students with a detailed knowledge of sustainable design. While this topic is too large to be properly handled in this volume, it is important to stress that future generations of designers will be required to take up the challenge of the sustainable management of the earth's resources, balancing social, economic and environmental concerns through their practice. In many Western countries, much that has been discussed at intergovernmental level since the 1980s has filtered down to become concrete. Modern practitioners will be dealing on a day-to-day basis with questions of sustainable design practice against the background of potentially rapid climate change and intense debate about the use of the world's scarce resources.

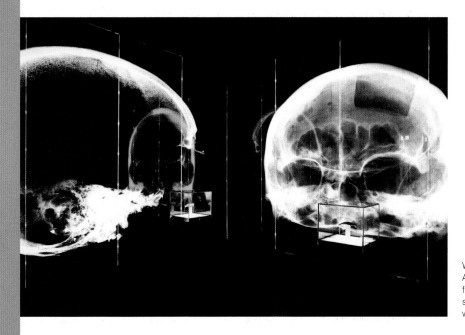

Westphalian State Museum of Archaeology, Atelier Brückner, Herne, Germany, 2003. Skull fragments in cases are displayed alongside large-scale projected computer-generated images, which explain the significance of the exhibits

How to use this book

The 14 chapters of this book examine exhibition design today and the key elements of the exhibition design process, from formulation of the brief through to construction and handover to the client. Each chapter refers to consecutive elements of the process, explaining the industry terminology and delivering key information.

The "Introduction" provides an overview of exhibition activity in the world today, and includes a short account of major historical milestones and influential practitioners in exhibition design. The roles and responsibilities of the exhibition designer in both trade and public exhibitions are described.

Chapter 1 "The brief" describes how a good brief should be formulated and the types of information that may usefully be included. This chapter also describes how the briefing language can influence the design process.

Chapter 2 "The visitor" describes how exhibition audiences are analyzed and includes discussion of branding and targeted audiences. It also describes how exhibition designers might address visitors who have varying levels of knowledge and diverse learning styles.

Chapter 3 "The site" looks at the opportunities and constraints provided by the exhibition site and their impact on design strategies.

Chapter 4 "Exhibition strategy" is a concise account of how exhibition designers work with a given brief to produce the strategy for an exhibition. Diagrams show how these strategies help to formulate visitor journeys.

Chapter 5 "3-D design skills" describes how exhibition designers generate ideas, research visual references and formulate exhibition plans. It includes illustrations of models, sketches and visuals used in the initial stages of the three-dimensional design process for trade fairs, museums and galleries.

Chapter 6 "Graphic design skills" looks at the use of text and imagery in the exhibition environment. The importance of legible and readable text and text–image scale is discussed, with practical advice on large-format printing and production issues.

Chapter 7 "Lighting" discusses lighting strategies specific to exhibitions. It describes how lights can be positioned over exhibits and the use of lighting to model objects (such as sculptures), as well as backlighting, edgelighting and spotlighting, with illustrated examples.

Chapter 8 "Interactives" describes the guiding principles of interactive design and gives some key examples.

Chapter 9 "Sound and film" considers how sound and film can be used to support an exhibition storyline, and includes advice for designers wishing to commission audiovisual experts, as well as practical information about installation.

Chapter 10 "Materials" looks at the considerations designers must take into account when they specify materials, such as fire safety, durability, suitability for purpose and sustainability. Illustrations in this chapter include examples of the material sample boards that are used for presentations to clients.

Chapter 11 "Portable exhibitions" discusses temporary exhibition equipment that can be easily erected and dismantled, with useful illustrations.

Chapter 12 "Technical drawing" looks at the role of technical drawing in the delivery of exhibitions, with examples of plans, sections, elevations and three-dimensional drawings by leading practitioners.

Chapter 13 "Construction and delivery" describes how designers and exhibition-design firms structure their production process and work with contractors to achieve successful results. It includes information about the role of the project manager and the implementation of green design.

Chapter 14 "Conclusion" describes how exhibition design has evolved as a discipline, and how green criteria are set to change the industry. It also describes the economic importance of exhibitions in countries with little tradition in this area, and some of the responsibilities of the exhibition-design profession.

1.

This chapter describes the ideal brief, how it is formulated and the various aspects of exhibition planning that it should cover. These include the target audience, the context or narrative in which exhibits will be seen, and the way in which the theme of the exhibition should be interpreted. A brief also highlights the need for the client to provide the designer with all the information necessary to achieve a successful outcome.

At the beginning of every project, designer and client need to develop a shared understanding of a project. This understanding needs to be both creative and practical, describing what is expected, as well as the creative opportunities. Typically, a good brief is recorded and provides a reference point for future developments, helping both client and designer understand whether, as a project moves forward, they have strayed from the initial intentions, or whether assumptions have changed. Successful projects start with a good, clear initial briefing, but this will often evolve as client and designer explore the potential of a given project.

Ultimately, the mark of a successful brief is a successful and creative project. The skill of the client in creating a design brief cannot be underestimated—the better the brief, the better the working process and the realized project. Accurate attention to information such as budgets, costs and programme is essential, while similar attention to less tangible elements such as themes and content will likewise lead to relevant, thought-provoking creative responses. Brief-writers often ask how prescriptive a brief should be. Good projects can be achieved with both loose and tightly prescriptive briefs. However, if the designer is to meet the expectations of the client, it is really important that the client is clear about what those expectations are. If a brief does not communicate intentions clearly, the designer will likely waste a lot of time and effort trying to discern them.

How specific should a brief be?

Some briefs can be too prescriptive. If the client specifies what they would like to see in their exhibition too precisely, they effectively take design decisions into their own hands and deny themselves the opportunity to use the designer's expertise. A brief that is too vague, on the other hand, runs the risk that the designer may waste time working on issues that are not relevant to the task in hand.

All in all, if the client has good ideas that they feel should be considered, they should put them up for discussion at the outset, but be willing to take the designer's advice on whether they are appropriate. This saves time and avoids the common situation where the client has an idea but waits to see whether the designer comes up with the same one, and is disappointed when they do not. The best briefs are specific about objectives, learning outcomes and available assets, such as collections—this leaves the designer free to inflect the content in the best way, and consider which delivery techniques might be best for which type of content.

A business-to-business exhibition held by mobile-phone suppliers	Primary audience	Secondary audience
	• Mobile-phone retailers (existing customers) • Mobile-phone retailers (potential new customers)	• Mobile-phone customers • Trade customers in related businesses • Mobile-phone support technicians
A public exhibition	Primary audience	Secondary audience
	• Children aged 6–12 • Parents of children aged 6–12	• Children below 6 and above 12 • Independent adults of all ages • School and educational groups

As a designer, it is essential to test your understanding of the brief by questioning the client, investigating scenarios and generally probing the brief's soundness. If the client has not described the nature of the task properly and some aspects do not make sense, ask questions, even at the risk of appearing naive.

What kind of language should a brief use?

A brief usually contains lots of dry factual information, such as scope, budget and programme, and there is no point in dressing this up. However, it should also always contain some emotive language to convey the importance of the project—why it is exciting and worthwhile. Creative design often thrives on the association of words and images, so clever, funny and evocative language can be used to stimulate the designer's imagination. The language used can also provide the designer with valuable insights into the client's frame of mind, which can, in turn, shape a better working process and indicate the most appropriate forms of communication. For example, formal clients may prefer well-prepared materials, presented less frequently, while less formal clients may wish to see working sketches and early ideas at more regular intervals.

The briefing process is not limited to written documents, however. Creative immersion in the idea of a project is essential. A visit to a museum vault, a client's factory, cultural visits undertaken together and joint workshops will all help convey ideas and feelings, and enable a designer and client to develop a successful working relationship.

Strategy

There are myriad ways to set out the necessary components of a brief, and these are listed below. Large projects may feature all of these elements and more, but smaller projects will often omit any number of these if they are not relevant.

Institutional or company objectives

Most companies and museums have a list of written objectives or institutional goals tailored to their overall mission, and it is incredibly helpful to see these, particularly when working for a client for the first time, as these will govern the development of the experience. These objectives will have been carefully considered, and will often have a strong influence on the daily work of the client body. These aims often benefit from some explanation, though—who originated them and how they evolved. For museums, these statements are a key point of difference, indicating to staff and visitors how they distinguish the experiences they offer from their competitors.

Messages and outcomes

Most exhibitors have values and ideas—often referred to as "key messages"—that they want to communicate to their audiences as part of an overall strategy. These are typically altered and updated more frequently than institutional objectives, and they often mirror short-term campaigns. Museums can use these messages to help them pursue, for example, strategic educational initiatives to enhance students' understanding of science, natural history or history. Commercial exhibitors will often have strategic goals that explain the competitive strengths and unique advantages of their current offer. Related but slightly different are visitor outcomes. These describe the ideas of impressions the client wants the audience to take away from their visitor experience. For example, a natural history exhibition about insects might be intended to leave schoolchildren with the idea that "the bugs in my house are really interesting", or "science can be fun". It can be really helpful to state intended "visitor outcomes" as well as "visitor messages", as there is a critical difference between delivering messages (saying that "science is fun") and designing an experience that creates an understanding in the mind of the visitor (having visitors say "science is fun" after their visit). The former is more straightforward; the latter is a more complex outcome to achieve, but ultimately a more rewarding result. Visitor outcomes can be tested through audience surveys, which can help designer and client understand how close they are to reaching their targets.

The subject or content of an exhibition is sometimes tied to a wider campaign or, in the case of commercial exhibitions, to wider branding strategies. A coordinated approach that enables an exhibition both to gain publicity and to help broaden and deepen a wider branding strategy is sometimes required. This kind of thinking is less relevant for museums than it is for commercial exhibitions, where the explicit aim is to enhance brand perception. Commercial exhibitors often have extensive reports detailing areas where they need to heighten or shift visitor perceptions of their brand. This information can be especially useful, and should be included in briefs for commercial exhibitions so that the designer can maximize any opportunities for linking with existing branding, marketing or communications. Exhibition content also often connects with, or gives insight into, topics on school or university curricula. For many national institutions, particularly museums of science and natural history, these links are very carefully considered. If an exhibition subject directly addresses an aspect of learning—say "optics" or "how machines work"—the museum can play a powerful role in expanding and deepening student learning through live demonstrations and showing key historical objects that may have been previously explained or introduced in the classroom. Where the client wants to make these links, it is important to explain in the brief exactly what the links are, and what students are expected to take away from their experiences. This kind of information has an impact not just on the spatial storytelling aspect of an exhibition, but also on design features, such as gathering spaces for groups, or capacity for live demonstrations, to give two examples.

Sustainability

Sustainability features in many exhibition design briefs, so it is a good idea to establish from the outset what this means in the context of the project. Sustainability can relate to two distinct areas in exhibition design: environmental and financial. Environmental sustainability affects the materials used in constructing the exhibition, and may even affect the working process, impacting on travel, for example. Financial sustainability refers to the business plan or business objectives a client may have when developing an exhibition, and will impact upon such factors as how many visitors can occupy the space at any one time, or whether there is a retail or café space.

Ambitions for sustainability should be defined early on in the project, ideally by the client—how they expect sustainable principles to be applied, and to what level. There are a number of official bodies that provide benchmarks for environmentally sustainable projects: BREEAM (Building Research Establishment Environmental Assessment Method) in the UK and LEED (Leadership in Energy and Environmental Design) in the US are examples. Whereas architects have become familiar with sustainable working practices and standards, examples of the application of sustainable exhibition design practices are fewer, although large project teams often include sustainability consultants to help realize sustainability criteria.

Masterplanning

Very often exhibition designers are asked to create "interpretive masterplans". These address the need to plan links between disparate content/gallery areas, and often encompass an entire site, or a large section of a site. A completed interpretive master plan shows potential visitor routes between galleries, illustrates logical content sequences (such as a chronological or thematic approach) and might illustrate a range of costed options to help the client decide how best to use their buildings and galleries within a given budget. These studies are necessary to make integrated visitor experiences that are consistent with a pre-determined, logical, carefully devised narrative.

Interpretive masterplans might also make recommendations for the placement of cafés or gift shops along the route to maximize the client's revenue and provide comfort for visitors. As the planning of new facilities and the re-thinking of existing facilities often requires new marketing or operational strategies, these masterplans can be accompanied by marketing or operational plans produced by external consultants.

Marketing

Exhibitions are undoubtedly more successful when they are accompanied by large landmark events such as lecture series, book launches, and radio and TV programmes. If events are planned around the opening of an exhibition,

Ralph Appelbaum Associates, London, UK, 2014. Creative and rich design environments stimulate ideas and creative solutions.

it is helpful to make exhibition designers aware of this as it may affect the focus of the exhibition. Increasingly exhibition content is shared across a number of platforms, including social media, providing new ways to gain public attention for museum content and attract new audiences. Forward-thinking exhibitors have also begun to mix virtual and physical encounters that enable people to share in the experience of being in the exhibition, and allow visitors at the exhibition to see digital input from outside. Key visitor attractions from a museum or exhibition experience provide leverage for marketing and social media, and can sometimes be designed to provide maximum exposure to social media. If a client has these expectations, they should be communicated in the brief.

Costing

Any thinking about the scale of an exhibition will require an understanding of cost levels. For larger projects, specialist exhibition cost consultants are essential in helping project and client teams understand what they can expect for the funds available. Generally, highly interactive or audiovisual experiences tend to be the most expensive, while simple graphic or object displays are less costly. However, some up-front information about overall budget is important as a guide for all parties.

Public funding

Many exhibitions can only be achieved with the help of public funds. Specific funding bodies, such as the Heritage Lottery Fund in the UK, the European Commission in Europe, or the National Endowment for the Arts in the US have criteria that must be met through exhibition design. Briefs should be clear about these criteria, as designers often have experience of navigating these successfully, whereas a client can be facing them for the first time. Some funds may involve a series of applications, and briefs should be clear about the dates and requirements for each stage. This way client and designer can work together to ensure any submissions are successful.

Content and assets

The brief will then need to establish the details of the proposed exhibition's actual content—the storyline or themes underpinning it, as well as the assets and physical conditions available to achieve the desired visitor experience.

Storyline

A number of design practices and museums routinely use the language of "narrative" when designing and devising new exhibitions. Narrative design dictates that exhibition content be put together into a story sequence, with a beginning, middle and end (*see also* Chapter 3). The introductory component helps visitors to understand the context and characters in a story, and the museum exhibits are then arranged as if to tell an unfolding narrative.

The logic of this approach is strong, as stories are the most elemental way we have as humans to convey and recall information. Briefs will therefore ideally include a broad narrative for the exhibition experience. A storyline need not be long—a couple of pages of text is sufficient—but this will help by suggesting dramatic turning points, and putting the relative importance of parts of the story into perspective.

Themes

Visiting museums is a distracting business and rarely are visitors able to give their undivided attention to complex and unedited information. Consequently, like a good travel guide, exhibition curators spend a great deal of time working out how to flag interesting aspects of their exhibition content by highlighting thematic links and illustrating parallels between seemingly unrelated subject areas. This impacts how content is grouped and how those subject areas are called out in exhibition graphics and multimedia devices. Briefs should state the main themes of the exhibition, or ask that the designers draw their own thematic conclusions.

Content

Curators and subject specialists, however knowledgeable and thoughtful in their approach, often benefit from the assistance of specialist exhibition content developers, usually working for a design company. Content development, or the art of working with an exhibition subject to help make content comprehensible to visitors, is a specialist skill. It requires considerable knowledge of best practice in the treatment of content by parallel institutions, as well as a methodology that enables a client to look at their own subject matter from a host of differing perspectives. Through intensive workshopping and consideration of options, content development can provide new insights and opportunities—even radical changes—in the way a subject can be displayed and arranged.

Exhibition assets

The motivation for staging an exhibition can spring from many sources: a desire to sell or market products, to show an existing collection of artefacts and objects, or to share an idea with a new audience. In exhibition jargon, the stuff of an exhibition—the cars in a transport museum, for example, or fossils in a natural history museum—are known as "exhibition assets", and these are sourced and displayed according to how important they are in telling the narrative (see above). This approach has not always been the case. Many museum displays were once built around the enthusiasms of curators, with less consideration of how visitors would understand them.

Assets can also refer to other features of a museum or exhibition. These might include different kinds of archive, such as film or photography, the museum's location, its buildings and architecture, a strong visitor base or volunteer group, or, for corporate projects, brand awareness.

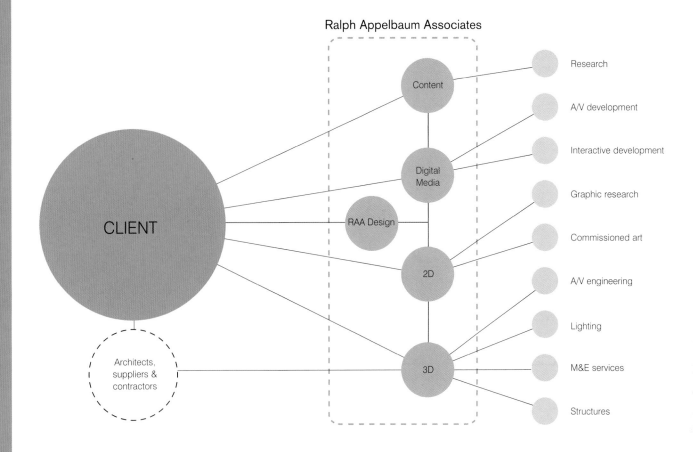

Ralph Appelbaum Associates

CLIENT

Architects,
suppliers &
contractors

Content

Digital
Media

RAA Design

2D

3D

Research

A/V development

Interactive development

Graphic research

Commissioned art

A/V engineering

Lighting

M&E services

Structures

Where possible during the briefing process, designer and client should work together to make a full assessment of the available assets. A broad overview mentioning key assets is fine to begin with. This will then be refined and expanded upon as the project progresses.

An "organogram", a hierarchical diagram setting out the roles and responsibilities of the staff designing an exhibition.

Cataloguing and recording

Meticulous recording and transfer of information about exhibition assets from the client to the designer is also critical to the success of an exhibition. Spreadsheet templates with comprehensive information about the height, width, depth, weight and display conditions are standard tools for tracking and recording objects selected for exhibition. Image and film assets should be recorded with detailed information on image resolution, size and relevance to a particular content area. Exhibition databases will usually have a unique catalogue numbering system that identifies every object, graphic image, sound or film asset intended for display. This may differ from internal systems already in use by the museum or client, and is intended to enable effective communication between designer and client. At the briefing stage, it is worth making sure that both client and designer understand the different database documents that will be used during the project, and how these documents will be shared between them.

Conservation

Long-term display of any exhibit requires the consideration of trained conservators to determine the optimum conditions for display and to prevent harm to often valuable and irreplaceable objects. Creating the appropriate conditions for each object requires an understanding of the collections but also needs the collaboration of a number of professionals, including lighting designers, services engineers (responsible for regulating the atmosphere of a gallery) and architects, who should provide galleries that are as sympathetic to conservation as display. If the client wishes to borrow objects from other institutions, they will often be asked to guarantee that environmental conditions are suitable. Good briefing material should always include mention of conservation policy.

Site and building

Exhibition briefing material will usually be accompanied by comprehensive information about the site of the exhibition and detailed floor plans that indicate how visitors might arrive and exit, amenities such as gift shops and cafés, and any adjoining spaces. Power, data and other services drawings will also be necessary and should be made available directly or through collaborating architects, facilities managers or services consultants.

Legal requirements

Exhibitions need the scrutiny of appointed experts who have legal and/or advisory powers to scrutinize and, where necessary, amend designs to ensure that they comply with the law. These might include fire, accessibility and health and safety specialists. Where important constraints are known—for example, fire exits or important access points for wheelchair users—it can be helpful to include these in the brief. This helps the designers to integrate these constraints from the beginning and may save time later in the process.

Audience

Increasingly, exhibition clients and designers research the needs of their intended audience before beginning a project. This is known as "formative evaluation". This can be done through an analysis that takes into consideration, amongst other things, proximity, wealth and size of local audiences, as well as motivations for visiting. Naturally, major exhibitions in big cities with large local populations and good transport links tend to attract larger numbers of people. However, an exceptional attraction with unique appeal to a wide section of the population can sometimes exceed expectations—in the UK, for example, the Eden Project in Cornwall is a remote visitor attraction that nevertheless attracts over a million visitors per year.

Audience studies can provide the designer with a lot of useful information. Peak and low-season visitor assumptions help architects and designers to work out, for example, the capacity of circulation spaces, cafés and restaurants. A study that helps predict the origin and number of foreign tourists will help designers and clients to determine the kind of written information they will portray in the exhibition, and whether translations will be needed.

In addition to a purely statistical analysis, museum experts have devised classifications of likely visitor types, based on less tangible things such as motivation. This kind of research is helpful for designers because it describes why different types of visitors might want to go to a museum and, by extension, how the designer might best meet their needs. In this context, some visitors might be described as "refreshers" (those who go to exhibitions to "restore" themselves, replenish their minds and who gain a spiritual satisfaction from learning). Others might be "experience seekers" who want to visit the "latest thing", and be able to tell others that they have done so. Motivation classifications are useful design tools, but they require some understanding and analysis (see, for example, Falk, J. H., Heimlich, J. and Bronnenkant, K., "Using identity-related visit motivations as a tool for understanding adult zoo and aquarium visitors' meaning-making" in Curator vol. 51, no.1, pages 55–79).

If such research has been carried out, and is deemed relevant to the type of experience the client has in mind, it should be included as part of the briefing materials. The more the designer knows about the existing or intended audience, the better the experience will be.

Time and money

Any brief should be accompanied by some reference to an approximate budget, together with a rough idea of when the exhibition should open, and the project's scope and responsibility. Variations in programme and budget can be disruptive to exhibition programmes, and designers find it difficult to work with frequent changes to either of these constraints.

The following table provides an outline of the usual division of responsibility between client and design practice.

Client responsibilities	*Planning*	*Consultants to client*
	Exhibition premise	Architecture
	Briefing	Market research
	Curation	Accessibility
	Audience research	Film-making
	Accessibility	Health and safety
	Education	Fabrication and installation
	Marketing/PR	Planning consent
	Conservation	Security
	Education	
Design practice responsibilities	*Planning*	*Consultants to design*
	Masterplanning	Translation
	Narrative design (includes graphic and 3D design)	Interactive design
	Scriptwriting	Sound design
	Artworking	AV hardware design
	Content development	Structural engineering design
	Content coordination	Film production
	Multimedia development	

DO…

- Be clear about what you are required to do.
- Make sure the brief allows for creative interpretation.
- Research the subject of the exhibition.
- Anticipate potential problems at the briefing stage.
- Share briefing information with important project workers as required.

DON'T…

- Move forward on the basis of a purely oral brief.
- Start to design the exhibition without exploring the brief adequately.
- Start the project without properly defining the roles and responsibilities of the client, the design team and other project workers.

2.

This chapter discusses the vital topic of visitor engagement with an exhibition. It describes how layers of information can be created for diverse audiences, and how modern learning theory has influenced the way designers create displays for visitors with different levels of knowledge. It also includes information about interpreting a company's brand in the context of an exhibition.

Engaging the visitor

"Engagement" is significant in the world of exhibitions, and in any book on the subject the word pops up consistently. It describes the process of addressing visitors directly, stimulating them, turning their attention towards something, creating lasting positive memories of a display and giving them new insights. Significantly, there is a real difference between showing exhibits to a visitor and engaging him or her with them. Engagement is a much deeper and more profound experience that changes and deepens understanding and is the aim of good exhibition design.

To engage visitors in an effective way, exhibitors spend a great deal of time and energy researching their audience's interests and motivations and classifying it by age, sex and socio-economic group. Like all events that cost money, exhibitions involve competition. For a show aimed at consumers, this might take the form of attractions such as shopping, leisure complexes and garden centres. For business-to-business exhibitions, each stand at a trade fair competes against its neighbours and a host of alternative exhibits. By trying to understand what motivates a particular audience, a designer can develop designs that address target groups and engage and develop visitor involvement.

Alongside the research required to create engaging displays that speak to the designated visitor group, the designer also has to consider the physical and intellectual barriers that prevent audiences engaging with exhibits. At a simple level, this may mean examining the physical environment to ensure that wheelchair users, the visually impaired and members of other disabled groups have access to the displays. But there are also less tangible barriers to explore. Visitors may stay away from an exhibition if they feel it does not relate to them, or that they do not "fit in". Daunting and confusing reception areas don't make visitors feel welcome. These are all factors that can be controlled by the designer.

Opposite
"IBM 100: THINK", Ralph Appelbaum Associates, New York City, USA, 2011. Located at New York's Lincoln Center, this exhibition features a giant interactive wall where visitor movement creates visualizations in dynamic shapes and colour.

white light festival
More Savings, More Flexibility Than Ever Before
SPRING 2012

The Visitor Bill of Rights

1. Comfort: "Meet my basic needs."
2. Orientation: "Make it easy for me to find my way around."
3. Welcome/belonging: "Make me feel welcome."
4. Enjoyment: "I want to have fun."
5. Socializing: I came to spend time with my family and friends."
6. Respect: "Accept me for who I am and what I know."
7. Communication: "Help me to understand and let me talk too."
8. Learning: "I want to learn something new."
9. Choice and control: "Let me choose; give me some control."
10. Challenge and confidence: "Give me a challenge I know I can handle."
11. Revitalization: "Help me leave refreshed, restored."
[Black, Graham, *The Engaging Museum* (Abingdon: Routledge, 2005), p32]

The USA Visitor Services Association Bill of Rights. This Bill of Rights for visitors spells out the main obligations of exhibitors. Note that interaction between visitor and exhibitor is explicitly encouraged by point seven. Point ten emphasizes the need to understand visitors and their level of understanding about a subject.

Understanding a target audience means research—on the one hand asking questions about the motivations, preoccupations and ideals of the visitors an exhibition aims to attract, and on the other reflecting on the physical and intellectual barriers that would prevent them engaging with the display. With this knowledge, the designer can work out strategies to stimulate visitor interest and involve viewers in the display by relating these to the exhibition content.

For some topics of broad interest, diverse visitor groups will be expected to attend. For example, sports cars might appeal to a number of different age and socio-economic profiles, though perhaps with a predominantly male bias. The designer is therefore addressing a diverse audience that might approach the exhibition from a wide range of perspectives. On the other hand, displays, such as those for children, have to be extremely well researched and targeted. What appeals to a five-year-old will not necessarily appeal to a ten-year-old, and a display that is intended to address both groups could prove to be a costly mistake if it is poorly researched. The greater the sum spent on an exhibition, the more exacting the research must be. In some cases, the client will test aspects of an exhibition such as posters and interactives by showing them to evaluate their effectiveness with the desired audience.

The process of creating engaging displays usually involves a representation of the target audience. To reach the exhibition's designated visitors, the designer links its subject to something they know, understand and have a positive connection to, usually researched visually using inspirational moodboards. So, if the target group is young professionals aged between 30 and 40, the designer should try to represent them and their interests on the board, making that representation as stimulating as it can be. The aim is to dynamically visualize key inspirations. Moodboards have a dual purpose.

They help to stimulate the designer's imagination while providing interesting precedents that demonstrate the direction of his or her thinking to the client— a kind of visual mindmap. The client can compare the images on the board with their own understanding of the market in which they wish to operate.

To draw the desired visitors into an exhibition, it has to be made clear through advertising, graphics and the physical environment that the display is for *them*. Traditional audiences may be comfortable with the routine of visiting exhibitions. For groups to whom this does not apply, the designer has to demonstrate clearly through appropriately designed posters, literature and marketing a feeling of welcome and a sense that there might be something in the exhibition to engage a range of visitors.

Inspirational moodboards or precedent studies have a further purpose: they help the designer and client to study and refine the language and tone of the exhibition. The images on a board can highlight an appropriate design language for conveying messages and ideas about the show to the target audience. They are often key inspirations for the experience of the exhibition, visually and spatially, and demonstrate how its key objectives can be translated into a three-dimensional experience.

Scott's Last Expedition, Natural History Museum, Land Design Studio, London, UK, 2011. This immersive exhibition recreates and interprets the science legacy of the Antarctic expedition by Captain Scott in 1912.

The Arctic Study Center, Anchorage Museum of Art and History, 2010, Anchorage, Alaska
Design: Ralph Appelbaum Associates

Smithsonian Arctic Studies Center is a new cultural-center model that serves, and is served by, Alaskan Native communities. The collection, is interpreted in consultation with Alaskan Native scholars, curators and community elders representing fourteen communities. Through updatable digital stations visitors uncover multiple layers of discovery for each object, including oral histories, historic photographs, artistic depictions, and a growing body of Native and scholarly commentary.

Above
The showcases are easy to open and enable staff to facilitate easy access to culturally important artefacts including clothing, tools, carvings and ceremonial art.

Left
Special detachable object mounts allow objects to be easily removed for study.

Above
Multimedia installations immerse visitors in the story of the Arctic through recordings of Alaskan Native storytellers and sounds from the natural environment.

Left
A series of related objects describe the context of life in the Arctic.

Layering for diverse audiences

Every large exhibition addresses a wide range of visitors, some with more knowledge of its theme than others. To accommodate their varied needs, designers and exhibitors create layers of information. Any exhibition can be layered in a great variety of ways. For example, there could be a layer for lengths of visit—short, medium or long—or for different interest groups: a display of aeroplanes might have separate layers for engineers, school children and pilots. Below are four types of visitor with differing levels of knowledge, who might be catered for.

The expert

This is the specialist who knows the terrain well and wants to supplement his or her detailed map of the area. They may have covered most of the ground before, so they are interested in some of the least trodden paths. They are looking for exhibits or information that will further their existing knowledge, though much of what they see will be familiar to them. He or she might need a research facility, perhaps a screen or a database of reference material, to explore some aspects of the exhibition more deeply. They may wish to sit down, especially if they have an enquiry that could be time-consuming. Their eye may be caught by a number of exhibits, and they need to have the facilities to enable them to delve deeper into the provenance, type, date and background of any one of them.

The frequent traveller

This person is familiar with the main landmarks and would like to discover more about the terrain by exploration. He or she has a reasonable foundation of knowledge and wants to increase it, but is motivated by general curiosity rather than the need to pursue any specific information. To satisfy the needs of the frequent traveller, the designer has to plan for an informed level of enquiry. This may be conveyed in a number of ways: explanatory text, audiovisual displays or other interpretative media may be appropriate. For some exhibitions an extensive catalogue would be useful for a generalist to read and explore at leisure. The frequent traveller may also benefit from a website with further details of the exhibition.

The scout

The scout does not know the terrain but wants to pick up on the main landmarks. The exhibition designer must ensure there is legible signage and labelling that identifies a clearly defined path. The trail of information he or she lays out should transmit sufficient information for the scout to understand the main thrust of the exhibition with minimum confusion. This visitor needs a highly organized and rigorous "top layer" of information.

2.

The orienteer

The orienteer often doesn't know where to go in an exhibition. He or she looks for something that is meaningful to them, some light they can navigate by. They may have been brought along by another visitor who has more understanding of what is being shown and has abandoned them. Really good interpretative design should include a wide range of activities and options for the orienteer. In science exhibitions younger children, who are unlikely to understand a series of exhibits intended for adults, might be provided with displays that thrill them as well as delivering a subtle message. For example, a static display of dinosaur bones might satisfy an adult with an interest in natural history. For a child, a simulated ride on the back of a dinosaur would be much more fun, while still communicating many of the important aspects of dinosaur behaviour.

Churchill Museum, Casson Mann, London, UK. A central interactive table allows visitors to click on individual elements of a Churchill archive. The top layer of information is general, but by clicking through a series of windows, visitors can access detailed information including primary sources such as letters and memos written by Churchill.

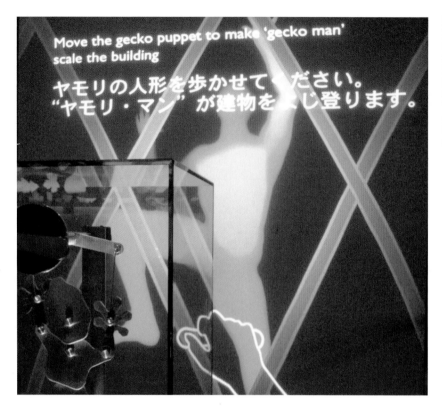

Move the gecko puppet to make 'gecko man'
scale the building

ヤモリの人形を歩かせてください。
"ヤモリ・マン" が建物をよじ登ります。

UK Pavilion, International Expo 2005,
Land Design, Aichi, Japan. This exhibit
engages a wide spectrum of the audience
through a mixture of visual, auditory and
interactive stimuli. The visitor is encouraged
to learn about the ability of a gecko to
climb vertical surfaces by making a virtual
"gecko man" scale a building. The exhibit
also demonstrates how humans can
develop technologies by studying and
emulating animals.

Learning styles

Modern learning theory emphasizes that learning is a varied process.
By borrowing some of its terms it is possible to divide the visitor's mode
of engagement into three differing categories—visual, auditory and
kinaesthetic—each of which describes one of the most common ways
to learn about exhibits. These categorizations can be useful to the designer
as they emphasize the varied types of stimulus required to engage a broad
range of audiences.

The visual learner

This type of learner requires visual stimulation in order to help engage with an
exhibition. Typically, he or she is most moved by eye-catching displays and is
less likely to read text. They like visual rather than written explanations of
phenomena and technical data, so diagrams, timelines and flow charts suit
them best. No visitor is exclusively driven by the visual, but their interest in
exhibits will be stimulated by images, film and three-dimensional sculpture.
Any subsequent examination of text is driven by the initial visual impact of
the display. Designers and artist tend to be visually driven and can easily
empathize with the visual learner.

The auditory learner

The auditory learner is the least suited to traditional exhibition display. He or
she learns best through verbal communication and discussion, and likes to

interpret the meaning of things through speech. To reach them, the use of sound is essential. Interactive screens, voice recordings and audio guides are the interpretation tools of choice for this type of visitor. Discussion with curators, gallery talks and presentations are also useful ways of engaging auditory learners.

The kinaesthetic learner

This type of visitor learns best through a hands-on approach that allows them to actively explore the physical world, and steers clear of traditional museums and exhibitions. For the kinaesthetic learner, who is interested in objects or artefacts that can be touched, a display of objects behind glass would simply be too detached; there would be nothing to hold or do, and he or she would soon get bored or look for distractions. The interactive display particularly appeals to the kinaesthetic learner, who likes the feedback and involvement of electronic and analogue interactivity. This active style of engagement is rarely catered for in art galleries, but is well understood in interactive science exhibits.

Left and below left
Ford VJ Experience, Imagination, Detroit Auto Show, Detroit, Michigan, USA, 2007. This experience was devised in order to increase the emotional resonance between visitors and the Ford brand. Visitors were filmed answering questions about what would make a difference in their lives. The filmed visitor responses were collated and then compiled by VJs (video jockeys) in visual sequences with soundtracks for broadcast on a large LED screen. A central hub featured the VJs at work, while low-level screens encouraged visitors to contribute to the experience. The screen content was, therefore, generated by the visitor and was intended to inspire a new form of interaction between the visitor and the brand.

Branding

All clients are concerned about how they are perceived by the public. When they hold an exhibition, this perception is altered, rethought and reconstructed by how visitors react to the show. It is the designer's job to meet the client's requirements to strengthen, alter and reinvigorate visitor perception through the experience of the exhibition. To achieve this, the designer needs to know two things.

First, he or she has to understand how the client is currently perceived in the marketplace. If the client is well known—a major car brand, for example—the designer or design company may carry out their own research into the target market, depending on their resources and the budget available from the client. With less well-known organizations, much of the information will be provided by the client. For small exhibitions, the research may be a cursory glance at the Internet and a leaf through the information provided by the client.

Second, the designer has to find out what the client wants to achieve, and their thinking about the market in which they operate. The client will often have an array of brand information: diagrams such as the "brand wheel", a brand manual with corporate logos and brand statements, and a host of other brand information generated by the marketing department. It is important to ask the client how the exhibition fits into the overall marketing strategy.

The designer's job is to interpret the client's brand values in terms of a real exhibition experience. For many companies, their brand is entirely two-dimensional, played out through advertising and corporate literature. Exhibition designers are tasked with taking the brand out of the graphic realm and interpreting it as a series of spatial experiences. The first rule is that all corporate signage must be scrupulously reproduced; normally no company or institution allows their corporate logo to be altered. However, beyond the obvious strictures of corporate graphics, the further interpretation of the brand is in the creative domain of the designer. As long as he or she can argue convincingly that their ideas coincide with the client's brand values, there is often scope.

Large public institutions have begun to dabble hesitantly with the idea that how an exhibition audience perceives their brand is instrumental in their long-term health. However, for trade exhibitors brand perception is central to a show and taken very seriously. For them, a thrilling and delightful exhibition can be useful only if it is consistent with, and supportive of, an overall brand message. Some clients will rely heavily on their design company for advice about brand strategies and brand communication. Care must be taken in this arena because, though many designers are familiar with brand issues they cannot be said to be truly expert. Where necessary, they hire marketing and brand consultants to deliver specialist branding advice to their customers.

Guinness Storehouse, Imagination, Dublin, Ireland. Designers Imagination used a broad palette of media to create an "immersive" brand experience for the makers of Guinness. The all-encompassing design was effective in communicating a series of brand values in a modern and engaging way and the Storehouse has proved a popular visitor attraction.

The brand environment

Although there is nothing new about multisensory displays, designers of commercial exhibitions often use them to match the exhibition experience with the brand values of the client company, with the aim of making the visitor "feel" a "brand experience". The term was coined by the design group Imagination at the end of the 1990s, and the systematic communication of brand values through sensory means has been an established practice since that time. Part of the motivation for "sensory" brand environments is that the visual saturation of the modern world has blunted the effectiveness of visual communications, and to reach visitors effectively full use should be made of sound, touch, smell and taste.

What this means can best be described by an example. In a traditional commercial display of, say, computer chips, the exhibitor would display the chip neatly on a specially designed pedestal, with high-quality lighting and a well-edited graphic panel to describe its use. The designer of the panel would take care to highlight key advantages such as the number of calculations the chip could perform, the ease with which it could be installed and after-sales

Above
"Fast and Fabulous from Beijing to Shanghai with Bombardier", Migliore + Servetto, Milan, Italy, 2005. This "brand experience" conveys the essence of the brand of train and airplane manufacturer Bombardier through an experiential approach to the design.

Below left and below
A rendering and sketch of the display.

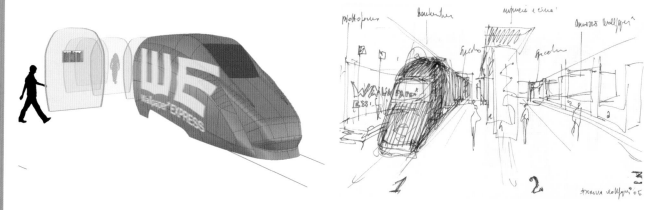

support. For many professional buyers of computer chips this information might be sufficient, though the display would undoubtedly have a similar feel to countless others.

The "brand environment" approach, on the other hand, is to appeal to the consumer on an emotional level, by creating a heightened perception of the client's brand that goes beyond the qualities of a single product. To do this the designer uses all the means at his or her disposal to create an enveloping environment in which the brand values, which in the case of the computer chip might, for argument's sake, be described as "speed", "professionalism" and "support", are played out through every aspect of the display: sight, sound, touch and smell. The architecture of the exhibit reflects the product's brand values, with its form, the tactile qualities of the materials, and the sound and smell of the environment specifically chosen to amplify and reflect the brand message.

National Museum of Ethnology, Opera Design, Leiden, the Netherlands. A device such as this "Magic Carpet" can transform a child's experience of a museum visit.

Children and exhibitions

Of all visitors, children are possibly the most critical. Unlike adults who can empathize with most exhibitions, however mediocre, children can be damning in their appraisal of exhibits that do not engage them. The words "boring", "dull" and "pointless" are often used. Moreover, they will not spend time on these displays, and are prone to play games, mess around and generally cause mayhem. Parents, teachers and museum demonstrators have a great interest in creating exhibitions that engage children and absorb their attention.

Like all other exhibitions, shows for children of all ages have to be well researched. Designers are generally too old to fully appreciate what children like, and though they may have memories of what it is like to be a child, these memories should be refreshed through thorough investigation. The most helpful sources could be educational psychologists, teachers, parents and,

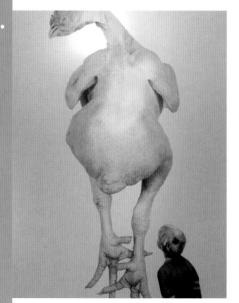

most importantly, children themselves. Ask questions. "What games do you play?", "What television programmes do you watch?" and "What makes a good day out?" are a good start. Taking small children to an exhibition can provide real information about how they relate to displays. Their reactions are very different to those of adults, and the designer can learn far more by seeing children in the exhibition environment than through reading or other forms of research.

Designers of science exhibitions stress how important it is for children to have fun when they visit them. Po-faced and overserious displays are likely to put young ones off visiting exhibitions for good. Dusty exhibits in sealed cabinets with no interactivity are anathema to children, and lead to boredom, which is the enemy of any good show. How often have you heard a child say, "That was really boring"? It takes only a few such experiences for children to be completely turned off by museum-based learning. Good design and a thoughtful approach to the exhibits are the best ways to prevent this. However, it cannot be assumed that children are not willing to learn. They can be the first to say "What was the point of that?" if they think a fun exhibit serves no purpose.

Children have a very incomplete picture of how groups of knowledge relate to each other. Teachers describe how they can come away from an exhibition with numerous misunderstandings; they may not realize that the ancient Greek or Roman civilizations date from after and not before, say, dinosaurs. They have been heard to say the Vikings were at their height during the ice age—and, given their background knowledge, might have good reasons for thinking this. As children get older, areas of their knowledge map are filled in and the task of explaining context becomes easier. For most learning exhibitions, the designer should consider how the background to them is communicated and plan their flow accordingly.

Above left and above
"Food: Traditions, Taboos and Delicacies", National Museum of Ethnology, Leiden, the Netherlands. Designed by Opera Design, this exhibition about the taboos and traditions of food from around the world was highly interactive. Oversize wall-mounted graphics show familiar foods in a new light.

The audience for most exhibitions aimed at children will include a large number of families, often with two or more children of differing ages. This gives rise to the problem of designing displays for several different age groups at once. This is an issue that many museum designers and science centres have given thought to. The answer is to pitch the design towards slightly older children. They will not interact with displays that seem too young for them, but young children are drawn to ones aimed at an older age group because they aspire to having the same experiences as older children. To a greater degree than most adult visitors, children enjoy group interactions with exhibits and are social in their approach. They may stand back from a display until they see another child exploring it, and join in only when they feel it is acceptable to do so. For the designer, this means displays have to be designed with social groupings in mind—for example, so that only one child plays on a machine but there is space for several others to see what he or she is doing. When the first child has finished playing the other children will take their cue from the reactions of their peer group. If the feedback is good, they are often keen to become involved. In some instances parents will demonstrate how to use a display and the child will join in with their guidance.

Children enjoy the freedom exhibitions allow them. They often do not have much choice in other aspects of their lives—at school, for example—and in most cases they would not have chosen to visit the show in the first place. Ideally, the designer should think about how they can exercise this freedom, and provide them with lots of options without creating a rabbit warren in which no teacher or parent will be able to find them if they get lost.

Most exhibition designers agree that activity is the key to successful exhibits. For example, it is useful to show European children how Japanese women dressed traditionally by displaying a kimono on a mannequin, but much more fun (and educational) if they can try one on. Similarly, Japanese children might be impressed by seeing a medieval knight's armour, but might be far more excited to try on a replica suit of armour.

Children's Project & Discovery Centre, Damascus, Syria
Design: Damascus Consultants and Cultural Innovations

As part of an educational initiative in Syria, Cultural Innovations was asked to develop a framework for learning in a proposed museum in Damascus. The aim of the museum was to open up the possibility for self-initiated exploration of related exhibits for young visitors. The initiative marked a departure from the traditional authoritarian school system and aimed to open the way for a more active, participatory and self-directed form of education. The expressed aim was to create critical questioning and to free human minds and developing capacities for work, while both adapting and contributing to change.

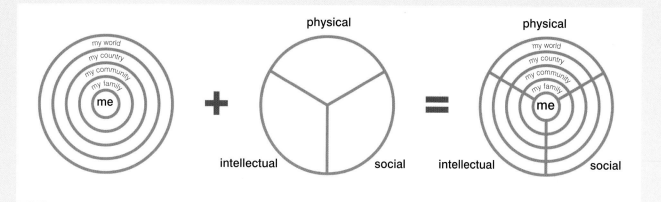

Above
The world of the child is represented by a series of concentric circles, from the personal to the global. The second circle breaks down these connections into physical, social and intellectual. The combination of these connections is the stated aim of the museum's learning philosophy.

Below
A policy document describes how the learning environment is represented developmentally, isolating learning goals for differing age groups.

Age Group	Curiosity	Channel	Explore (Experiment and Gather Facts)	Create (Hypothesis)	Share (Me+++++)
5 to 7	What happened to the dinosaurs?	Material	Exhibition about dinosaurs and theories about their life and death	There are several ways in which the dinosaurs may have become extinct. Scientists have been wrrong in the past and are still searching for more answers.	What is the lifecycle of other animals that I know about? Are they threatened with extinction? What can I do about it?
		Material	Programme about the life of dinosaurs, baby dinosaurs, etc		
		Experiential	Hands-on mock dinosaur dig		
		Experiential	Demonstrations about fossil preparation techniques		
		Virtual	Online virtual tour of the SDC's dinosaur-related exhibits		
		Virtual	Newspaper article featuring factoids and a quiz		
8 to 11	What does "dinosaur" mean and how are they named?	Material	Exhibition about the types of dinosaurs discovered in the Middle East	To communicate we need to name everything and, in science, most often these names have meaning which can be learned.	What other resources are available to help me with my school project on Jurassic World dinosaurs?
		Material	Travelling exhibit about the origins of dinosaurs		
		Experiential	Discovery box about dinosaur teeth		
		Experiential	Demonstration of dinosaur DNA modelling		
		Virtual	Television special about dinosaur hunters in the Middle East		
		Virtual	Online list of suggested reading material and resources		
12 to 15	How does what happened to the dinosaurs tell us about our own world?	Material	Exhibition about form and function in the animal world	How an animal is constructed impacts what it can eat, how it survives, its very existence (form and function). All ecological niches will be filled.	What can I do to help save endangered species?
		Material	Programme about predators and prey		
		Experiential	Green Team session about ecological issues		
		Experiential	Mentoring sessions with an ecological expert		
		Virtual	Online writing competition about ecological challenges		
		Virtual	Web lessons about the importance of biological diversity in the world		

Science of Spying, Children's Museum, Indianapolis, Indiana and Science Museum, London
Design: Jump Studios

The exhibition presents children with the opportunity to become a spy. The first area is a "recruitment area" (below) where the visitor enters the show through the "secret" entrance in the back of a phone box. The visitor learns "spy skills" (opposite) like opening combination safes, disguising themselves, searching through waste bins for evidence and playing with computer interactives. In the "Tech Zone" (overleaf), children experience "face-scanning" technologies. In "Spyworld" some visitors find themselves in a spying corporation (overleaf) while other visitors are invited to spy on them through a two-way mirror. Visitors finally "escape" from the exhibition by crawling under an infrared beam at waist height. The designers used models and computer visuals with images of children to demonstrate how the children might interact with the environment. This exhibition engaged children through role-play and games, while communicating serious information about modern surveillance technologies and the near ubiquity of surveillance devices in modern cities. The ideas were tested with the intended audiences throughout the development.

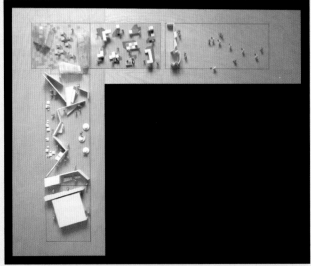

Above
Model of the entire exhibition. The entrance is at the top right of the model.

Left
Visitors entered the exhibition through 'secret' phone booths (shown on the right of the photograph).

Above left
Model of the "recruitment area"
at the beginning of the exhibition.

This page
Renderings and a photograph
of the "spy skills" area.

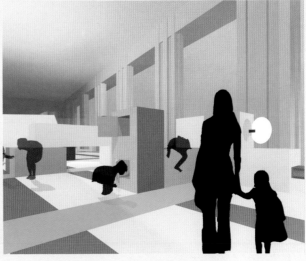

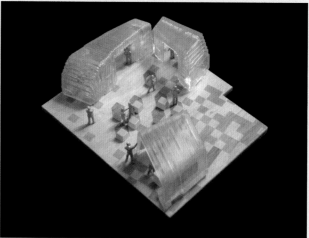

Top left and right
Photograph and model of the "Tech Zone".

Above and left
A rendering and model of "Spyworld".

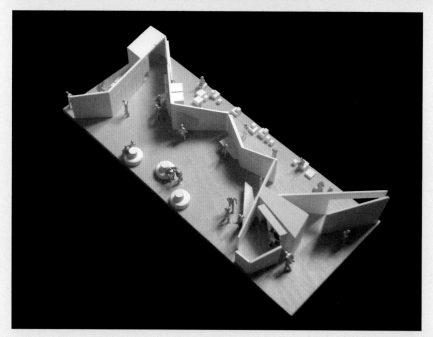

Teenagers and museums

Teenagers are often reluctant visitors to museums and are less happy to accept, as many younger children do, that the experience is "good" for them. A number of explanations are put forward by museum commentators. One suggests that teenagers generally lack curiosity about the world outside the bubble of their school, friends and immediate environment; others point to the pressures put on them to achieve extrinsic goals like exams, college entry and so forth. Teenagers themselves complain that museums are not relevant to them and that they find them alienating.

For many teenagers, a museum is a place where they are told how to think and behave, and anything apart from hushed reverence for the displays is frowned on. The presence of museum guards and anxious staff worried about the safety of their exhibits is a further barrier to a teenager's enjoyment of the museum environment.

Designing for disability/accessibility

For the last ten years, design for the disabled has been more happily described as "inclusive design" or "accessibility". This reflects a shift in emphasis from a perceived need to cater for wheelchairs users and the severely handicapped to a growing realization that disability is far more prevalent than was previously understood or allowed for. Campaigns by disability groups has caused governments to enshrine good practice in law, and made obligatory in many countries what was previously merely encouraged. As a result of this legislation, positive steps have been taken towards genuine accessibility, though much work remains to be done. The patchwork buildings, multiple levels and labyrinthine corridors of many major institutions continue to test the skills of the most able orienteer. For many disabled visitors, these institutions are often impossible to navigate without expert guidance and help.

Campaigners stress that good inclusive design should promote the integration of facilities, creating environments that can be used equally by all visitors without separating the able-bodied and disabled. By compartmentalizing disabled users, it is argued, exhibitors effectively promote the attitude that they belong on the margins. Certainly, many of the well-intentioned contraptions built in the past to help people with disabilities actually compromise their visiting experiences, and create an artificial separation that causes resentment and ultimately discourages exhibition visits. Designers should therefore aim to create not special "disabled" exhibitions but good public ones that the breadth of the visiting population can access by a number of devices, including "touch tours", induction loops and good circulation planning. Many measures that are motivated by accessibility also benefit the wider public. For example, by limiting the use of highly reflective glass designers are helping all visitors, not only the visually impaired, to see exhibits more easily.

There are a number of practices that make exhibitions more accessible for disabled users. For example, the Victoria & Albert Museum in London organizes sign tours for the deaf and "touch tours" for the blind. The latter enable blind visitors to read special labels in Braille and feel historical stone sculptures. By using their sense of touch, they are able to engage in a personal and intimate way with the museum's sculptures. The tours are only for the blind, to ensure the conservation of the sculptures; their by-product is that normally disadvantaged, visually impaired visitors feel that they are privileged.

Accessibility experts stress that any inclusive measures have to be well thought through. There is no point in installing Braille labels and exhibit-handling facilities in a room with an open staircase. However much blind users may want to touch a display, they would never want to risk plunging down an unbarriered stairwell.

The best way to understand the experience of people with disabilities is by personal experiment. The Royal National Institute for the Blind and numerous other organizations concerned with accessible design demonstrate what it is like to be disabled by asking design students or consultants to simulate disability by using a wheelchair, for example, or wearing dark glasses with a film over the lenses.

In a large group of visitors a proportion will be affected by other hidden disabilities, which should not be forgotten. For example, dyslexia is common and can be addressed by good graphic design.

DO...

- Ask your client to pass on information about their current audience and any new audiences they would like to attract.
- Research the audience carefully and try to find out what might attract it.
- Build up a visual archive of "moodboard" images from your research.
- Respond to visitors' diverse learning styles by providing a variety of ways for them to engage with exhibits.

DON'T...

- Assume your responses to exhibits or display devices are shared by everyone. Use research to understand others' needs and preferences.
- Put unnecessary barriers between visitors and exhibits. Allow viewers to get as close to displays as can reasonably be allowed.
- Design displays that alienate disabled visitors. Equal access for all users is key to good modern exhibition design.
- Expect visitors to understand and enjoy exhibits if the reason why they are being displayed isn't clearly communicated. If they fail to grasp the significance of an exhibit the failure is in the interpretive design.

3.

The site

This chapter looks at the variety of approaches designers can take to a site, depending on whether an exhibition is permanent or temporary, and whether the space in which it is held is open or closed. It discusses the importance of a building's structure in determining how and where exhibits are displayed, and also provides information about choosing sites at trade fairs.

The permanent exhibition site

For visitor centres and permanent exhibitions that are tied to a particular geographic position, the first step is an analysis that takes in routes to the site, and its topography, sightlines and other relevant factors such as the prevailing wind direction and sun orientation. Exhibitions that are intimately connected to their site, such as sea-life centres or natural history exhibitions in woodland, are particularly sensitive to, and their success depends very largely on, these factors. If a new building is involved the designer, in conjunction with an architect, may be able to manipulate environmental constraints and opportunities to deepen the visitor experience. A number of sustainability factors also come into play. Careful positioning of building elements, particularly windows, in respect of prevailing wind directions and the movement of the sun will enhance the energy efficiency of the building and reduce the need for air conditioning and central heating.

Manchester Art Gallery signage, Holmes Wood, Manchester, UK. This wayfinding signage in the Chinese district of Manchester welcomes the local community to the art gallery.

Signposting the exhibition site

There are a number of opportunities and pitfalls:

- Where possible, ensure that posters and signage are consistent in style with the advertisements for the exhibition. If it has been advertised in magazines and newspapers visitors will be looking for signage in the same style.

- Ensure that the signage can be followed from the first poster or pick-up point. Visitors hate to follow a trail of signs only to make a wrong turn some way along the route and find that they have been abandoned.

- Iconic structures or landmark sculptures outside an exhibition can be effective advertising, especially when visitors link them with the show.

- Where possible, iconic structures or signage that can be seen by passers-by should be lit at night. Even if the museum or gallery is closed, many people might be persuaded to come back the next day.

"The Cult of Beauty", Victoria and Albert Museum, Opera Design, London, UK, 2011. This introduction uses sculpture, painting, graphics and projected light to convey the theme of the exhibition.

Signposting trade fairs

For most trade fairs, the organizers use a site plan to mark out aisles and corridors in empty halls, then subdivide the remaining spaces into pitches. These are sold to the exhibitors, who choose a pitch based on its size and position in the hall. The wealthiest and most important exhibitors are usually given first refusal on the most visible pitches, while the remainder are sold to companies with smaller marketing budgets. Halls are usually big— some are massive—with few obstructions. Each hall is like a mini city with large companies on the favoured sites, surrounded by smaller boutique-sized stands. Occasionally, the organizers try to spread the main sites around the hall to ensure fewer "dead spots", encouraging visitors to pass the smaller exhibitors on their way to the larger ones.

For any company choosing a site, it is important to ask about the relationship of the stand space to the entrance. A prominent position close to where visitors enter a hall will get more traffic than sites that are further back and, as in a town centre, such prime locations are often sold to exhibitors at a premium. If there are several halls it can be useful to be on a main route between them. Like many large museums, big trade fairs have their main roads, side streets and quiet courtyards. The closer a stand is to the main road, the more likely it is to be seen.

As in many towns, large trade fairs have "zoning" laws that force exhibitors to build below a certain height to ensure regularity, and often impose "setbacks" to make sure that all substantial structures are away from the edge of a stand in order to clear sightlines. The laws may also involve creating

Ford/Aurora project, Imagination, Berlin, 1998. This event gave the designers the rare opportunity to make their own entranceway. The ramp was at the beginning of an experiential journey, creating anticipation and expectation in the visitor's mind.

Rendering of exhibition stand for Shell, Imagination. Exhibits within a trade fair environment need to be clearly signposted, with signage visible along the aisles of the exhibition hall. These tall signage totems bearing the company logo are orientated to attract maximum visitor traffic.

pathways between exhibitors and ensuring good circulation through the hall. These regulations are stated in a manual and should be closely followed as many organizers force exhibitors to take down any construction that breaches them. Companies sometimes buy stand space that has an obstruction such as a column within its boundaries. The organizers of the fair should be able to provide exact details of its positioning within the space, to the nearest centimetre, to aid the designer with his or her planning.

"Open" exhibition spaces

Some galleries are designed to show exhibits in the context of the surrounding landscape; for the sake of clarity, let's call them "open" exhibition spaces. They have large areas of glazing with views to the exterior. The pleasure of an exhibition in an open gallery is the interplay between the exhibits and their environment. For the designer, this type of gallery has some drawbacks. First, the exhibits have to compete with whatever visitors can see out of a window and it is more difficult to manipulate the viewer's attention. Open galleries are also affected by fluctuating daylight, and the designer has to take its shifting emphasis as it changes daily and through the seasons into consideration. There is a long tradition of daylit display spaces. The Great Exhibition of 1851, the forerunner of the World Expo movement, was housed in a huge, glazed temporary structure: the Crystal Palace. This was transparent to the outside world, and its interior spaces were visually connected with its surroundings in London's Hyde Park.

Open galleries are unsuitable for displaying objects that may be harmed by ultraviolet rays and high lux levels. Fabrics, watercolours and books, for example, are severely affected by daylight, and can deteriorate visibly during the course of an exhibition. When it is well controlled, daylight leads to a comfortable visitor experience, though one that is perhaps a little less intense than in galleries where all the lighting is artificial.

Craig Thomas Discovery & Visitor Center, Jackson Hole, Wyoming
Design: Ralph Appelbaum Associates

Craig Thomas Discovery & Visitor Center, Jackson Hole, Wyoming, is an exhibition and visitor center for the Grand Teton National Park. Noted for its spectacular landscape and wild life, the park currently has more than four million visitors a year. These images show how the designers have sought to create an open exhibition space by integrating the exhibits with the landscape outside the display area. The architectural and design teams worked together to employ the building as an orientation device for visitors to the park. Seven peak identifiers embedded in the floor radiate out to features in the landscape. Portions of the exhibit floor come alive with slow-moving media, called the Video Rivers. Inspired by the geologic processes that formed the Teton range, a landscape of uplifted graphic surfaces and dioramas and plinths rise dramatically out of recessed areas of the floor.

Left and bottom left
Section and plan showing sightlines radiating out into the landscape.

Below and bottom
Photograph of the completed exhibit area with the park landscape visible in the distance, and a computer rendering of exhibit area.

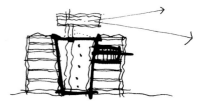

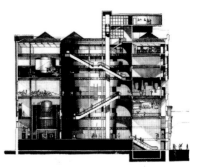

"Closed" exhibition spaces

Closed exhibition spaces with no daylight give far greater control to the designer. Where there are no competing views of a gallery's surroundings, the visitor is forced to focus purely on the exhibits and their message. For so-called immersive environments, where the designer aims to profoundly affect the visitor's state of mind, closed galleries allow him or her to construct a narrative using sound, film and interactivity without external distraction. Where lighting cannot be disturbed by fluctuating daylight, designers have a much freer hand to emphasize the relative importance of the exhibits through subtle changes in light value. From the perspective of conservation, temperature, humidity and ultraviolet rays can be carefully monitored. Most projectors and video screens rely on relatively low light levels (with the exception of very powerful daylight projectors and screens) and a closed environment is therefore ideal for multimedia displays.

After roughly an hour the closed environment, especially where light levels are very low or there are dramatic contrasts between light and dark, can become oppressive for visitors. The designer should therefore plan rest stops in areas where general light levels are higher. Long exhibition journeys in windowless environments can be tiring, and daylight helps to ease the sense of claustrophobia engendered in many large galleries.

Many of the most interesting galleries have a mixture of closed and open spaces. The Guinness Storehouse in Dublin is a mostly closed narrative journey that progresses up the building and ends with a high-level panoramic view of the city. The narrative implicitly ties the visitor's emergence from the closed, multiple levels of the exhibition to the open "brand experience" of sitting with a pint of Guinness and looking out over Dublin.

Above left
Guinness Storehouse, Imagination, Dublin, Ireland. The Guinness Storehouse is designed as an immersive brand experience in a mainly "closed" space. Video, projection and images are more effective when daylight is excluded.

Above, centre and top right
Guinness Storehouse, Imagination, Dublin, Ireland. Visitors to the branded experience finish their visit at the top of the building in a glass viewing room with a 360-degree panoramic view over Dublin. This room is visible from vantage points throughout the city and visually connects Dublin with the Guinness brand.

The Centre Pompidou in Paris, designed by Renzo Piano and Richard Rogers, was designed to be more "open" than traditional exhibition spaces in a number of ways. The ground-floor gallery has numerous public entrances to the street and is visible to passers-by through a long glass façade adjoining a public square. The entrances allow visitors to use the whole ground floor as a thoroughfare, creating a marketplace-like atmosphere that is less formal and more open than traditional galleries. Less pompous and authoritarian than its predecessors, the Centre Pompidou is a landmark in the development of exhibition spaces.

Internal organization: architecture

In traditional museums and galleries visitors circulate through a series of interconnected rooms. These create natural divisions for showing the subject matter of an exhibition but, particularly in old buildings, the display surfaces are supporting walls and are permanent and unmovable. This means that, for curators, rooms tend to be inflexible vehicles for displaying exhibits. Modern galleries generally have far fewer structural dividing walls, and therefore provide more freedom in the way that exhibitions are delivered. For example, the Centre Pompidou has an "open" or "free" plan with no internal structural columns and walls; its huge floors are supported by lattice steel beams. Exhibitions at the Pompidou are designed from scratch on a flat, level floor with few impinging walls. Although each show has to accommodate visitor flow up escalators, the building structure provides remarkable scope for matching the design of the exhibition to its content over a large floor area. In free-plan environments the designer controls navigation as well as the mounting and display of objects.

In many historic museums and galleries, collections are acquired piecemeal, and interpreted variously as curatorial ideas change over time. Walls are moved and spaces are refurbished according to immediate needs, often without any consideration of the overall effect. The result is a disjointed and fragmented experience for visitors. If a design requires changes to the structure of a building, a structural engineer must be employed to advise on the details and structural integrity of any proposed construction work.

The designer must consider possible circulation routes and how the exhibition will be approached, and get an impression of the length and quality of the visitor experience within the constraints of the site. Disability laws in many countries (see also Chapter 2) specify that exhibitions should be accessible to disabled visitors, and changes in level therefore have to be considered at an early stage to ensure that wheelchair users, for example, are not excluded. Staircases cause delays and if a show is on several floors it is necessary to plan the best way to move from one to another. For many exhibitions, especially lengthy ones, consideration should also be given to refreshment facilities, spaces for sitting down and access to toilets.

An initial assessment of light levels will enable the designer to consider how light will be controlled, especially where there are windows. Similarly, any

Opposite
Natural History Museum of Utah, Ralph Appelbaum Associates, Salk Lake City, Utah, USA, 2011. This 3-D floorplan illustrates how collection types are arranged throughout the museum; A multi-level floorplan illustrates how content is dynamically arranged along a visitor circulation path and across a simulated landscape.

3.

Collections

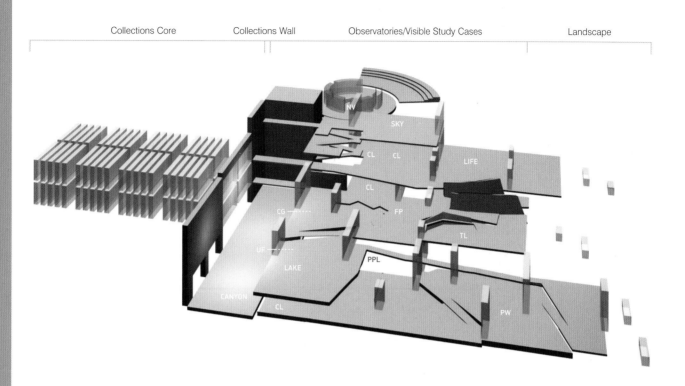

Collections Core Collections Wall Observatories/Visible Study Cases Landscape

Circulation

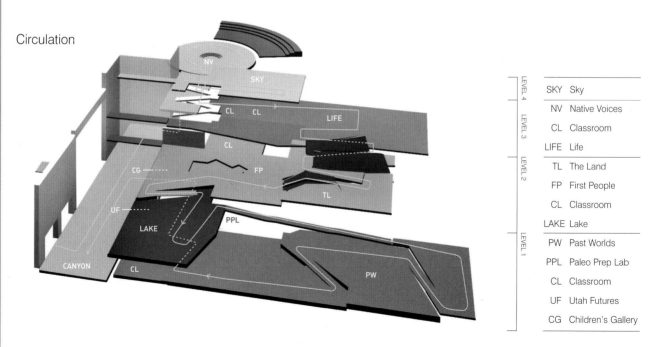

LEVEL 4	SKY	Sky
	NV	Native Voices
LEVEL 3	CL	Classroom
	LIFE	Life
LEVEL 2	TL	The Land
	FP	First People
	CL	Classroom
	LAKE	Lake
LEVEL 1	PW	Past Worlds
	PPL	Paleo Prep Lab
	CL	Classroom
	UF	Utah Futures
	CG	Children's Gallery

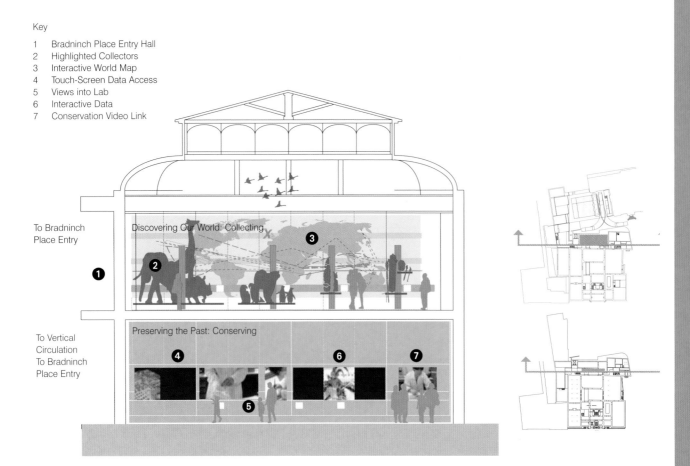

Key

1　Bradninch Place Entry Hall
2　Highlighted Collectors
3　Interactive World Map
4　Touch-Screen Data Access
5　Views into Lab
6　Interactive Data
7　Conservation Video Link

To Bradninch
Place Entry

To Vertical
Circulation
To Bradninch
Place Entry

Discovering Our World: Collecting

Preserving the Past: Conserving

Above and opposite
Royal Albert Memorial Museum, Ralph
Appelbaum Associates, Exeter, UK, 2011.
Section drawings for this masterplan are
intended to give a provisional impression of
content and visitor experience in advance of
full concept design.

variations in heat may have to be resolved—if not by the designer, then by those responsible for managing the building. Detailed technical drawings are often available from building managers, showing the original architect's blueprints and subsequent amendments to the structure, though these should always be checked against the space itself.

If a list of exhibits has been issued, the designer can start to think about what will be displayed in relation to the site. It is helpful to see the list at an early stage in the design process as some exhibits may be so large that there is only one place where they can be accommodated. Exhibits will also often have to be moved from a delivery bay into the exhibition space, and in an initial survey the designer should trace this movement, checking that displays can be easily offloaded and taken through any necessary doorways. As the relative humidity, temperature and light levels of the site can affect the exhibits themselves, it may be necessary to assess their possible environmental impact, too.

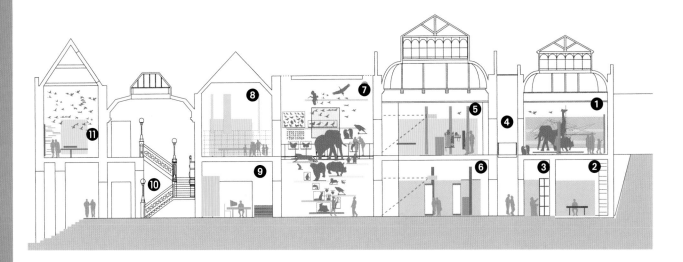

Internal organization: content

Frequently, particularly in older buildings, the designer's task is to unite fragmented exhibition spaces and link them to make a coherent story. There are many ways of doing this. Traditionally, gallery designers have organized content by discipline. So if the topics covered in a museum encompassed, say, the history of Australia, these would be broken down into separate disciplines—natural history, social history, decorative arts, fine arts, etc. This approach follows the departmental expertise of the curators, and usually leads to objects being subdivided and distributed amongst galleries accordingly; displays of rocks and minerals end up in one gallery dedicated to geology, plants and animals are housed in another, and newspapers, pictures and paintings are placed in yet another.

The current, and most popular, method of arranging content uses "narrative" design—the scripting of a single over-arching "story", broken down into a number of individual sub-chapters that include a mixture of disciplines and gallery experiences. Returning to our Australia example, the story might be the arrival of settlers in Australia and their first adventures in unfamiliar lands. A first gallery, "Arrival", might involve marine science material (the fish

London Transport Museum, London, UK
Design: Ralph Appelbaum Associates

These images show how the visitor journey is mapped in sketch form in a designer's notebook through an overview diagram (right) and individual sketches of the detailed program (below). This visitor journey is then translated into a three-dimensional drawing (opposite, top left) that demonstrates progress from the reception, up to the second floor in a lift, descending on a staircase. This total journey was then mapped onto a foam board model and inserted into the structure of the exhibition building (opposite, top right). The arched structural members of the model help to show the relationship of the exhibition to the host building and the relative position of the largest exhibits. Daylight studies show the movement of sunlight as it changes throughout the day

(opposite, centre). Exhibits that are likely to be affected by harmful UV rays can be grouped in areas not affected by daylight. After the design is refined, a CAD rendering shows the design with materials applied and human figures (opposite, bottom left). A photograph of the finished project (opposite, bottom right).

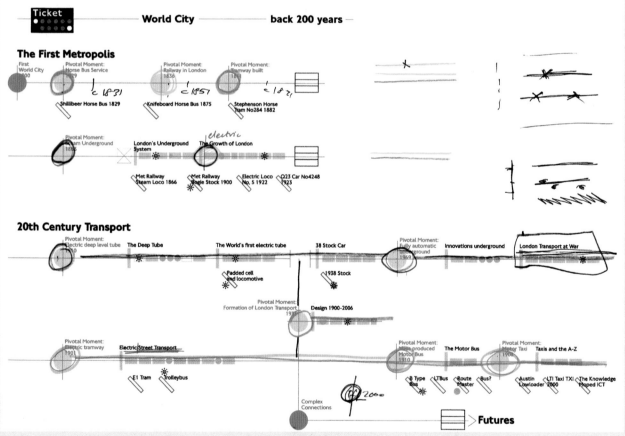

Above and top
Initially the visitor journey is mapped out in an overview diagram and detail sketches.

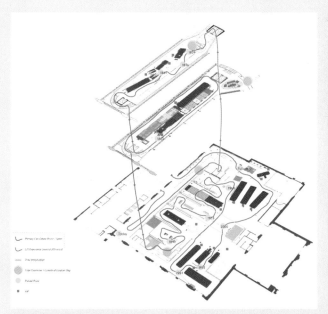

Above left and above
An axonometric diagram and a three-dimensional model show how the exhibition fits into the existing structure.

Left
Computer image showing daylight studies.

Below
Photographs of the completed exhibition space.

they ate on their journey), ornithology (the birds that followed the same migratory paths), human biology (how they used nature to survive), decorative arts (their paintings, drawings and body art) and geology (the siting of the first settlements on volcanic material). Narrative ordering of material can be chronological (following events in time), although it need not be. Stories can be told backwards, for example, or through dramatic episodes that lead the visitors to make narrative connections. This cross-disciplinary approach is perceived to be more visitor-friendly as it uses the intuitive mechanism of a story to order experiences rather than the more abstract division of material suggested by the departmental boundaries of curators. It also opens up the potential for interpretation through a variety of media rather than just a collection of things—once you have described the content as a story, then it feels natural to use a variety of storytelling media (film, sound, tactility, etc.). In addition, the narrative approach offers the opportunity to create chapters of

Natural History Museum of Utah, Ralph Appelbaum Associates, Salt Lake City, Utah, USA, 2011. This huge showcase gives the visitor an early glimpse of this museum's varied and rich collections housed in surrounding galleries.

create chapters of the story that match the physical envelope of the exhibition, thereby facilitating a collaborative relationship between exhibition designer and content developer.

In 1996, the Dutch design consultancy Opera was given a rare opportunity when it was commissioned to work with the entire collection of the National Museum of Ethnology in Leiden, the Netherlands, and redesign all its internal displays. Opera used a continuous internal wall "like a ribbon" to visually connect all the displays over a number of floors. The ribbon represented a journey around the world, and acted as a navigational tool for visitors as well as being an important unifying design element. This solution thus combined physical factors (the internal wall used as a navigational device) with a narrative device ("journey around the world") to organize both content and physical space-making.

How to survey a site

The purpose of a survey is to record the size, structure, details and visual appearance of a site so that accurate drawings can be prepared to scale. These are used as a basis for the redesign and planning of interior space. Site surveys are often carried out by surveyors, using extremely accurate equipment. However, it is useful to know how to survey a site without electronic aids, particularly when designing small, temporary exhibitions.

Site surveys are best done by two people, one to measure and the other to note down the measurements.

Equipment
Cameras; pens; pencils; A3 paper pads (tracing/detail or graph); clipboards; scale rules; extending steel measuring tapes (approx. 8 m/26 ft); 100 m (328 ft) tape; 2 m (6½ ft) folding measuring rod.

The survey
- Photograph the whole site. The best way is to take photographs in a long sequence, so that when you get back to the studio you can knit them together and create a collage that shows all the wall surfaces. Additional wide-angle shots will help you remember the layout of spaces. Don't take photographs at random; you may find it impossible to remember how the images relate to the site.
- Take photographs of mains boxes, air-conditioning units and floor sockets to remind you of the services available.
- Even if you have good CAD drawings it is essential to check their accuracy. If there are no drawings you will have to do a full site survey by drawing and measuring the space.

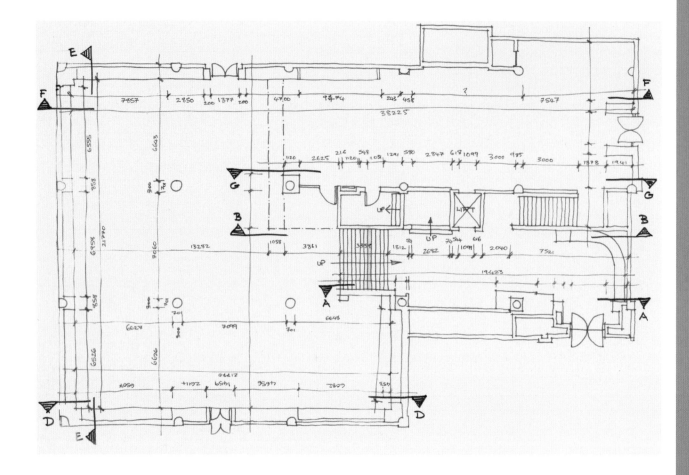

In the studio

- Draw a plan of the whole space.
- Draw all the walls/elevations, one by one, with all the doors, fire equipment, air-conditioning and wall-mounted sockets marked.
- Draw section lines on the plan. On separate sheets draw the wall elevations that correspond to the section lines.
- Take overall measurements of the space at a number of places and draw them on the plan.
- Measure the elements that make up a whole wall length and put them on the plan. If the measurements don't add up, check them and work out where the discrepancy lies.
- By taking measurements diagonally across corners you will be able to work out whether a room is square. If the diagonal measurements are not roughly equal, you will have to do additional measurements to calculate the angles of the walls.
- When you have measured the major elements on the site, start to work on the details. Record additional details at a larger scale on separate sheets and note their location on the plan.

Above and opposite

These drawings show how a site survey can be sketched out on an A3 size sketch pad. Note that the plan (above) shows the overall organization of the space. The wall elevations (opposite) correspond to the sections marked on the plan: A–A, B–B, etc. It is useful to take photographs of all of these views in the existing building so that when drawing individual elements, the designer can check visually whether the drawings seem correct.

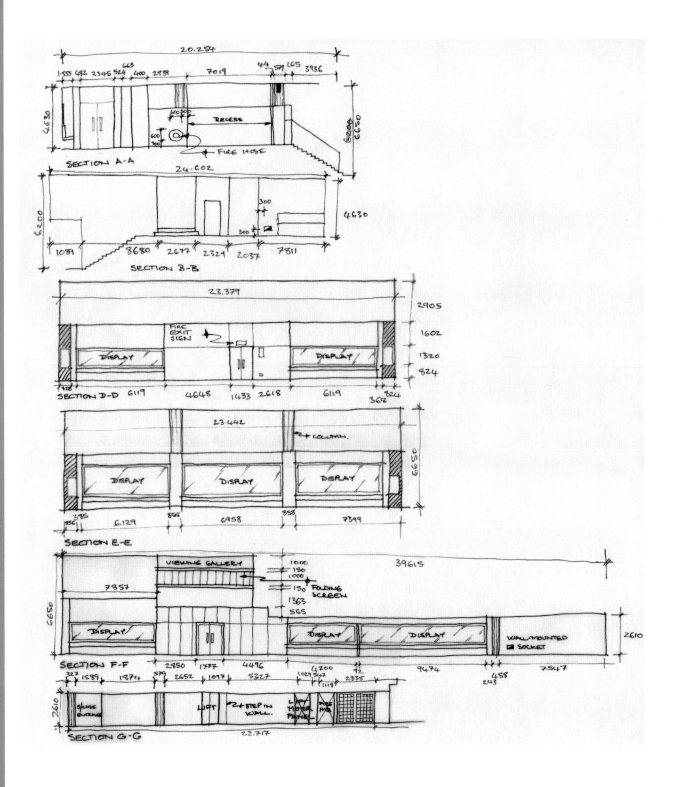

- Take care to mark all the wall- and floor-mounted sockets on all plans and elevations. If you are intending to build free-standing units that need power, you will have to work out carefully where the power will come from. Ensure that cables won't run along the floors where they will create a hazard.
- When you get back to the studio use the top of a drawing board to make a long sequential collage of all the data. Then transfer the data into your computer or on to your drawing board.

DO...

- Thoroughly investigate the spaces you are designing for by taking photographs, drawing and measuring.
- Measure loading bays and delivery doors to determine a maximum size for exhibits and display devices that will be taken through them into the display area.
- Analyze and develop exhibition content to see how it might best work within the physical constraints of the exhibition area.
- Determine which walls and internal structures can be moved to facilitate displaying the exhibits.
- Examine the route from the building entrance to the exhibition space.

DON'T...

- Install ramps or steps that deter wheelchair users.
- Deter visitors through poor signposting.
- Place fragile exhibits that are affected by ultraviolet rays and high light levels in galleries lit by daylight.
- Forget to consider the effect of daylight on the mood of the exhibition.

4.

This chapter shows how an exhibition strategy evolves, based on the initial brief and formulated by the client and designer. It describes how exhibits can be classified, the ways in which they can be viewed by the public, and the importance of creating experiences, rather than traditional displays, for visitors.

What is an exhibition strategy?

Every exhibition begins with a premise or rationale. This may be very simple, such as "Things I have collected recently" or "Our products", but in most cases it is a complex story supported by scrupulous research. The premise should explain the background to the exhibition and provide a reason for including some objects and excluding others. Along with the other briefing information, such as the storyline, context document and visitor profile, etc. (see chapter 1), it forms the basis for an exhibition strategy. While the brief is nearly always authored by the client, the exhibition strategy is formulated jointly by client and designer.

The exhibition strategy determines how the premise will be played out in detail in a given space or location. As such, it requires consideration of a whole range of factors, including the content of the show, how exhibits are divided or classified and how to engage visitors with the displays. There may be some key determinants that need initial consideration; perhaps the nature of the site, the nature and size of the exhibits or the need to attract particular audiences, but an exhibition is mostly a compromise between a number of factors. The exhibition strategy always responds to access and sustainability issues, and must respond to a given budget. It is not the design per se, but an approach to the design. It can often be best described through images showing the types of activities and moods the designer wishes to create, without too much detailed design information.

Classifying the exhibits

The drafting of an exhibition brief often involves deciding how to classify the exhibits. There are innumerable ways of doing this—chronologically, alphabetically, by subject, by theme, etc—just as there are for arranging books on a shelf. The designer has to consider the coherence of the classification and how it will impact on the visitor experience. For historical displays, classifying exhibits by time period is the most common, from the oldest artefacts to the most recent. This kind of schema is intuitive and easily understood by the majority of visitors, with little explanation needed. On the other hand, product displays are usually thematic, classified by generic type, so an exhibition of electronic goods is divided into cameras, phones and televisions. The choice that is made is often based on assumptions about the visitors to the exhibition and which categories they will best connect with. Exhibitors differ in their classifications; in most museum exhibitions the content is divided into a number of chapters. Though opinions vary as to the total number of these, most concur that more than seven discrete areas in an exhibition would confuse the majority of visitors. Sometimes the classification system is affected by where the exhibits are displayed; if an exhibition is housed in four rooms it would be difficult to divide its content into three subcategories.

Exhibits can also be classified in a mixture of ways, so an overall historical exhibition may initially be divided into time periods—for example,1700–1800, 1800–1900, 1900–2000—and then into thematic subdivisions such as clothes, furniture, art, etc. All classificatory systems are necessarily arbitrary, and there are bound to be displays that do not fit neatly into categories. Given the above time periods, if particular types of clothing were worn between, say, 1850 and 1950, it would be difficult to determine in which one they should properly be displayed without inventing a series of subrules. Visitors are often less concerned with the exactitude of a classification and are looking for a snapshot of a historical period based on scholarship rather than detailed definitive information. Some exhibitions are not divided into discrete categories; instead, ideas are communicated by juxtaposing the exhibits.

Devising a path

Devising how exhibits are viewed sequentially in a space is a major part of the designer's task. Approaches differ: some exhibitions offer visitors a very open exploration of exhibits and some are very prescriptive, forcing them to work their way along a predetermined path.

The single path

A single path ensures that all visitors have similar experiences and allows the exhibitor to plan their approach to them in detail, so that they encounter a succession of exhibits in a preconceived fashion. This may be important where the objective is to build a platform of knowledge in the visitor's mind. For example, if a museum is creating a science exhibition it might decide to show explanatory material at the start of the path to introduce visitors to scientific ideas. Later exhibits will be better understood once a basic understanding has been established. This process of introduction and preparation is called "scaffolding". The same technique is employed by trade shows. For example, before they see any of the exhibits visitors might be ushered into a cinema to watch a film which would immerse them in a series of inspirational stories intended to communicate the brand values of a particular company. If the film is effective, visitors are usually more receptive to the company's marketing and products, and altogether more suggestible.

It should be noted that the single path approach is not always a matter of choice: some exhibition buildings, particularly historic ones, are simply too small to allow for individual exploration. Single path displays often involve visitor management problems and "dwell time" needs to be strictly managed.

Single path

The multiple path

A multiple path exhibition causes fewer traffic management problems as visitors can select alternative exhibits to engage with when a particular display is busy. This approach also allows for greater freedom, and provides visitors with the possibility of following their own interests and preoccupations. Multiple path exhibitions nevertheless require signposting and orientation information; although visitors follow self-determined paths they still need to know where they are within the overall schema of the exhibition and its environment. In a museum, multiple paths provide a wide range of themed visits. Designers often devise alternative routes through displays, and guided groups, interested in different subjects, can take separate paths. For example, in a museum of natural history, there might be a choice between tours of, say, animals, plants and human biology.

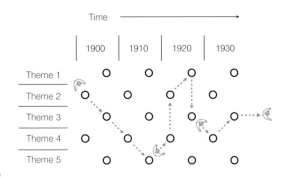

Multiple path

The radial pattern

The radial pattern was devised by the nineteenth-century English museologist and explorer Henry Pitt Rivers, but was never implemented. In the 1960s, the scheme was revived and new proposals were produced for the Pitt Rivers Museum in Oxford, England but, again, it was never put into practice. Pitt Rivers envisaged a display of Paleolithic artefacts in the centre of a series of concentric circles each devoted to objects from a subsequent era— Palaeolithic, Neolithic, Bronze Age and so forth—up to the present day. By walking along paths from the centre visitors would be able to see how a series of artefacts had evolved, and could trace the history of specific objects. The circles would have increased in circumference with an increasing diversity of artefacts in the outermost displays. The radial pattern was the forerunner of the visitor journey, often used in museum exhibitions to represent the world in microcosm.

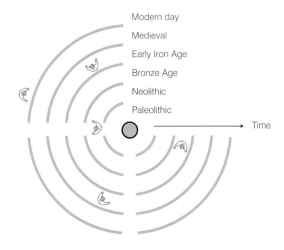

Radial pattern

"Star" exhibits

Exhibitions can be arranged predominantly around outstanding objects when the exhibitor wishes to engage visitors with "star" exhibits before drawing their attention to less immediately striking ones. This type of display is important when other classification systems might entail a dull visitor experience. The Victoria & Albert Museum took this approach when it redesigned its British Galleries in the late 1990s. Before this reworking, artefacts had been classified in a variety of ways, none of which, in the opinion of the museum, engaged visitors sufficiently. The displays were redesigned to maximize visitor enjoyment and to highlight the most dramatic and exciting examples in the collection. Star exhibits have

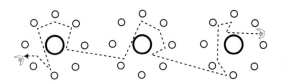

"Star" exhibit

a dual role: they enliven the areas around them, and also tend to draw visitors through a gallery and create a sense of expectation throughout the journey.

Areas of affinity

As it is usually difficult to make absolute classificatory distinctions, some exhibitors create "areas of affinity", placing exhibits as near as possible to similar artefacts. This approach has its own logical problems and demands that exhibitors make subtle judgements about how close one object should be to another. However, it does allow visitors to make immediate visual connections between exhibits, compare them directly and follow a thread of exploration from one artefact to another. This system was used very subtly by René d'Harnoncourt at the Museum of Modern Art in New York for "Arts of the South Seas", to show the distinctiveness of artworks from different Polynesian islands. Individual areas of affinity were divided with walls, and gaps in the walls created vistas through the exhibition that allowed visitors to make cross-comparisons between discrete but related displays.

The fan pattern

The fan pattern is usually favoured for business-to-business trade fairs. This allows visitors to take in immediately all that is on display at a show, and works very well for anyone who has little time and wants to see a particular stand without delay. Trade fair customers have less interest than exhibition visitors in lengthy "experiences"—this applies especially when small businesses are involved—and need to move quickly and directly to their area of choice. For them, a stand with everything on display visible as they approach it is often preferable. It is important to orientate trade fair stands towards their busiest approaches.

Map orientation

An interactive map is often the hub of an exhibition. Visitors can consult it and follow the route through the show that it suggests. If they wish to find out more about the subject of the exhibition, they can go back to the map to find new ways of exploring the displays.

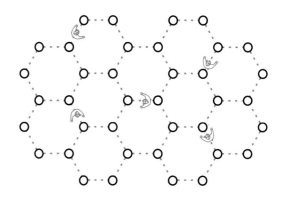

Areas of affinity

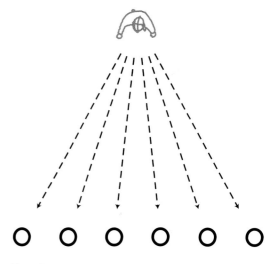

Fan pattern

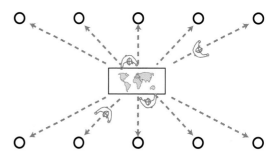

Map orientation

The importance of experiences

Modern designers stress that exhibitions are concerned with creating experiences rather than displays in a traditional sense. This distinction is important because it moves the boundary of the design task from physical display—the mounting of objects for visitors to see from a safe distance—to the more demanding task of altering and engaging the visitor's perception of the exhibition subject. Increasingly, designers are concerned with creating galvanizing and transformative events that provide memorable impressions. This often involves the new staples of art and design practice: film, multimedia and interaction.

DO...

- Investigate the premise for the exhibition.
- Construct an interpretive strategy to bring the premise to life.
- Create a storyline that can be divided into chapters to suit the exhibition space.

DON'T...

- Start the design until the premise is settled.
- Allow the design to deviate from an agreed strategy.
- Create strategies that are too complicated for visitors to understand.

5.

This chapter describes how the ideas that determine the overall concept of an exhibition are generated to evolve an exhibition strategy, and how sketches, models and computer visuals are then used to develop the final design plan. Important considerations during this process are how visitors will move through the exhibition, and how their experience of displays can be improved by the dynamic use of heights.

Generating guiding ideas

As with any design project, it is important to develop guiding ideas that respond to the brief. Once they are formulated, the designer will have a rationale to support his or her design proposals and be able to show the client, through models, drawings and computer visuals, how they will be implemented. The ideas will link the storyline, audience and site context, and will be the basis for the design approach to every aspect of the exhibition

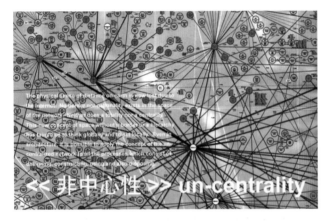

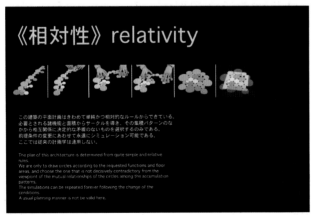

Tomihiro Art Museum, aat+ makoto yokomizo, Architects Inc., Azuma Village, Japan. Three boards are used to describe the architects' approach to the design of this museum dedicated to the work of the artist Tomihiro Hoshino. Each concept board and principle helps to describe how the solution was arrived at. The clear communication of the principles helps the designers and the clients to unite around a series of agreed ideas.

from external advertising to construction details. Once they have been accepted by the clients, they will form part of a shared understanding that helps the individuals involved in the project to work together in pursuit of a common goal.

It is perfectly true that many design schemes with very little conceptual content are put forward and accepted. It is very easy to spot them—they are dull and repetitive. The very best ones are packed with interesting ideas about learning, interaction, lighting, materials and design. Ideas for exhibitions come from a huge range of sources, not all of which are directly related to art and design. However, there are some standard ways to find inspiration:

- Researching previous examples, known as precedents, helps the designer to understand current developments in exhibition design. Precedents are taken from magazines or books and are carefully sifted before being presented, sometimes mounted on boards, as part of the analysis of the brief and to show the client that relevant approaches have been considered.
- Where the client is a commercial entity, designers try to discover as much as they can about the customer's experience. Most clients collect information about how their brand is perceived and often have clear goals for improving brand perception. Designers will also usually do their own research, by attempting to document and research typical encounters with a brand, often using photography, interviews and image research.
- Mindmapping exercises or brainstorms draw out ideas about a brief very quickly. Mindmaps are usually created by a group of designers in short intensive sessions, and are a time-efficient way to obtain a number of perspectives on the brief. It is important for all participants to express their ideas and thoughts quickly without censoring them—everyone says the first thing that comes into their minds and concepts are developed through word association.
- Ideas are developed through observation and experience. Designers are enriched by inspirational events and places, which can be recorded through drawing, photography and video. Exhibition design is very much a synthesis of related disciplines and designers are frequently influenced by, for example, art practice, theatre design, architecture, product design and production design for films.
- Every exhibition has a basic thesis or storyline which the designer needs to research with the aim of translating it into displays visitors can engage with. Too much research can be a handicap as the more the designer learns about the subject of the exhibition, the less he or she is able to empathize with visitors who are encountering it for the first time. However, it is necessary to understand the theme of the exhibition well enough to work with the storyline.
- The guiding ideas for a design can be written in a design rationale, but they are more often set out on a series of illustrated boards, with key words or brief annotations.

Evolving a design

When all the preparatory work is complete, the designer will start to develop a design for the exhibition (see chapter 4) that addresses the intended audience, works with the exhibits and can be delivered for the available budget.

The approach for exhibitions of contemporary art will be very different to that for other types of show, such as those concerned with history or science, or trade fairs. The nature of the exhibition and many of the display methods will already be determined by the choice of artists and by curatorial direction. In this case, the designer has a more discreet role as an enabler and facilitator whose judgements are made in cooperation with the curator and artists. There has to be a clear understanding that the artists', and not the designer's, work is paramount, though individual artists will have to compromise for reasons of space or the phrasing of the show. Living artists, like living playwrights, like to have a hand in the staging of their work. However, if an artist is dead, curators and exhibition designers—much like theatre directors and production designers—have a greater say in the interpretation of his or her work for new audiences.

Outside the world of art, designers have more scope to fashion the content of an exhibition. Modern exhibition design tends to be interventionist and is fully alive to the possibilities of sound, film, texture and smell. Like art, design has a great many new tools at its disposal, and the best exhibitions use these tools to create experiences that communicate on an emotional as well as intellectual level. Stephen Greenberg of exhibition designers Metaphor (formerly DEGW) has described this as being similar to a three-dimensional movie, in which the audience participates actively, that uses sound, light, film and other media to convey a story through a process that is part drama, part scenography. These new methods open up new possibilities for storytelling in which the exhibition environment is reconceived as a narrative with a number of parts in which the drama of the story is relived by the visitor. Every aspect of the exhibition is then interpreted in the light of this narrative, using materials, lighting, film, physical layout, graphics and a range of other media to reinforce the storyline. To achieve this complex mix, the designer needs to work with other creative professionals and technicians to achieve a seamless experience in which all the elements combine to reinforce the same message.

For many designers, interaction is the key to a good exhibition. A proportion of the visiting public is not content to look at displays and admire them through a thick layer of glass. Children in particular, but many adults as well, like to interact with exhibits. Many visitors, after all, would prefer to "fly" a plane on a simulator rather than simply admire the buttons and levers in a purely static display.

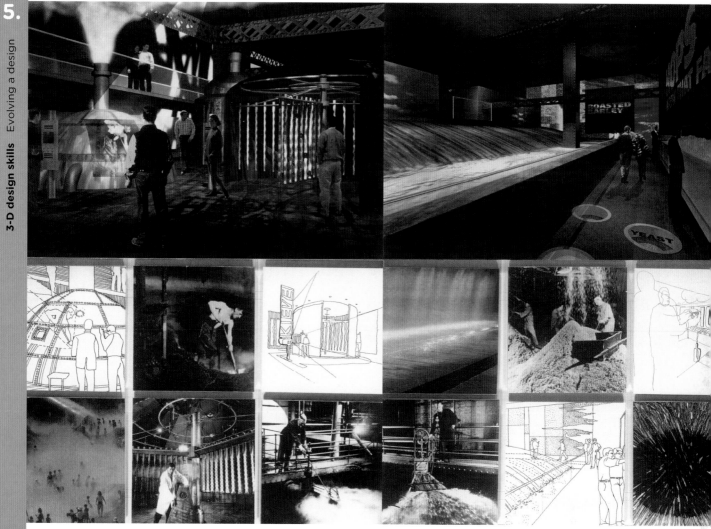

Guinness Storehouse, Imagination, Dublin, Ireland. These moodboards show images chosen by the designers as key inspirations for the design. Some of the images relate directly to the storyline, while others are purely experiential, intending to convey the kind of experience the designers are aiming for.

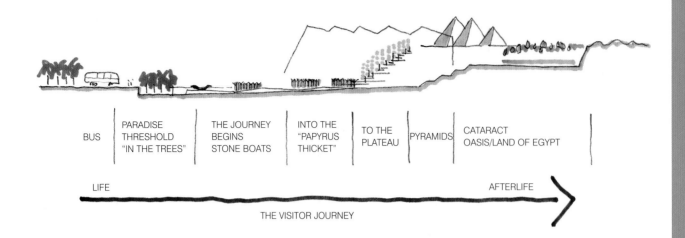

| BUS | PARADISE THRESHOLD "IN THE TREES" | THE JOURNEY BEGINS STONE BOATS | INTO THE "PAPYRUS THICKET" | TO THE PLATEAU | PYRAMIDS | CATARACT OASIS/LAND OF EGYPT | |

LIFE   AFTERLIFE

THE VISITOR JOURNEY

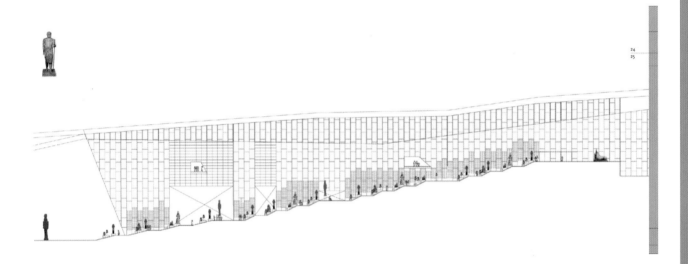

Grand Egyptian Museum, exhibition design by Metaphor, Cairo, Egypt.
The museum is situated near the Great Pyramids of Giza. The museum
building, by Heneghan Peng Architects, is organized as a "running stair"
design inclined towards the pyramids. The exhibition design, by Metaphor,
organizes the displays along a single timeline covering more than 3,500
years, with the most recent exhibits at the base of the incline. The visitor
walks up the running stair in the direction of the pyramids, encountering each
subsequent period and ending at the oldest exhibits of the prehistoric era.

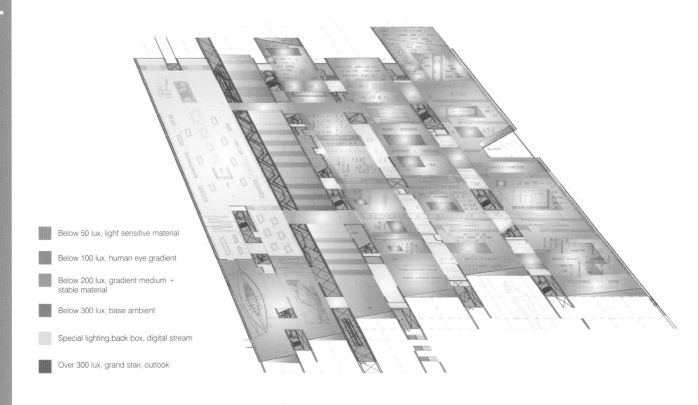

Below 50 lux, light sensitive material

Below 100 lux, human eye gradient

Below 200 lux, gradient medium +
stable material

Below 300 lux, base ambient

Special lighting, back box, digital stream

Over 300 lux, grand stair, outlook

Developing the design using sketches, models and plans

Once an exhibition strategy has been decided on, most designers start to develop their designs using scale models, sketches and rough drawings of layouts. If the exhibits are listed it is useful to draw all of them to scale and put them on the plan, which should have been checked against a survey of the site. Where key exhibits fit only into certain spaces, it is useful to position them first and compare their size with that of the other exhibits in the overall plan. At this stage, it is important to be aware of all obstructions and height restrictions in the exhibition space. The next phase is drawing and modelling, to create and test three-dimensional solutions. Some designers make rough conceptual models with a sculptural bias that help to inform the design concept. The models are preparatory exercises, which free up the designer's thinking and help him or her to intervene in a space without being too hidebound by its existing structure. Spatial ideas are continually developed through a series of sketched plans, and sketches and models; these are quite rough to start with, but are gradually refined until they are workable documents that can be discussed with the client and other project workers.

Grand Egyptian Museum, Cairo, Egypt. This site diagram shows light levels in the display areas. The diagram is instrumental in helping curators and designers to place light-sensitive exhibits within the display area.

Great North Museum, Newcastle upon Tyne, UK.
Design: Casson Mann

This museum combines a varied collection that incorporates natural history, antiquities and decorative arts. The natural history displays shown here are ingeniously organized using stacked display containers. The animals in this display seem to be playing in and among the containers, mimicking their behaviour in the wild. Contextual graphics and interactives complete the interpretive design.

Below left Gallery plan showing arrangement of specimens

Bottom left Section showing vertical arrangement of specimens.

Below Display containers communicate the habitats of different species.

Section A-A

In-depth displays within the rear of the display containers including:

- Habitat
- Survival
- Feeding habits
- Adapting to environments
- Camouflage
- Skeletons and bio-mechanics

Investigation including:

- Investigation drawers
- Images and film
- Microscope investigations
- Live animal exhibits
- Boxed alcoves for visitors to enter
- Closed box with a peephole

Predators roam the spaces between the display containers

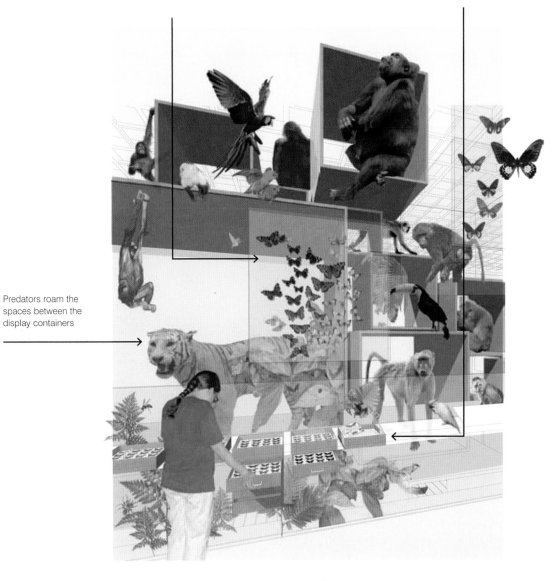

Rear view of the Diversity of Life gallery from the first floor balcony

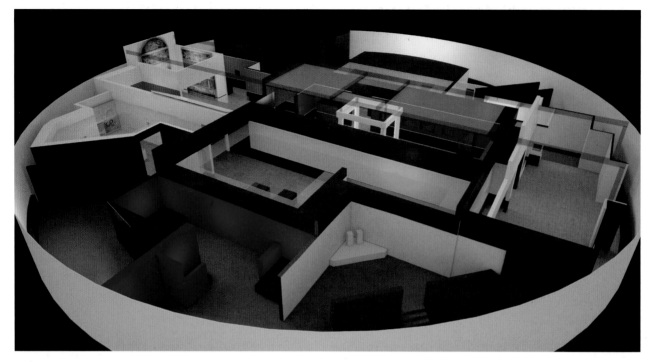

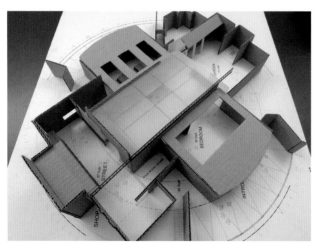

"Pompeii & Herculaneum", the British Museum, Land Design Studio, London, UK, 2013. (Clockwise from top) CAD layout of the space clearly communicates visitor experience and materiality of proposed design; photograph of completed exhibition; cardboard model constructed on CAD layout of exhibition; CAD wall elevations are mounted onto foamboard to give an impression of the visitor experience.

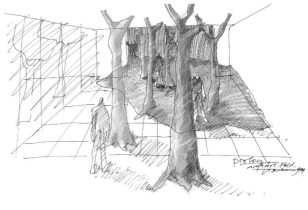

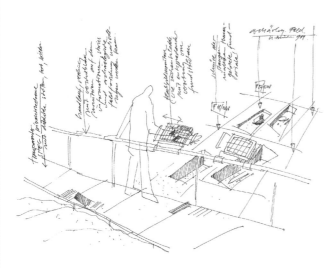

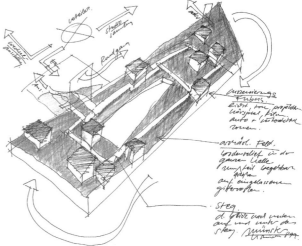

During the early stages of the project it is important to show ideas quickly and intuitively to clients and collaborators without going too far down the wrong track. Models are the preferred method of most schools of architecture and design, because they allow students to explore three-dimensional solutions quickly and can be turned around in the hand to be analyzed from multiple viewpoints. They tend to create design solutions that are truly three-dimensional, as any intervention can be judged in plan as well as elevation. Scale human figures glued into models help the designer to appreciate how individual visitors will experience the exhibition. Individual interactions with single exhibits are best developed through sketches; these can provide a great deal of detail and can be annotated to show the client that a number of factors have been considered. Models and computer visuals should always be produced in such a way so as to communicate the experience from the visitor's viewpoint. Eye-level drawings and models that can be peered into are helpful for anyone who wishes to examine a scheme.

Top left and right

Westphalian State Museum of Archaeology, Atelier Brückner, Herne, Germany, 2003. The prologue to this display of archaeological artefacts is the "Forest of History". The trees, dating back 5,000 to 14,000 years, are described by Uwe Brückner as "silent witnesses" to our archaeological history and set the scene for a walk back into Westphalian history. A final photograph and sketch by Uwe Brückner are illustrated here.

Above left and right

Westphalian State Museum of Archaeology. Brückner organized the display along chronological lines. Thematic content was picked out at various stages through a number of "theme cubes" that convey time-spanning themes. The sketch on the left shows the intuitive relationship of the visitor to the archaeological field and the exhibition content, while on the right an overview shows the "archaeological field" with the "archaeological path" and theme cubes.

Once the rough sketches and models have been made, the final plan will begin to take shape. The plan is very important in spatial design and shows all the elements involved in the exhibition. Their layout is crucial to a successful scheme and governs a host of factors including visitor navigation, how the exhibits relate to each other, the ease and comfort of visitor circulation, the duration of the exhibition and the ease with which fire exits can be found. The layout is amended regularly in most museum and gallery projects, through discussion with the client, health and safety officers, access specialists and fire officers. It is often possible to make small amendments to the plan without changing the look and feel of the whole design. However, if there are major amendments the designer may have to start again from the beginning and reconfigure the whole scheme. It is his or her responsibility to ensure that the final result, despite any compromises, is a harmonious and ergonomically successful whole.

"Water: A Unique Resource", Expo Zaragoza, Ralph Appelbaum Associates, Zaragoza, Spain, 2008. This Pavilion was both a pedestrian footbridge and an exhibition pavilion.

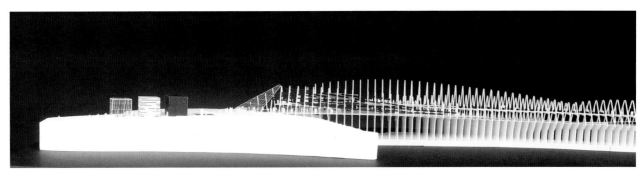

Top
Photo of model showing view of pavilion from the river.

Middle
Photo of model shows pavilion approach.

Lower
Photo of model shows integration of interpretive elements within architectural envelope.

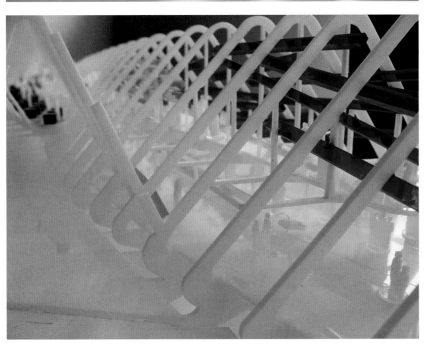

Churchill Museum, London, UK
Design: Casson Mann

This project was very constrained by a grid of heavy structural steelwork which limited the size of the displays and the width of the aisles. All the disparate elements of the display were effectively tied together by a very consistent geometry throughout. Graphics, artefacts and multimedia displays were integrated into a series of waist-level counters which depicted parts of Winston Churchill's life. Each counter was clad with a material that communicated an aspect of the statesman's life. For example, a "Chartwell Chintz" patterned laminate, which referred to Churchill's childhood home, was used for the counter that showed his early life, while the "War Years" plinth was clad with an aluminium that referenced a World War II fighter plane.

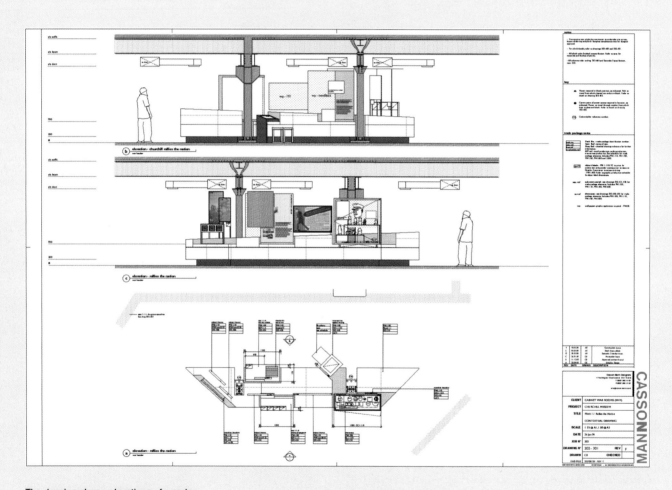

The drawing shows elevations of a series of exhibits. These drawings are essential to communicate the detail of exhibit display to contractors and co-workers.

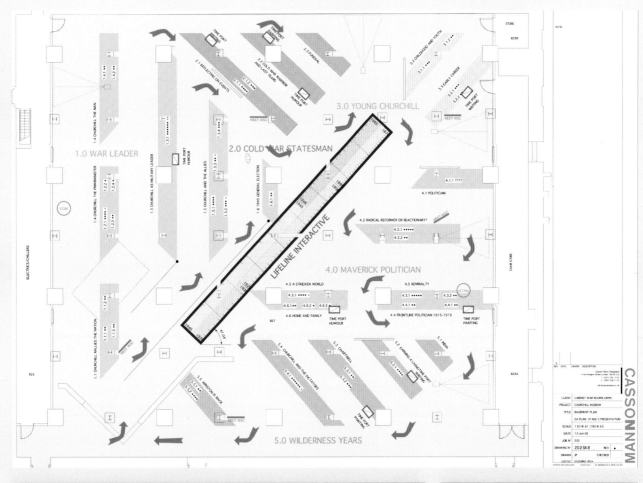

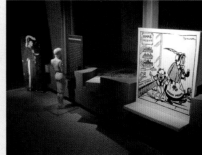

Top
An early overall layout made to outline the size of the display area, the circulation and the general organization of exhibits.

Left and above
Model of the waist-high display structure (above) and photograph of the completed exhibition (left).

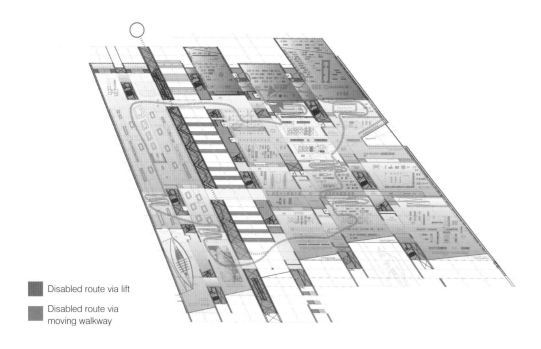

■ Disabled route via lift

■ Disabled route via
moving walkway

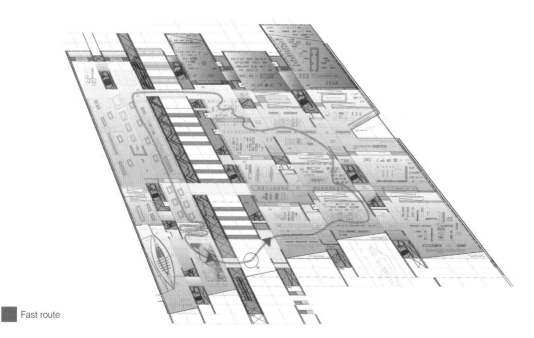

■ Fast route

Grand Egyptian Museum, exhibition design
by Metaphor, Cairo, Egypt. The top image
shows how the exhibition designers devised
routes through the exhibits for disabled users.
The pink route is via an elevator, and the
blue route is via a moving walkway. The
bottom image shows a fast route through
the major exhibits.

5.

Planning the circulation

Circulation planning enables the designer to determine what experiences visitors will have and the sequence in which they have them. Its quality has a major impact on visitor satisfaction and has to be carefully scrutinized. Many institutions rely on large numbers of visitors on public holidays and require sufficient circulation space to accommodate crowds on these days, even if they are relatively empty at other times. Coach parties arriving simultaneously at an exhibition also cause temporary peaks in visitor numbers.

It is often possible to plan a number of timed routes that can be tailored for particular groups. Separate paths through a display help to prevent too many visitors being in one area at the same time, while allowing museum staff to show different aspects of the display. The priorities are:

* Make sure large parties don't go through a display at the same time.
* Ensure visitors remove hats and coats that will interfere with a display.
* Allow sufficient room near turnstiles and cloakrooms to accommodate large parties.
* Create separate routes through a display to prevent guided groups from running into each other.
* Avoid "pinchpoints" and blockages. A pinchpoint that is too narrow or a single blockage will cause visitors to back up. They can be held up by obstructions in any part of the site, including the car park and shop.
* Do tests to see how many individuals can move comfortably through the exhibition at one time. If necessary, a timed entry schedule can be used to ensure that safety standards are met and visitor numbers are controlled.
* Work out how many visitors can view a display at the same time. Look at individual visits and estimate how far back viewers will have to stand to see it. This can be worked out by positioning figures on a plan.

When planning circulation routes it is important to note where exhibits face each other on opposite sides of a path—visitors will stand back to view them and block the path down the middle. If interactive displays are planned, the designer should anticipate that for every child interacting with an exhibit, several others may be looking on to see what is happening. Space should be found to accommodate these onlookers. Museums and galleries that expect visits by school groups often have briefing rooms and classroom spaces where museum staff give health and safety talks and introduce the children to the displays they are about to see. Space may have to be created for this and factored into visitor-flow planning.

At crowded and popular "blockbuster" art exhibitions visitors tend to create a lengthy conga that shuffles from one exhibit to the next. When very large visitor numbers are expected, the designers has to think carefully about how the exhibits are positioned and try to give viewers with restricted space something to see on every part on the route. Frequently, designers are asked to summarize visitor journeys, estimating the time that an average visitor will

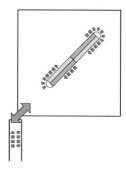

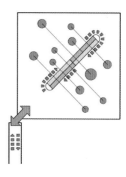

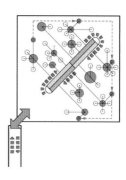

Churchill Museum, Casson Mann, London, UK. In the early proposal stages Casson Mann developed the idea of a clockwise circulation around a central interactive table reference area with separate islands around it. The top image shows the entrance to the museum and the desired direction of circulation around the exhibition and interactive lifeline table. The centre image explains the physical and intellectual relationship between the lifeline tables and the surrounding thematic display plinths. The bottom image shows possible alternative circulation routes as generated by the lifeline table and the thematic plinths.

spend in each area, known as "dwell-time". It is usually assumed that a museum experience will be approximately 1.5–2 hours and that the sum of all the individual dwell-times on the visitor route should add up to this figure.

Every circulation plan should anticipate the need for visitors to find toilets, buy things from the museum shop, and eat and drink in a comfortable and restful space with access to daylight. The width of the circulation routes should conform to local building regulations; most museums and galleries prefer at least 1.8 m (6 ft). To accommodate wheelchair users, a minimum of clearance of 1.2 m (4 ft) between obstructions is recommended.

Trade fairs

Displays for trade shows have to be very open to encourage visitors. Potential customers will avoid a stand if they have to jostle for space with the company's staff. Designers should aim to create 3 m (10 ft) between displays whenever possible, leaving lots of clear space. Trade exhibitors are prone to clutter their stands with too many exhibits, driving away potential customers. Open spaces with good circulation are an invitation to the user, and a clear signal that the stand is designed to accommodate the browser. Many exhibitors at trade fairs divide their stands into public, semi-public and private areas. While the semi-public areas can be compressed—visitors who are invited into them are happy to sit close to each other— the public ones at the front need to be widely spaced and inviting, with an easy means of escape. Visitors find small, enclosed spaces on stands forbidding, and often fear that a salesperson will trap them into an unwanted conversation or lengthy sales

Churchill Museum, Casson Mann, London, UK. This very long interactive table, called the "Lifeline", is activated by a pressure pad on its rim and allows visitors to access both general and detailed information about Churchill's life.

presentation. Many people prefer to browse before they express an interest in a product, and resent being persistently questioned by stand staff before they have had an opportunity to explore the display on their own. In this way, good exhibition stands are similar to well-designed shops: they provide opportunities for visitors to browse before they are approached by sales staff, with clear opportunities to escape if they have no interest in the products displayed. The better alternative to an enclosed display is usually an island installation with space around it on all sides that can be approached from any direction rather than a forbidding display wall that cuts off the visitors' exit. Very occasionally, some displays have the opposite effect and are too open. Although visitors like easy circulation, an empty space can be forbidding.

Developing elevations

Alongside the plan, designers usually work simultaneously on the elevation or height of the exhibition structure. Floor layouts that succeed in plan form are often less successful in elevation, so this aspect of the design may need to be developed: good schemes work in elevation as well as plan. Also, the heights of individual elements in an exhibition have to be carefully scrutinized to ensure that a range of visitors can access them adequately, including wheelchair users and children.

A number of factors are involved in developing successful elevations:

- The visitor experience can often be improved by the dynamic use of the height of exhibition spaces. Exhibits arranged along a single line with no deviation in height may appear too uniform.
- Large exhibits are navigational tools that help visitors to orientate themselves in complex environments. Careful placement of these can draw visitors from one area to the next.

Grand Egyptian Museum, exhibition design by Metaphor, Cairo, Egypt. The exhibition design uses very large "landmark" artefacts to signpost distinct areas of the display, with smaller displays placed around them. On the drawing, the designers have categorized artefacts by three scales: miniature, child size and gigantic.

Sonance exhibition stand Design: Pentagram

Pentagram Design was tasked with creating a range of marketing materials for Sonance, a company that sells concealed in-wall loudspeakers. After Pentagram created the corporate identity, the 3D designer Lorenzo Apicella designed an exhibition stand inspired by the logo. This series of sketches shows how the plan was evolved through sketches and computer renderings. The plan clearly shows how the public areas of the stand are generously spaced and leave plenty of room for the visitor to walk on the stand from the aisle. Exhibition stands have to fight for attention in a crowded environment and designers frequently build high to draw visitors' attention.

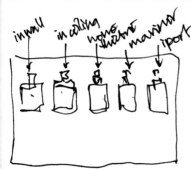

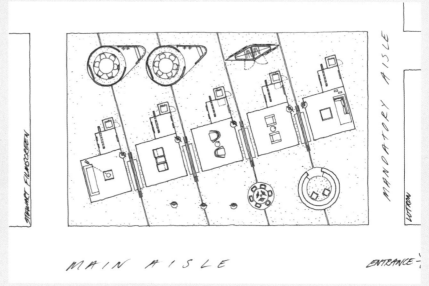

Above
This drawing shows how the plan was skewed on the rectangular site, as well as delineating the surrounding aisles and visitor approaches to the site.

Top
The Sonance logo, developed by Pentagram Design, was the inspiration behind the stand's three-dimensional design.

Above
A sketch shows how the designer of the three-dimensional aspect of the stand, Lorenzo Apicella, divided up the space into Sonance product areas, which are roughly represented by five blocks.

Right
Sketches show early designs for a meeting area with a sloping wall.

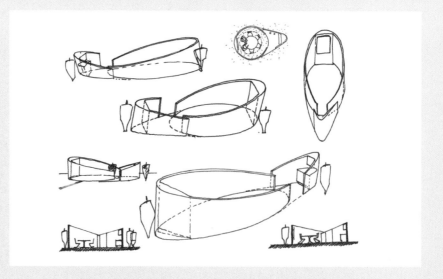

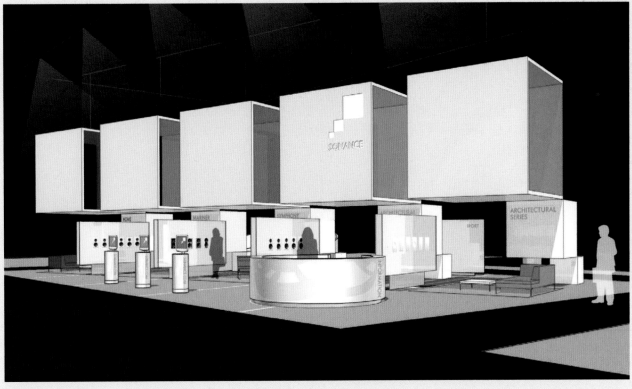

Above and below
A CAD visual block model rendered and refined in
Photoshop (above) and a photograph of the final stand (below).

- Designers often try to create an impression of orderliness and clarity through the use of consistent heights for plinths, display tables and signage. This enables visitors to read separate and diverse displays in the context of a common system. While it is often not desirable to create one height of display plinth to serve every objective, it is usually possible to cater for all artefacts through a handful of common elements of different heights.
- Visitors come in different heights and sizes. Displays have to accommodate these and must be designed so that all audience groups have equal access.

The direction of flow

As a rule, Western visitors follow the right-hand wall of an exhibition space, while studies suggest that in the Arabic-speaking countries of the Middle East visitors take the opposite route, and by instinct turn left when they enter a gallery. Other studies have shown that Japanese visitors usually occupy the centre of a room before following the exhibits around the space. This has an impact on the placement of exhibit labels and signage. For example, in Europe or America, if the designer wants viewers to see the label before they see a painting it has to be on the left side of the picture, and vice versa for a gallery in the Middle East.

DO...

- Generate guiding ideas through research, mindmapping and personal observation.
- Research and analyze relevant precedents.
- Refer to the exhibition strategy when you develop the plan.
- Use models, sketches and computer visuals to envisage how the scheme will work in practice.

DON'T...

- Leave too little room between display and create pinchpoints and queues.
- Consider your scheme purely from the standpoint of the plan or layout. All schemes should be considered three-dimensionally so that the elevations are as successful as the plan.
- Block fire exits and escape routes.
- Design displays that are inaccessible to people with disabilities.

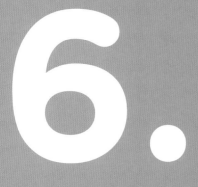

6.

Graphic design skills

This chapter explores how graphics play a key role in an exhibition, interpreting its theme and being a means of communicating visually with visitors. It provides information about the methods that can be used to reproduce them, and emphasizes the importance of readable, legible text that can be easily seen by the viewer.

The role of graphics in an exhibition

The graphics for an exhibition are an interpretation of its theme or storyline. They are an integral part of any show and are conceived in tandem with its three-dimensional design. Their role as part of the overall concept depends on a number of factors. Where budgets are low, or if there is an existing infrastructure of walls and partitions in the exhibition space, graphics tend to be the main element in the design process. For displays where all partitions and walls have to be built from scratch, their role tends to be smaller, though still significant. Graphics are a key part of the visual theatre of exhibitions and visitor communication. The appropriate treatment of text is essential to good exhibition design and, if mishandled, the most likely cause of difficulties for visitors.

Graphic designers who work for exhibitions are often also involved in other fields such as print or website design. Layout and typography skills learnt in one medium are transferable to exhibitions, though there are some obvious differences. Specialized large-format printers are used to reproduce exhibition graphics on a wide range of materials, which are different to those used for print, and which the installers—who have a jargon of their own—fix to existing and new walls using a number of methods that may be unfamiliar to non-specialists.

Directional signs to draw people into an exhibition are often called wayfinding graphics. These are intended to tease and entice visitors but they also serve the practical purpose of showing them where to go. Good wayfinding graphics direct visitors to the exhibition itself and help them to

This page and opposite top
"Stirling Wilford", Thomas Manss & Company, Royal Institute of British Architects, London, UK, 1996. Thomas Manss & Company used bright colours and cartoon-like drawings to make this architecture show accessible to a non-specialist audience. The common approach to invitations, posters, catalogues and structure helped to tie the disparate elements of the show together and present the visitor with a coherent single experience.

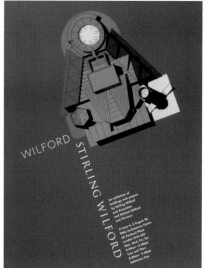

identify distinct spaces within it. It is important that the graphics can be read and understood from a distance and are sufficiently bold and noticeable to be seen in crowded areas. In many cases, graphic designers develop a hierarchy of signs of differing scales in a consistent style. The hierarchy includes large external signage, medium-sized area headings, subheadings and diminishes to object labels. The size and prominence of the text helps visitors to navigate through the exhibition and develop a map of its content.

Text for modern exhibitions is written and presented to connect with a diverse audience on an emotional as well as intellectual level, addressing different reading abilities, aptitudes and learning styles. The style is layered, allowing visitors to skim a top level of information when required, or to delve

Below
National Museum of Ethnology, Opera Design, Leiden, the Netherlands. The text on the wall is intended to lure visitors into the exhibition, though it is unlikely that the text would be read in its entirety by passersby.

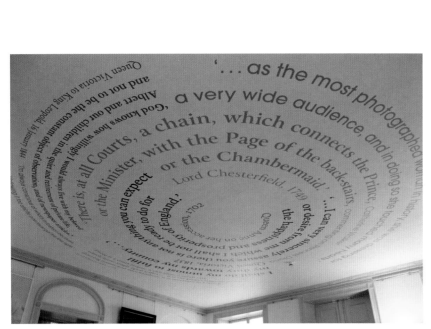

Kensington Palace, ACME Studio, Inc., London, UK, 2010. Screenprinted wall graphics invite visitors into this space.

deeper if they are seeking more knowledge. Typically, the text should work alongside other information cues and may be supported by sound clips, video projections and the scenographic treatment of the display.

Exhibitions, like illustrated books, are rarely "read" in a strictly linear fashion. For example, like readers, visitors may see a title and skim the contents until their attention is caught. Their behaviour can be unpredictable. They may read area or chapter headings after they have seen all the displays, and some go to the end of the exhibition to find out how it finishes before they inspect the first area closely. Typically, most visitors view a display before looking at a label or explanatory text, for the understandable reason that they are only interested if the display impresses them. Text is therefore conceived in the context of visitor behaviour, and it cannot be assumed that understanding of a display is informed by earlier labels or panel text.

Exhibitions thrive on publicity, and in the often short time they are open they have to create maximum public impact. Designers of all stripes agree that to be effective exhibition graphics, however imaginative or creative, should communicate a clear and consistent message through all media including banners, brochure design, websites and catalogues. This has many benefits, but at a basic level consistent use of imagery and text avoids confusion. For example, entrance signage that differs from an outdoor banner for the same show might easily mislead a potential visitor into thinking they were in the wrong exhibition. Graphic consistency helps to establish an exhibition in the mind of the visitor. According to graphic designers such as Thomas Manss, consistency does not mean dullness. Tricks, inventive layouts and vivid colours all have their place, as long as they are subordinate to a guiding idea that emanates from the designer's interpretation of the brief. Where the graphic content overwhelms the subject of the exhibition, or becomes noticeably divorced from the subject matter, the purpose of the exhibition is undermined.

Face of Fashion, National Gallery, London, UK
Design: Thomas Manss & Co.

The firm was approached by the National Gallery to design a book for the "Face of Fashion" exhibition at the National Gallery in London. The "Face of Fashion" logotype was first designed for the accompanying catalogue book and was subsequently used on posters, banners, invites and collateral such as make-up and badges. The consistent use of logotype and materials helps the visitor to gain a clear idea of the exhibition and its content.

Above
Exterior banners advertising the exhibition.

Below
Catalogue and cube-shaped invitation.

Above images
The exhibition's identity was extended to include carrier bags, press packs, books and badges.

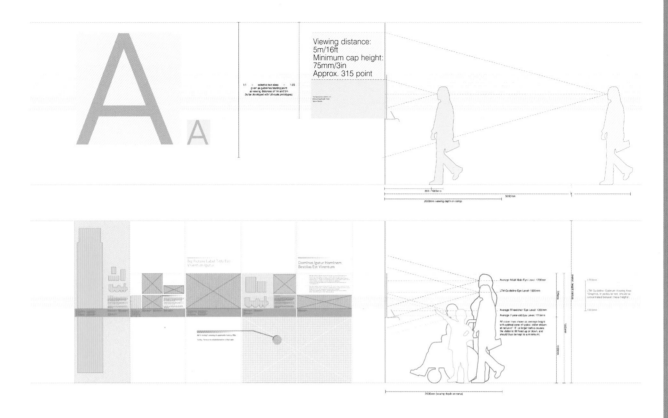

For graphic designers who generally work with printed documents, the main challenge posed by exhibition graphics is appreciation of scale. Print graphics are normally designed at a comprehensible scale and can easily be output through a normal printer, at A4 or A3, and carefully inspected for nuances in type size. Exhibition graphics, by contrast, are designed on scale drawings or elevations, typically of 1/10, 1/20 and 1/50. A line of type that looks tiny on a 1/50 scale drawing may look ridiculously large on a wall. It is also crucial to understand how far back viewers will be standing when they see the type. If they are trying to see it from a distance of, say, 20 m (65 ft), type that seems large when someone is close to it will be absurdly small. The golden rule, confirmed by numerous graphic designers, is to print the type at different sizes, put the printouts on a wall and use instinct to choose the size that is most appropriate. It is also important to read the architect's and designer's three-dimensional drawings for the exhibition space and visit the site to appreciate the graphic environment. Most graphic designers superimpose scale human figures on their drawings to demonstrate the relationship of any images or texts to the exhibition visitor.

Graphics diagram for London Transport Museum, Ralph Appelbaum Associates, London, UK. This diagram shows how designers use scale drawings with scale figures to determine the correct height of graphic panels. The height of graphic panels will be determined by the needs of the target audiences. In many cases this will be a compromise to suit as many visitors as possible without discriminating against disabled visitors.

Approaches to exhibition graphics

In many instances, the design of exhibition graphics is constrained by the client's "house style". Corporate clients tend to be wary of deviations from the strict brand interpretations outlined in their identity manual, and many marketing experts are steeped in the same culture. Where a house style is imposed, all exhibition text must use the corporate font and designers are often required to use standardized layouts and even predetermined corporate photography. Many major museums and all commercial clients take this approach. Their brand is a jealously guarded asset to be applied with consistency in any publication, website or exhibition. However, brand identity manuals rarely anticipate exhibitions and the creative task of translating the brand into a three-dimensional environment.

With a fixed typeface, logo and even suggested layouts there is a danger that the graphics could become dull and formulaic—less a creative enterprise than a layout task with no connection to the content of the exhibition. This dilemma has to be faced by the client as well as the designer. When there is constant pressure to create interest in a product or new service that is being launched at an exhibition, the typographical formulas from the brand manual, already familiar to the market, can seem staid and familiar. The challenge is therefore to create stimulating graphic work that enhances rather than dilutes the established brand equity.

Where there is no imposed house style, designers are free to use "contextual graphics" where typography, images and layout are in sympathy with the content of the exhibition. Using historical typefaces, colour combinations and substrates that have a relationship with the content, contextual graphics evoke the period of the exhibition, or least make reference to it. This approach is complex and the designer has to make a series of fine judgements about the appropriateness of the contextual references. Many exhibition subjects have powerful graphical associations. For example, period typefaces and layout styles might be used in exhibitions of Pop Art or Art Nouveau because both subjects have powerful and recognizable visual associations and typographical styles. These help the designer to use his or her skills to subtly evoke ideas in the minds of the visiting public.

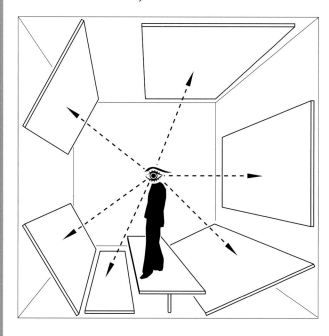

Herbert Bayer is the inspiration behind a great deal of modern exhibition design. His Extended Field of Vision diagram demonstrates the principle that graphic surfaces should be orientated towards the viewer for optimal effect.

House style graphics: London Transport Museum, London
Design: Ralph Appelbaum Associates

These final production drawings show the printing and material specifications for the graphic production company for the museum's labels, which were produced using Transport for London's own corporate font. Within this framework, the designer makes subtle use of colour, printing method and good layout to produce clear text panels.

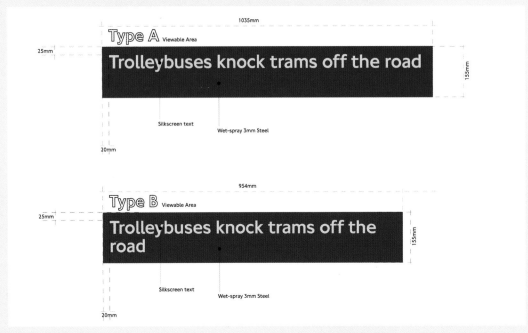

Above and below
Good layout and clear distinctions between header and body copy make labels easy to read. Well-written panel text allows visitors to skim a top layer of information and gain a sense of an exhibit by reading just titles and captions. If the visitor wants to learn more, they can read the longer explanatory texts below.

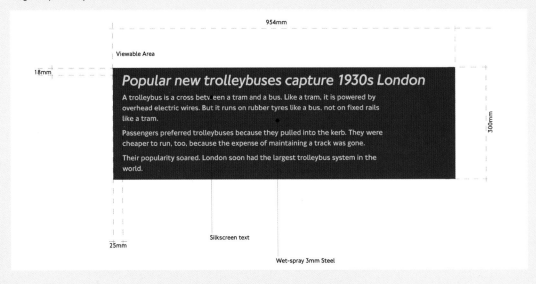

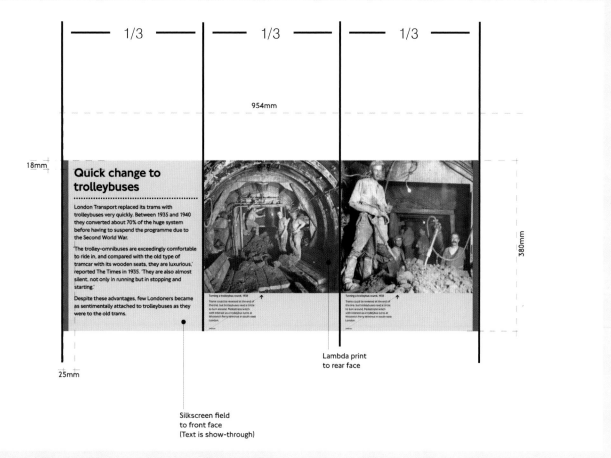

1/3   1/3   1/3

954mm

18mm

Quick change to trolleybuses

London Transport replaced its trams with
trolleybuses very quickly. Between 1935 and 1940
they converted about 70% of the huge system
before having to suspend the programme due to
the Second World War.

'The trolley-omnibuses are exceedingly comfortable
to ride in, and compared with the old type of
tramcar with its wooden seats, they are luxurious,'
reported The Times in 1935. 'They are also almost
silent, not only in running but in stopping and
starting.'

Despite these advantages, few Londoners became
as sentimentally attached to trolleybuses as they
were to the old trams.

380mm

Lambda print
to rear face

25mm

Silkscreen field
to front face
(Text is show-through)

Above
Designers use grids to give a sense of order and structure to graphic
panels. This panel grid divides the areas of the graphic into equal thirds.

Below
Accessibility experts recommend justifying text on the left only. The ragged
line on the right gives shape to the paragraph and helps the reader to locate
himself along the lines, making the panel easier to read.

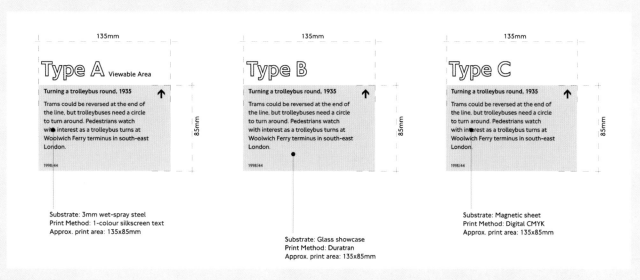

135mm   135mm   135mm

Type A Viewable Area

Turning a trolleybus round, 1935

Trams could be reversed at the end of
the line, but trolleybuses need a circle
to turn around. Pedestrians watch
with interest as a trolleybus turns at
Woolwich Ferry terminus in south-east
London.

1998/44

85mm

Type B

Turning a trolleybus round, 1935

Trams could be reversed at the end of
the line, but trolleybuses need a circle
to turn around. Pedestrians watch
with interest as a trolleybus turns at
Woolwich Ferry terminus in south-east
London.

1998/44

85mm

Type C

Turning a trolleybus round, 1935

Trams could be reversed at the end of
the line, but trolleybuses need a circle
to turn around. Pedestrians watch
with interest as a trolleybus turns at
Woolwich Ferry terminus in south-east
London.

1998/44

85mm

Substrate: 3mm wet-spray steel
Print Method: 1-colour silkscreen text
Approx. print area: 135x85mm

Substrate: Glass showcase
Print Method: Duratran
Approx. print area: 135x85mm

Substrate: Magnetic sheet
Print Method: Digital CMYK
Approx. print area: 135x85mm

Developing graphic installations

This series of images shows the development of a series
of graphic installations for the London Transport Museum.

Left
The initial concept of a gridded structure
with colour-coded graphics displayed at
different heights.

Below left
A detailed sketch showing a hierarchy of text,
header copy and body copy with illustrations.

Below
Elevation drawing showing experiments
with colour and tone.

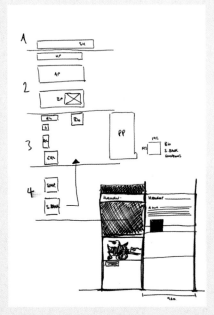

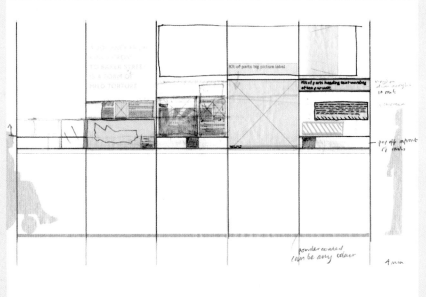

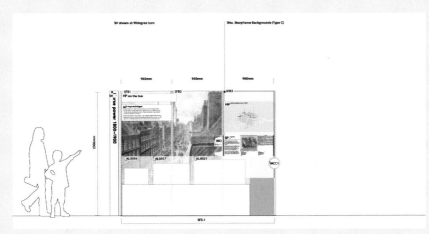

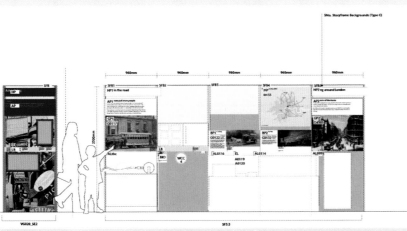

Left
In this elevation more colours and
developed illustrations are introduced
alongside scale figures and graphic
sizes indications.

Below left
Further developed panel ideas
with dimensions.

Below
Photograph of the completed design.

Churchill Museum, London, UK
Graphic design: Nick Bell Design;
Exhibition design: Casson Mann

This is an example of the contextual style discussed at the beginning of the chapter. The typefaces, colours, layouts and multimedia displays were chosen to evoke the Churchill period. There were three "voices" in the exhibition, a narrative voice, Churchill's own voice and a further voice that expressed the words of the generals and army staff who worked with Churchill. The Churchill "voice" was expressed in Clarendon, an English font that originated in 1845. The "voice" of generals and army staff was printed in a font called American Typewriter, while any other incidental text was expressed in Motorway, a sans-serif font used for road signage in postwar Britain.

The combination of static wall graphics and multimedia displays allowed the designers to create a very layered exhibition with many tiers of information. For example, handwritten notes with great historic value could be shown alongside typeset text, which would allow visually impaired visitors to see the content of the notes more clearly and with greater magnification. Nick Bell set out to evoke the atmosphere of a pre-digital age office, with its typewritten scripts and filing cabinets packed with information. All interactive elements of the show followed a style guide compiled by Bell to create consistency. In line with the spirit of the static wall graphics, Bell stipulated that all screen-

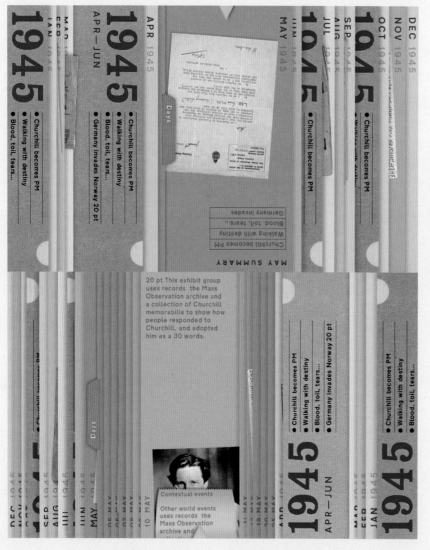

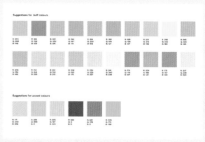

Left
Nick Bell was responsible for the overall graphic content, both static panels and interactive displays. This meant using consistent colours, layouts and typography, and an animation style that suited the content.

Above
Chart showing the colours to be used in the exhibition's multimedia displays.

based information should use the three typefaces as described, and restricted the multimedia designers to using very simple animation devices. As a result all presentations had to show pictures as if they were sitting on a desk in a wartime office, and all elaborate fades and "digital age" techniques were intentionally excluded. Movement on screens was restricted to the horizontal and the vertical, so images and text emerged perpendicular to the edge of the screen, and all diagonal movement of content was eradicated. These deliberate restrictions may not have been noticed by the general public, but are part of the stream of information that was imparted by the design subconsciously to the visitor.

The design gives an impression of richness and complexity with sufficient consistency to make the overall experience rewarding. The buff colour of the files and the green paper interleaved within the files evoked the display topic. The files were intentionally slightly disordered and were shown crammed with pieces of paper as a busy pre-digital age office might have been. The overstuffed appearance was also intended to communicate the fullness of Churchill's life and his extraordinary productiveness.

Below
Three typefaces were chosen to represent the three "voices" presented in the labeling. Quotations from Churchill himself are laid out in Clarendon (below left), quotations from his staff are in American Typewriter (below), and information labels in Motorway (bottom).

Adjust font sizes until
Both fonts are the
same Cap height

Churchill's quotes: Clarendon

I felt as if I were walking with destiny and that all my past life had been but a preparation for this hour and this trial.

Other voices: Typewriter display

'Randolph was irresistible. He had incomparably more charm, more wit. But Winston is by far the better fellow'

Motorway Bold
Text: 50pt / Leading 45pt
Tracking + 2

Numerals
Text: 47.5 / Leading 45pt

This exhibition begins in 1940
when Winston Churchill was 65 years old
and war was raging across Europe.

Return: 30pt

The Second World War
won Churchill his place in history.
As Prime Minister, he led Britain
from near-defeat to final victory.

Return: 30pt

In doing so, Churchill became an icon
of what strong leadership should be.

Motorway Medium
Text: 50pt / Leading 45pt
Tracking -1

Designing for legibility

Legibility refers to the clarity of letterforms, individually and when composed to form words and lines, and is of paramount importance in exhibition text. This aspect of graphic design is the one over which designers have the most control. They are able to space words and paragraphs, vary font sizes and compose words in groups that make them easily readable by visitors. In many countries, including the United States and those in the European Union, disability legislation means designers also have the responsibility to design textual information that is legible to the wider visiting public—including visitors with relatively poor eyesight or dyslexia.

Legibility is related to the environment in which the text is situated. Even well-designed text will not be easily read if the lighting conditions are poor, or if it is behind reflective glass that makes seeing it difficult. The designer must also take account of where text is positioned. Text that may be legible close up won't be clear if it is placed at the back of a display case, far away from the viewer. The same goes for signage text. If it is mounted high on a wall it must be bigger and clearer than text that is at eye level and can be read from close by.

Top
Designer Thomas Manss used individual grids to create an intriguing and deliberately puzzling graphic for the Psion Organizer at an exhibition of design innovations.

Above
This design by Atelier Brückner is invisible to the naked eye, but can be read easily with 3D glasses.

Left
Where there is insufficient contrast between the text and background, type becomes illegible.

The legibility of text is influenced by the contrast between the text colour and the colour of the background. If they are too similar the text will be difficult to read and present a problem for the visually impaired. Strong contrasts— and good lighting— can enhance legibility. Light-coloured text on a dark background is harder to read than dark text on a light background. The designer can compensate for this by making the type larger or, in some cases, bolder.

Accessibility legislation does not set down any rigid guidelines, but it is difficult to imagine a situation in an exhibition where a type size could be smaller than 18 points. However, this does not necessarily mean that 18-point text will automatically be acceptable for visitors who are visually impaired; in many cases, it will not be legible if the lighting is poor or the text is set too far back.

The designer can always check the legibility of text by printing out a sample and pinning it on a wall at the intended distance from the viewer.

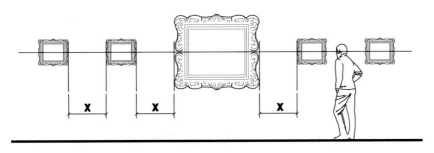

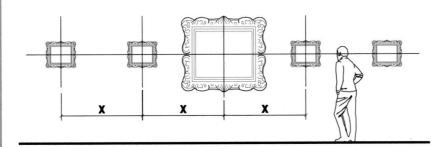

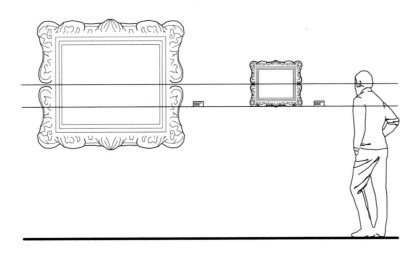

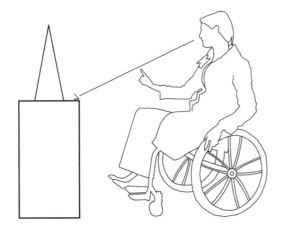

Left

Images on a flat wall can be arranged in a number of ways. In some cases, they will be given equal gaps between the images (top left). In other cases, the designer will centre the images at regular intervals (below left).

Centre left

Labels are often placed on an invisible line that continues around all the gallery walls. The height of the labels is usually set at the height of the bottom of the frame of the smallest image.

Bottom left

All plinth labels should be readable for wheelchair users. Many exhibitors use angled labels that can be seen equally by wheelchair users and standing adults and children.

Sparking Reaction, Sellafield Visitor Centre, Cumbria, UK
3D Design: Casson Mann; Graphic design: Nick Bell Design

The Sellafield Visitor Centre is sited at a nuclear power station in the north of England. The centre asked the exhibition designers to create a space for an open-ended debate that would allow visitors to express their views on nuclear reactors and fuel. Polemical animated texts are projected onto the walls and floors of the display area, provoking visitors to respond by writing on interactive screens.

There were no health disorders directly attributable to radiation exposure in the area affected by the Chernobyl disaster

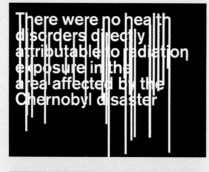

There is no safe dose of radiation

There is no country in the world that has found an acceptable solution for its radioactive waste

PEER DE RIJK, WISE (WORLD INFORMATION SERVICE ON ENERGY AND NUCLEAR INFORMATION), 2000/2001

The atom is for future

Designing for readability

Readability refers to the ease with which a piece of text can be comprehended and is influenced by the words used and the complexity of the sentence structure. Long, complex and specialized words make text less easily understood by the visiting public, though they may be justified in the right context. Some exhibiting institutions recommend in their guidelines that all texts should be readable by an average twelve-year-old. Studies show that even competent readers are less able to see and understand text in the often confusing environment of an exhibition, and reading ages are effectively lower for exhibition texts than for reading in less demanding surroundings, such as the classroom or home.

Some clients know how to write exhibition texts but many do not. Guidelines to the Ekarv method for writing readable labels are given below as an example of good practice, and designers should pass on these on to their clients if they feel the texts they are given are poorly written or too long for the exhibition environment.

The Ekarv method, named after Margareta Ekarv of the Swedish Postal Museum, is a proven set of guidelines, the effectiveness of which has been substantiated by research and has been widely adopted. This system addresses both legibility and readability issues, with recommendations for both text writing and layout. Trained graphic designers will know that these guidelines are only one of the many sources of information about readability and legibility, though Ekarv is one of the few devoted to the exhibition environment.

The most useful guidelines relate to line lengths and paragraphing. Very long lines are difficult to read and understand. The Ekarv method recommends that text is delivered in small, bite-size chunks. Designers, it is argued, should avoid long, densely written paragraphs. Research shows that small, clearly defined passages are easier to read and digest than long, dense passages. Users do not always read in a linear fashion, and they often make sense of text by picking out key words and phrases. Visitors are better able to pick out the shapes of individual words when they are written in small sentences, and are less likely to lose their place in the text. Small paragraphs allow visitors to navigate through a text panel at a glance, picking up key words easily and quickly. Museum specialists also emphasize the importance of including facts that may resonate with the audience wherever possible.

1. Use simple language to express complex ideas.
2. Use normal spoken word order.
3. One main idea per line, the end of the line coinciding with the natural end of the phrase. "The robbers were sentenced to death by hanging" is short and to the point.
4. Lines of about 45 letters; text broken into short paragraphs of four to five lines.
5. Use the active form of verbs and state the subject early in the sentence.

6. Avoid: subordinate clauses, complicated constructions, unnecessary adverbs, hyphenating words at the end of lines.
7. Read texts aloud and note natural pauses.
8. Adjust wording and punctuation to reflect the rhythm of speech.
9. Discuss texts with colleagues and consider their comments.
10. Pin draft texts in their final positions to assess effect.
11. Continually revise and refine the wording.
12. Concentrate the meaning to an "almost poetic level".

For example:

Ken Dixon commissioned this gold
necklace in 1800 as a present for his wife,
Elspeth. The jeweller Joseph O'Neill
manufactured it.

Thieves stole the necklace from Ken Dixon's
grandson in 1820. It was later restored
to its owner when the thieves were
caught attempting another robbery.

The robbers were sentenced to death by
hanging. One of the thieves said, "I wish
I had never clapped eyes on that
bauble" as he was led away.

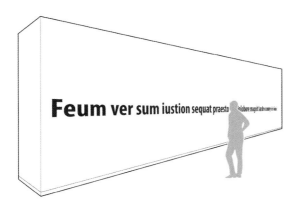

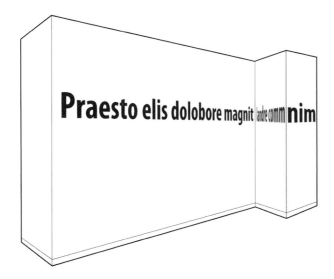

Left

In most cases, very long lines of text are avoided, especially at a low level.

Centre left

Area titles or chapter headings are usually mounted above the heads of visitors so that they can be seen from a distance.

Bottom left

It is important to check the viewable area available for a graphic to ensure that it does not run over or behind an obstruction.

Breaking the Rules: The Printed Face of the Avant-garde 1900–1937, British Library, London, UK
Design: Andrew Kellard Associates

The plan and elevation drawings were produced by the author for the graphic designer Kevin McKell at Andrew Kellard Associates. The graphic designer used these drawings to compose graphics that were later produced onto a digital vinyl wallpaper and applied to walling images created by the graphic designer and superimposed on graphic elevation drawings produced by the three-dimensional designer. The drawings are annotated with instructions for the graphic contractor regarding printing method and materials.

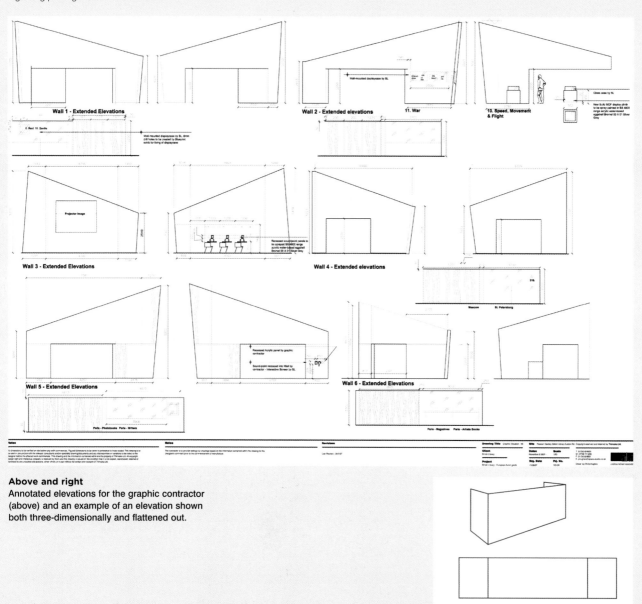

Above and right
Annotated elevations for the graphic contractor (above) and an example of an elevation shown both three-dimensionally and flattened out.

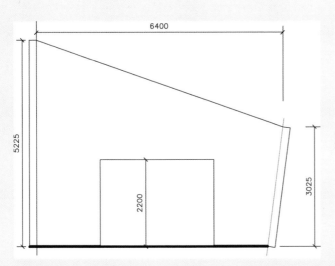

Above and above right
Scale elevation shown without and with the graphic treatment.

The design of the layout is usually done with low-resolution files. Before production, graphic designers will create high-resolution files for printing.

Above
Photograph of the completed elevation. The graphic was digitally printed onto vinyl, which was then applied to a timber backing sheet.

Reproducing graphics

Most exhibition graphics are printed by specialist large-format production houses. Traditionally, manual methods such as screenprinting were used but these are now relatively rare, and most exhibition graphics are produced from digital files. Digital printing is quick, convenient and accurate. However, there is no reason why graphics cannot be hand-applied when the creative strategy calls for this approach.

Table with detailed graphics specifications for an exhibition.

Ref:	Location	Size	Description	Quantity
1	Foyer	7236 mm (285 in) wide x 1500 mm (59 in) tall	Curved Wall: 2 mm (¹⁄₁₆ in) Foamex panel, wrap mounted, sealed and applied with UHB tape. 'Breaking the Rules' red text is fret-cut, 3 mm (¹⁄₈ in) Red Foamex, applied with UHB tape. Text height approximately 400 mm (15 in) tall. 16 fret-cut characters in total.	1
2	Foyer	TBC	Events & Credits Panel: Photographic prints, crystal sealed, mounted on 3 mm (¹⁄₈ in) Foamex. Applied to wall with UHB tape.	1
3	Foyer	TBC	Schwitters panel: Photographic prints, crystal sealed, mounted on 3 mm (¹⁄₈ in) Foamex. Applied to wall with UHB tape.	1
4	Foyer	TBC	Flickering images panel: Photographic prints, crystal sealed, mounted on 3 mm (¹⁄₈ in) Foamex. Applied to wall with UHB tape.	1
5	Foyer	TBC	Introduction Panel: Photographic prints, crystal sealed, mounted on 3 mm (¹⁄₈ in) Foamex. Applied to wall with UHB tape.	1
6	Manifesto text	TBC	Manifesto text onto wall: Pantone matched red vinyl title and body text is standard matt black vinyl applied directly to painted wall. Cap height of text is 15 mm (⅝ in).	1
7	Sound Poetry	900 mm (35½ in) wide x 600 mm (23⁵⁄₁₆ in) tall	Sound Poetry Panel: Photographic prints, crystal sealed, mounted on 3 mm (¹⁄₈ in) Foamex. Applied to wall with UHB tape.	1
8	Wall 1 (Front)	Approx. 3000 mm (118 in) x 3000 mm (118 in)	Large graphic on wall 1: Print graphic onto white vinyl, with matt seal to face. Then cut to shape. Apply direct to painted wall. The graphic will run around the side and back of this wall. Wall is 200 mm (7⅞ in) thick.	1
9	Wall 1 (Front)	Approx. 1000 mm (40 in) x 1000 mm (40 in)	Small graphic on wall 1: Print graphic onto white vinyl, with matt seal to face. Then cut to shape. Apply direct to painted wall. The graphic will run around the side and back of this wall. Wall is 200 mm (7⅞ in) thick.	1
10	Wall 1 (Front)	2625 mm (103½ in) x 375 mm (14¾ in)	Manifestos Section title: Vinyl matt black text. Text height is 375 mm (14¾ in) tall. Red arrow is fret-cut, 5 mm (³⁄₁₆ in) white Foamex, with "Cherry Red" vinyl to the front.	1
11	Wall 1 (Front)	425 mm (16¾ in) wide x 500 mm (19¾ in) tall	Body text is standard matt black vinyl applied directly to painted wall.	1
11a	Wall 1 (Front)	750 mm (29½ in) x 500 mm (19¾ in)	Wall 1 (Front) quote: Matt White and Pantone matched red vinyl text applied to painted plywood.	1
12	Wall 1 (Back)	See attached PDF for sizing	Wall 1 (Back) graphics: This wall will be covered in approximately 40 A1 individual blueback posters. Applied using wallpaper in an overlapping fashion.	
13	Wall 1 (Lightbox)	3700 mm (145¾ in) wide x 1350 mm (53¼ in) tall	Wall 1 Lightbox: Text printed onto Backlit cling film (measuring 3700 x 1350 mm/145¾ in x 53¼ in) and applied to the front of the Lightbox acrylic.	1
14	Wall 1 (Lightbox)	900 mm (35½ in) wide x 500 mm (19¾ in) tall	Wall 1 Lightbox quote: Matt White and Pantone matched red vinyl text applied to painted plywood on the back of Lightbox.	1

Vinyl text

Commonly used for signage, vinyl text is cut out of a roll of vinyl film with an adhesive backing and is applied by pressing it carefully on to a wall. This is a tricky process and is usually undertaken by graphics installers. Traditionally, all the text was cut out of the film by hand, but a digital cutting machine linked to a computer is now almost universally used. Vinyl cannot be used for long paragraphs of small text because the internal parts of the letters still have to be picked out by hand. This process which involves, for example, extracting the circle in every letter "O", is called "weeding". It is possible to print directly on to vinyl, which is then applied directly to a wall or surface. There is a huge range of vinyl films, including a frosted version which gives a sandblasted appearance when it is applied to glass, and coloured translucent films.

Above
Rolls of coloured vinyl with adhesive backing.

Left
Cut-out vinyl text on paper backing before application.

Below
Lettering applied directly to a wall is often produced as a "rubdown". The text is printed on a backing sheet and literally rubbed onto the wall, after which the backing sheet is peeled away.

"Rubdown"/dry transfer

"Rubdown" or dry transfer is a method of applying whole paragraphs of relatively small text to a wall. The text is printed on a film in reverse and the installer applies it directly to the wall by rubbing the front surface of the film. This method is more convenient than vinyl for long paragraphs of small text. It is also possible to apply rubdowns seamlessly to painted walls with no need for a backing panel. Rubdowns are often used in museums and galleries.

Cut-out lettering

It is possible to specify lettering that stands out from a back panel in relief. For low-relief letters (up to 10 mm/ ⅜ in thick), foamex is commonly used. Other materials include steel, brass, aluminium and Perspex. Metal letters tend to be expensive and are unsuitable for temporary exhibitions. It is possible to cut letters out of transparent or semi-transparent materials that glow when they are backlit, similar to shop signage. Modern sign-makers use a variety of computer-controlled machines for cutting out letters in relief, including water-jet cutters, laser cutters and milling machines. Letters can also be engraved in a solid material.

Inkjet printing

The large-format inkjet printer is the workhorse of the digital printing industry. It works in the same way as the domestic A4 version, but the carriage is wider and can accept rolls of material rather than single sheets. Inkjet printers can be up to 6 m (19 ft 6 in) wide (very exceptionally) and are used with materials such as paper, film and PVC. The maximum size of the print depends on the length of the roll used, usually 30 m (98 ft). The prints are usually laminated on to panels made from MDF (medium density fibreboard), foam core or foamex, to give them stiffness. They should be sealed with a film to give the finish— glossy, satin or matt— specified by the designer. A textured over-laminate is often used, to give a strong and durable finish.

Digital photographic printing

The most expensive of the large-format printing methods, photographic quality printing is less grainy than inkjet printing and more akin to a standard photograph. Digital photographic prints are sometimes given the name of the manufacture of the print machine, and so may be called Cibachome or Lambda prints. Photographic prints are produced on paper sheets, the maximum size of which is determined by the type of print machine used. Photographic prints are finished with glossy, satin, or matt seals—the choice is made by the designer.

Above left
The cut-out lettering shown in this image is made from polystyrene and then rendered in concrete by an exhibition model maker. Designed by Philip Hughes, Andrew Kellard Associates.

Above and top
Text cut from metal sheet with a computer-controlled milling machine.

Above
An inkjet printer printing on canvas.

Direct-to-media

Direct-to-media is the process of printing directly on to a substrate such as timber, board or plastic. The technology is relatively new and is developing fast. New machinery makes it possible to print on surfaces up to 3 m (10 ft) wide at high resolution (600 dpi or more). Reproduction varies according to the substrate, but it is relatively easy to produce a wide range of effects by printing on surfaces such as corrugated card, open-grain plywood, fluted plastics and Perspex. In most machines the maximum thickness of the substrate is about 40 mm (1½ in). The system used to feed panels into the machine allows the designer to create a design over a number of panels, which are fed in consecutively. Up-to-date machines are capable of spraying spot varnish to give a glossy finish to specified areas of the graphic. The prints are not usually sealed. Direct-to-media allows for seamless prints on very large panels.

Below
Examples of graphics printed onto recycled card using a direct-to-media machine.

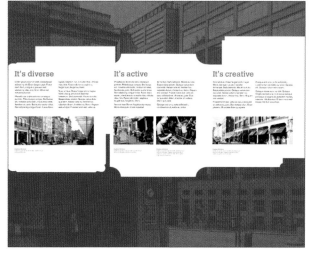

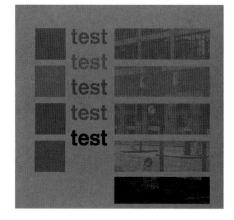

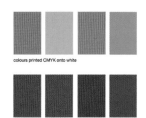

colours printed CMYK onto white

Dye sublimation is a computer printing process that uses heat to transfer dye to surfaces such as fabric or card.

Dye sublimation

Dye sublimation was commonly employed for many different types of material, but in exhibitions it is now used almost exclusively on fabrics. It is durable, long lasting and permeates the weave of a fabric extremely well. Open-weave banners, thick fabrics and gauze-like materials can be printed by dye sublimation with excellent results.

Silk-screening

Silk-screening is a non-digital process and, as such, is relatively rare. It involves making a type of stencil, a "screen", through which ink is forced on to the substrate. If multiple colours are required, a new screen is created for each ink. Silk-screening can be useful for applying graphics to an unusual substrate that won't fit between the rollers of a digital machine.

Mounting techniques

Inkjet or photographic prints can be mounted "flush" on a board, leaving the sides of the board exposed, or "wrap-mounted", which is a little more time consuming and expensive, and involves wrapping the edges of the print over to the sides. Where children are likely to pick at the edge of the board, it is essential to wrap-mount all graphics.

Where graphics are intended to go on a wall, the designer can specify that the panels are attached with Velcro tabs, so that they can be removed after the exhibition without damaging the graphics. If double-sided tape is used,

Left
Backlit duratran images applied to solid acrylic
panels emitting light from the side.

Below left
A duratran image applied to glass with
fluorescent backlighting.

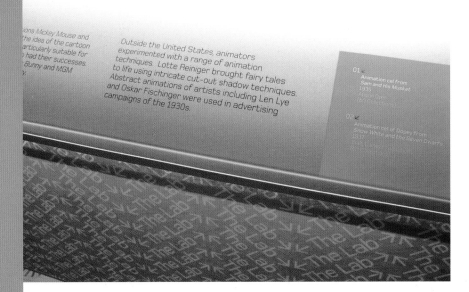

panels are usually destroyed when they are taken off the wall.

It is possible to fix thin graphics mounted on thin (2 mm/ 1/16 in or less)
foamex around a curved wall. Thicker panels usually crease when they
are forced around a curve and this harms the graphic.

New techniques enable a magnetic layer to be applied to the reverse
of the graphics, which fixes them to a metal subframe or panel and allows
them to be changed if necessary.

Outdoor applications

Most graphic production companies use printing inks that are resistant to weather and the harmful, degrading effects of ultraviolet rays. If there is any doubt, this should be specifically requested by the designer. All exterior graphics must be printed on a weatherproof substrate—for example, PVC, aluminium, glass or stainless steel. Paper and many fabrics are unsuitable as they rot or degrade.

Above all, outdoor graphics must be fixed to something stable. Large ones are likely to be subjected to strong winds, and have been known to bend or break steel supports if the wind factor is extreme. Very large banner graphics can act like sails and wrench façades from buildings. In some cases, the designer may have to consult a structural engineer to check the viability of large outdoor graphic banners.

Pop-up displays

Small pop-up stands that fold down into portable carry cases are common at trade shows and many clients are familiar with them. They can be kept in the client's office and transported to exhibition venues as necessary or, in some cases, they may be set up by a specialist installer who will also store the client's other exhibition equipment. The displays can be purchased through agents or graphic suppliers, who will usually supply a drawing of the stand showing its overall dimensions and the materials used. Most pop-up displays are clad with special roll-up panels attached to a framework with magnetic strips. Designers should familiarize themselves with how the panels are arranged, and the kind of graphics that work around this arrangement. It is important to take care when designing text or logos that straddle the panel joins. They will look odd if the edges of the joins do not meet precisely.

DO...

- Look at models, drawings and sketches of a proposed scheme to understand the placement of graphics.
- Work out the scale of 3-D drawings so that graphics can be reproduced at the appropriate size.
- Print out graphics at full size and look at them from what will be the visitor's viewpoint in the exhibition environment; adjust the size of text or images as necessary.
- Discuss readability issues with your client and avoid long passages of text.

DON'T...

- Forget that visitors have differing skills and abilities, and are frustrated by text that is at inappropriate scales.
- Display text or images at heights where visitors cannot see them.
- Design lines of text that are too wide to be easily read.
- Specify graphics without a proper investigation into the materials on which they will be reproduced or the printing methods that will be used.

7.

This chapter looks at the key role lighting plays in exhibitions, and the different effects it can have on exhibits, and on the exhibition space. It describes the types of light that are used, and also provides information about developing a lighting plan, and the set-ups that are available for trade fairs.

How lighting is used in exhibitions

The visual perception of exhibits, spatial relationships, surfaces and graphic treatments is governed by how they are lit. In the highly artificial environment of an exhibition, the designer uses lighting to interpret displays and to shape visitors' perceptions of their experience. It plays a central role in exhibitions, and every scheme is considered from this perspective.

Many contemporary designers of exhibition lighting learnt their trade in the theatre, and the parallels between the two disciplines are obvious. In both, lighting is adjusted to emphasize changes in mood and tone, and important dramatic elements are highlighted or banished to the shadows when necessary. Surfaces can be bathed in coloured light, dramatic sequences can be created with video projections, and objects can be modelled with angled lights. As in the theatre or films, exhibition lighting creates hierarchies, concentrating the richest pools of light on the strongest exhibits or suggesting equivalence through equal lighting.

The human eye

Interpretative lighting design relies on understanding human perception and some physiological considerations. Once the receptors in the human eye have adjusted to a general light level they can discern very small differences in tone and accent. However, eyes and brains are not designed to accommodate sudden changes in light. Going into an exhibition is often like entering a cinema. At first everything seems dark, but after a period of adjustment it is possible to make out subtle differences in luminance so that individual people, seats, clothing, etc., can be picked out. Emerging from a cinema into the midday sun can be dazzling, so that it is difficult to distinguish one object from another—though after a few minutes the human eye adjusts, and forms, colours, etc., are recognized. The exhibition experience should be comfortable on the eye, and the designer should carefully consider transitions from light to dark spaces and vice versa. Once the visitor has adjusted comfortably to a low light level, subtle changes in the lighting can be effective, but large, unplanned variations are tiring and unpleasant. The designer has a key role in ironing out these problems which, though often unnoticed by casual visitors, do have a negative impact on the overall experience of an exhibition.

"Amosphere: Exploring Climate Science", Science Museum, lighting design by DHA Designs, exhibition design by Casson Mann, London, UK, 2012. Lighting design with extensive use of coloured light evokes the earth's delicate atmosphere.

What's
the
Causing
Warming?
Turn the pages
to find out
what might happen
our future choices
02
Our Atmosphere

Magna Centre, Rotherham, UK
Design: DHA Designs

At this interactive science centre in a former steel processing plant, a sequence of light displays called "The Big Melt" is staged at 30-minute intervals. The light show uses programmable moving lights to stimulate the steel furnace processes. Speakers project a recorded sound track synchronized with the light display.

Concept storyboards for the lighting sequence of "The Big Melt" contain handwritten notes to explain the lighting and accompanying sound requirements.

Slag gone so furnace is tipped and steel 'tapped'.	Big red moment (more orange than red). Smoke billows. Strobes. End!
MAGNA	Old Furnace–concept storyboard for lighting–November 1999

As the metals melt slag and combustion can occur.	Special effects: pyro sparks shooting upwards and gas flame spurts out of burners set into lip of furnace top and furnace door. Sound: as before with slight modification to suggest 'melt'. Also cracks and bangs for sparks and fire.
MAGNA	Old Furnace–concept storyboard for lighting–November 1999

"The Big Melt" light show.

Surveying the site

The approach to lighting is determined largely by the nature of the exhibition venue. There are a number of factors that should be established before any scheme is embarked upon. Chief among them is the presence of daylight. Daylight is very powerful compared with most artificial light and will therefore change the designer's approach dramatically. Although the movement of the daily and annual movement of the sun is predictable, daylight varies with weather conditions. Low cloud cover will make a dramatic difference to the intensity of the light entering a space. The human eye is able to adapt to the changes in light levels, but where there is strong sunlight there may be deep shadows that affect displays.

Until artificial electric lighting became readily available at the beginning of the twentieth century, nearly all museums and galleries were lit through skylights above the exhibition hall, with light often filtering through a central atrium to the floor below. In many cases, this can be very successful. Sir John Soane pioneered this method in the United Kingdom's first purpose-designed public art gallery, the Dulwich Picture Gallery, founded in 1811, which still uses it very successfully, though artificial lighting has since been added to supplement daylight when external light levels are low. The use of skylights to light painting galleries continues to inspire architects. Schemes by Rafael Moneo (the Stockholm Museum of Modern Art) and Richard Meier (the Getty Center in Los Angeles) rely on toplight, though in these examples daylight is controlled by movable electric louvres that open and close according to the time of day. Modern lighting designers use a daylight study to examine the likely effects of the sun, and the findings from this study have a large impact on the lighting scheme proposed.

Trade fairs are particularly dogged by daylighting problems. New exhibition halls are often clad with glass, with occasional roof lights. The nature of temporary shows dictates that, at least where small ones are concerned, designers rarely conduct a proper site survey to inspect lighting conditions. This makes the lighting unpredictable for exhibitors. The relative strength of daylight means any artificial light is washed out by direct or indirect sunlight, especially when the sun is at its lowest and shines directly through windows. Where possible, it is helpful to perform a site survey. Like a department store with a number of competing franchises, most exhibitors try to outdo each other in light output. The lighting designer Dan Heap describes this as a "lux war" ("lux" is a measurement of illuminance). Most trade fairs are strongly lit and use a great deal of artificial light.

Daylight is normally totally excluded if there are conservation considerations. The sun emits ultraviolet rays that are harmful to many materials—plastics, for example, will often degrade. The usual approach, therefore, is to blank out windows and create a completely artificial environment. Ultraviolet-resistant film can be used to cover windows in some circumstances, but has a limited impact on fluctuating light levels.

National Museum of Scotland, Ralph Appelbaum Associates, Edinburgh, UK, 2011. The re-introduction of heavily filtered natural light through glass panels on the ceiling was part of a highly successful refurbishment of this iconic space.

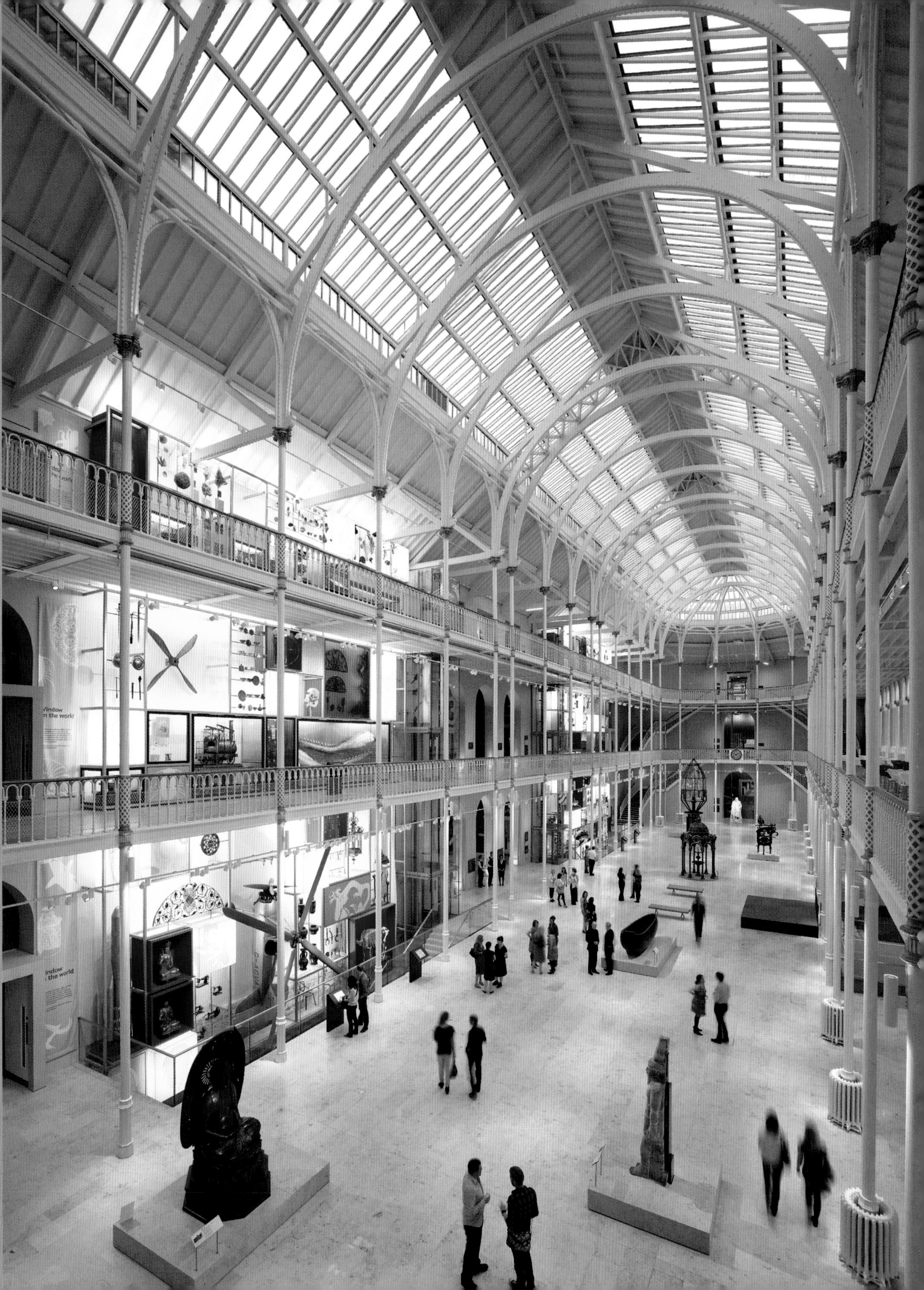

The site survey should reveal something about the fabric of the exhibition space, and the designer should check whether there is a lighting infrastructure, lighting track or suitable downlights. Enquiries should also be made about the adequacy of the power supply and the routing of cables to the lighting. If an exhibition is held on a heritage site, it is necessary to take great care with the existing fabric of the building to ensure that any new installations do not damage its original features.

The lighting plan

Once a survey has been carried out, the designer can begin to design the lighting. As with all aspects of exhibition design, the interpretation of the brief is the key. If it demands that a particular exhibit is a focus of the show, that exhibit will often be the starting point of the design. The lighting design is recorded on a lighting plan and may, in some circumstances, be demonstrated with a three-dimensional visual rendering generated by a computer package, or a rendered sketch. In some instances, it will show a series of events in sequence, over a prescribed period; the designer will produce a storyboard to demonstrate how the lighting changes during this sequence (see page 135).

Exhibit-focused lighting

For most exhibitions, the light focused on displays (known as "accent light") is brighter than the general background light (known as "ambient light"). The relative contrast between the exhibit and the background gives the exhibition its drama and focuses the visitor's attention on the display. The designer has the scope to create a tightly focused or "contoured" pool of light on the exhibit, or create a wider beam that lights the area around it. The widest-beam spotlight available, the Wall-wash, enables the designer to light a whole wall relatively evenly. A series of Wall-wash lights installed in sequence makes it possible to create a wide, fairly continuous spread of light over a long wall.

In a windowless space, the designer can use a single focused area of light to highlight a single display, allowing everything else in the room to vanish into the shadows. When multiple exhibits are lit, visitors perceive the journey between the displays, each of which is highlighted in a pool of light. Each exhibit also reflects light, spreading it throughout the display space. This reflected light is often sufficient to light doorways and paths between the displays. Where it is insufficient, extra lights must be added to ensure that visitors can circulate safely around the exhibition.

The effectiveness of exhibit-focused lighting varies in spaces lit by daylight. When it is dark outside, accent lights work effectively and visitors subconsciously perceive the contrast between the well-lit displays and the darker environment. If the sun is shining brightly, the ambient light levels rise and the space surrounding the exhibits becomes as evident as the displays themselves.

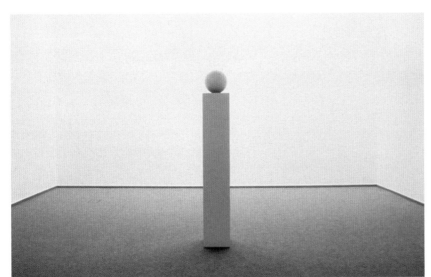

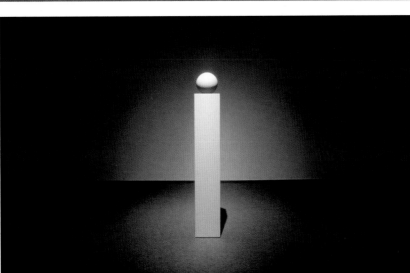

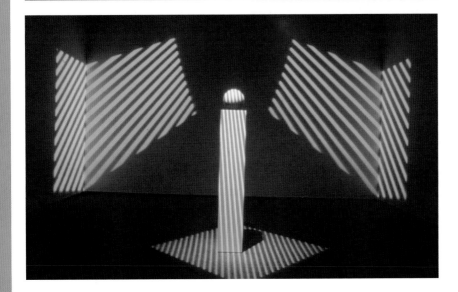

Left
"Ambient light" describes light thrown onto walls creating an overall brightness.

Centre left
"Accent lighting" describes an object illuminated while the surrounding room is in relative darkness.

Bottom left
"Sparkle", a third category, describes special coloured or accented light features intended to create a spectacle.

Types of exhibit-focused lighting

Spotlights

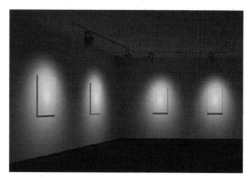

Wall-wash

 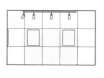 

Contoured spotlight

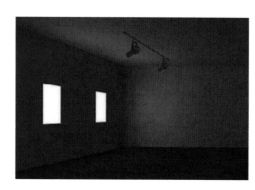 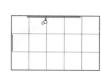

7.

Environmental lighting

In some cases, it may be important to create an even distribution of light throughout a space, regardless of the displays. Relaxation and teaching areas, and important circulation routes where visitors need more light, are examples. Where there are very large exhibits, such as rockets or aeroplanes, it may be almost impossible to light each one separately and distinctly, so a high ambient light level with few or minimal accent-lighted displays may be preferred. It is also helpful where visitors are expected to do a physical activity, such as interacting with a mechanical device, playing team games or dressing in historical clothing.

Visitors tend to find high ambient light more comfortable than accent lighting, though less dramatic. Lit walls and ceilings create a more pleasant atmosphere than individual pools of light, particularly for longer visits; for this reason, offices and public buildings tend to have high ambient light levels. Dark spaces with low light levels are wearying for visitors, and if they are expected to spend, say, an hour and a quarter at an exhibition, it is important to provide areas with higher ambient light levels, where they can rest their eyes. As stated earlier in this chapter, the transition from low ambient light levels to areas of high ambient light or daylight must be carefully managed, to avoid sudden increases in light levels that are uncomfortable to the eyes.

White Cube Gallery, lighting design: Dan Heap, London, UK. This gallery is lit from above through a translucent textile layer called Barisol. The light source is mainly daylight, but daylight fluorescent lamps give additional illumination when natural light is insufficient. This arrangement gives a very general ambient light.

Feature lighting

Feature lighting accentuates the contours of the three-dimensional form of a design scheme—for example, when the top edge of a wall is outlined with fluorescent tubes recessed into a purpose-made rebate. Its advantage is that it allows the designer to emphasize the shape of a three-dimensional structure or area, unlike accent lighting which tends to break three-dimensional spaces into disparate pools of light. Feature lighting can take the form of an illuminated outline, or a backlit structure similar to a light box. It is also used in nightclubs and bars.

Developments such as the use of LED lamps to make walls or surfaces, and materials with illuminated edges, have made feature lighting easier and more flexible. New control technologies have enabled designers to create programmable illuminated surfaces that change colour or pattern as required. Backlit surfaces can be effective, especially for transparent exhibits, but backlit walls often create light behind the object being shown, with the result that the background to the exhibit is much lighter than its front surfaces making it look like a silhouette. Perhaps the most famous example of a backlit exhibit is Lenin's embalmed body in Moscow. It lies on an underlit glass surface and the light from underneath it shows some details, but the strong contrast between the illuminated surface and Lenin's face makes it difficult to see the texture of his skin. Since he died more than 80 years ago, this serves a useful purpose.

Above and above left
"Great Expectations", Casson Mann, Grand Central Station, New York, USA, 2001. A giant light table acted as both the exhibition display structure and the main source of illumination while other sources of light came from coloured wall-washes and period chandeliers.

7. Coloured lighting

Lights for most art exhibitions have to be white, though lighting designers are careful to select either warm or cool tones, depending on the exhibits. Where the treatment of the subject allows, colours can be used as lavishly as in any bar or nightclub with spectacular effects. There are several key concepts to be considered when choosing coloured lighting.

Colour temperature

Colour temperature determines whether light appears warm or cool. Warm light is reddish, similar to a fireside glow, while a cool light is bluish. Colour temperature is measured by the kelvin (K) scale, which relates to the colour of a piece of metal heated to a particular temperature. For example, the colour of an incandescent lamp is similar to that of metal heated to 2,700°K. A fluorescent light might be the colour of metal heated to 3,500°K. The kelvin scale runs from around 1,800°Kelvin (red), through 2,700–3,000°K (yellow) to 20,000°K (very blue) at the upper end. Colour temperature is neutral at 3,500°K.

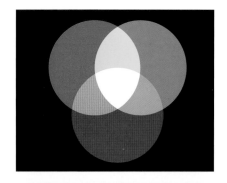

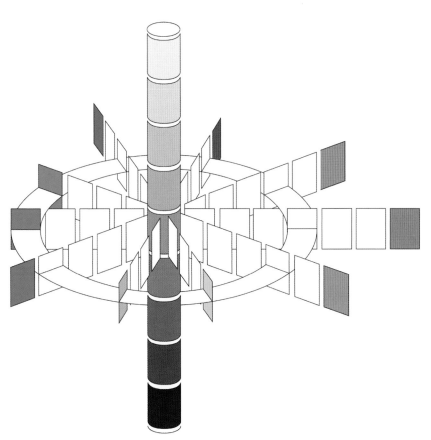

Above and top
Environments are tinted by a combination of coloured lights and coloured surfaces. When a coloured light strikes a coloured surface, the result is a third colour, which is a combination of both. For example, a red light directed at a green surface produces a yellow body colour.

Left
Diagram illustrating the Munsell System. In this system, body colours are classified according to criteria of brightness, hue and saturation to produce a complete sample catalogue in the form of a three-dimensional matrix. "Brightness" refers to the reflectance of a body colour and "hue" refers to the actual colour, while the term "saturation" expresses the degree of colouration, from the pure colour down to the uncoloured greyscale.

生活必需 NECESSITIES

Colour rendering

Colour rendering describes how well lighting shows colour on a material. Its scale is from 0 to 100—100 is excellent and 0 is awful—and its properties are most often experienced by shoppers. Large warehouse-like discount stores use cost-efficient high-output lighting with poor colour-rendering properties. This is usually fine for anyone buying tools or other hardware, but if they were buying a sweater it might well look different in daylight. Boutique shops usually use halogen or metal halide lights, which have better colour-rendering properties. Good colour rendering is important for exhibitions.

Coloured filters and gels

Coloured filters or gels can be added to some spotlights and most theatre lights to change the colour of the light output. If the beam of the light is projected on to a white surface, that surface takes on the colour of the light. Light reflected from a coloured surface takes on the colour of the surface. Any colour can be created by combinations of the basic three—red, blue and green—though a large number of purpose-made gels are available in a wide range of colours. Coloured lighting effects are also often created by covering fluorescent lights with coloured sleeves.

Hong Kong Wetland Park, design: Met Studio, lighting design: DHA Designs, Hong Kong, China. Recessed lighting features above and below this graphic panel accentuate the curve of the room. The graphic panel is lit from overhead spotlights trained around the wall.

Above
Hong Kong Wetland Park. Coloured lighting can
be very dramatic, especially when the exhibits are
picked out of virtual darkness as in this display.
Left
Hong Kong Wetland Park. Blue light is often more
effective than red light and is used more
frequently. Bright red lights often appear pink.

Modelling a three-dimensional object

Most three-dimensional objects need special attention during the lighting process. A single accent light accentuates the face of an exhibit, leaving its back and sides in relative darkness. Two lights positioned at the front model its face, leaving no obvious shadows. However, the exhibit will look relatively flat and two-dimensional until a third light is added at the rear. Photographers use a similar process to light portraits.

Spotlight – front elevation

Spotlight – side elevation

Spotlight – isometric

Spotlight – underside

7. Lighting for comfort

It is very much part of the designer's job to ensure that there is sufficient light for visitors to navigate through an exhibition, negotiate doorways and—particularly in an emergency—find exits. In many countries illuminated exit signs are obligatory, and it is a legal duty to ensure that they can be seen from all angles. Visitors should also be able to read textual information clearly. Where light levels are low this may require the designer to devise lighting solutions to make sure the words on a display are legible, often a considerable task. This obligation extends to serving the needs of the wider population, not just the young, fit and healthy. In many countries, this obligation can be enforced by disability legislation (see chapter 2).

Reflective surfaces often cause reading difficulties and the designer should avoid pointing lights at glass, especially at a height where their reflections will dazzle visitors. Problems are often caused by highly polished surfaces which reflect light into their eyes, and can be solved by avoiding glossy materials, especially for graphic panels.

Conservation

In most museum and galleries, the exhibits are examined by conservation experts who make recommendations about the conditions in which they should be displayed. These include the temperature and humidity in the exhibition space, and the brightness of the illumination striking the exhibits (measured in lux). Conditions may vary with each and every display. Fabrics and exhibits made of paper, such as books, watercolours and manuscripts, are exposed to a maximum of 50 lux in most European countries and the United States. Oil paintings are hardier and are frequently displayed under 200 lux. Many materials, such as plastics, are vulnerable to ultraviolet rays and need to be protected from sunlight. Loans to exhibitions are usually made with a number of strict stipulations about the amount of light the exhibits are exposed to for the duration of the show. The harm to an object depends on the length of the exposure: two days' exposure to 50 lux is equivalent to a one-day exposure to 100 lux.

Lighting specifications

The designer records the fittings (luminaires) and bulbs (lamps) he or she wishes to use on the lighting plan and, possibly, visuals. The luminaires are chosen to work seamlessly with the overall design philosophy. This means that antique fittings may be chosen to fit in with a historical show, though most exhibition luminaires are modern in design. For temporary exhibitions many institutions and trade fair contractors own a stock of lighting equipment which the designer will be expected to use.

Luminaires are chosen with a number of considerations in mind, including ease of installation, performance, flexibility, maintenance and external appearance. Once they have been chosen, the lamps are selected. Lamp choice is affected by factors such as lamp life, colour temperature, colour rendition, power output and control options. The designer may also look at dimming and adjustment options. It is usually part of his or her brief to provide the client with controls they can understand and are able to use without supervision. The options will vary according to the project. Some controls may be programmed through a lighting desk, and others may be manual and simple.

If the client takes responsibility for maintaining the lighting the designer may have to create a maintenance schedule. In some cases, his or her lighting subcontractor may carry this out while the exhibition is in progress.

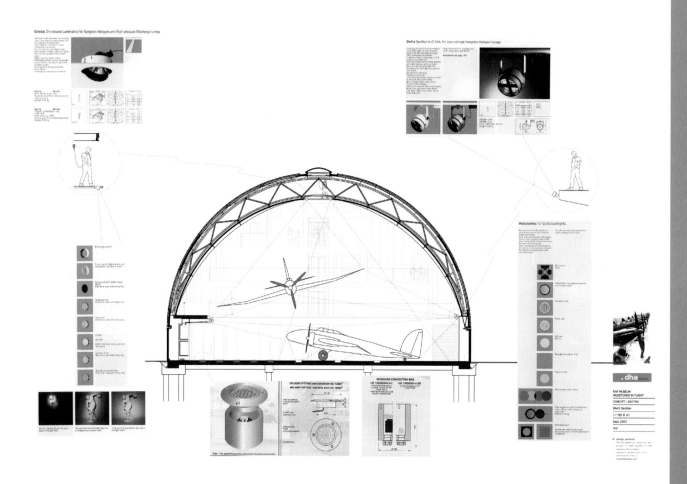

Royal Air Force Museum, lighting design: DHA Designs, London, UK. Concept drawing showing the proposed treatment of displays. A section drawing through the exhibition space is surrounded by detail images of types of light.

REFERENCES					NOTES				
Project: Heron Marketing Suite Date: December 2007—read with Drawing 3541ga Revision 05 Ref:									
Fitting Type	Fitting Ref	Area		Manufacturer's Reference	Description & Control Gear	Lamp Type	Finish	Accessories	Supplier
low voltage downlight	D1	Ceiling	Light Corporation	TYRELL 50 2035-802	Downlight. Use MODE ET-C dimmable electronic transformers (to suit circuit loadings i.e. ET-055-C for single lamps & ET-105-C if in pairs)	See Lamp list	White	8021-000 Honeycomb —and see Accessories list	Light Corporation
low voltage downlight FIXED	d2	Ceiling	Light Corporation	STARLIGHTS B 2001-802	Downlight. Use MODE ET-C dimmable electronic transformers (to suit circuit loadings i.e. ET-055-C for single lamps & ET-105-C for pairs)	See Lamp list	White		Light Corporation
Xenon strip cove lighting	tx	Ceiling Coves & Model Plinths	Light Projects	Tokistar Advantage Flexible Xenon Covelight on 75 mm (3 in) centres	Cove lighting system, Contractor to determine lengths—liaise with Supplier re: Mounting and transformers, etc. Note straight runs should be fitted in a mounting channel	5w cool white Xenon		24v	Light Projects Ltd. Charlie Wadsworth
wall light	w	Wall mounted – low –	Kreon	Small Square Side kr972823	Wall mounted side light— light downwards. Mains	100w qt-de 12 R7s		Millerghe reflector kr770802	Light Years
low level marker	g	Wall mounted – in base board – SURFACE MOUNTS	iGuzzini	B603	iGuzzini GLIM CUBE single wall BLUE 1w with DIMMABLE DRIVER	Integral		Note—fitting to be mounted with Ribbed Lines on front lens running up and down	iGuzzini Terrance Goode
GLASS WALL	NS	Mounted behind glass wall on floor	ACDC	20 mm (¾ in) 18/250 High Output Cold Cathode	COVELITE IN 1500 LENGTHS—HI OUTPUT— 1V to 10V DIMMABLE— NEMESIS 10 GEAR— BLUE 246			Individually controlled with 1v–10v Ballasts (1 per tube)	ACDC Lighting Systems Ltd
GLASS WALL	LH	Mounted behind glass wall on floor	Light Projects		Floor mounted Remote Integral Birdy with 1 m (3 ft) lead & barndoor	GE Exn	Black		Light Projects Ltd. Charlie Wadsworth

Example of a lighting schedule by DHA Designs. The schedule lists luminaires and lamps. These fittings would also be shown on accompanying plans and elevations.

Projector lights

Projector lights are used to project signs, patterns and images. Some have a digital feed that enables the designer to change the image, though most have a static image or "gobo" (see below) attached to the face of the light. With the advent of digital lighting, it is now possible to use a computer to create a pattern on the lens of light.

The gobo

This is a small metal plate out of which a pattern or shape—for example, a logo—is cut. The gobo is then placed in front of a projector light. The light shines through it to create a pattern or shape on the floor or a wall.

Fibre optics

In most major museums showcases are lit internally by a bundle of fibre-optic cables. A source lamp outside the showcase is used to transmit the light through the cables. The light shines from the end of the cables and is directed on to the display. The advantage of this system is that the heat source (the lamp) is at a safe distance from what is being shown, therefore preventing heat build-up near the display.

Moving lights

Very rarely seen in museums, moving lights are a staple of commercial exhibitions and, when appropriate, are used to create vibrancy and dynamism. Motorized lights are commonly used for product launches

Above
Martin stand, Euroshop 2008, Dusseldorf, Germany. Computer controlled projector lights by the Danish company Martin Professional are used to create moving flower patterns on the floor.

Above
London Transport Museum, Ralph Appelbaum Associates, London, UK. Images of advertising are projected directly onto the floor in this display.

and event lighting. Large ones are programmed on a desk by a lighting designer, who controls how the light moves and creates a sequence of movements. When the sequence has been set, the desk is removed and a programmable memory chip that records the sequence worked out on the lighting desk is connected, which continues to deliver the lighting movements when the desk is removed.

Backlighting

Many exhibition designers create "glowing" surfaces by lighting translucent materials from behind. The designer fills a box behind the surface with light, using soft diffuse lamps like fluorescent tubes. Boxes used for this are usually painted white inside, to give maximum reflection. In some cases, the designer may create a hot spot of light on the front of the surface so that the backlighting forms a frame. Sometimes, he or she may want to produce a very even light like that in a photographic light box.

Edgelighting

Lighting designers often place a lamp, usually fluorescent, parallel to the edges of a translucent glass panel to create a glow around a display. If the panel is engraved, the facets of the engraving glow as they pick up the light emitted by the lamp.

Parcan

The parcan is literally an open-ended "can" around a lamp, with a frame in front of the can for filters, and is used in the theatre where it delivers an intense light to a stage set or scene. Parcans are usually power hungry, and often have flaps in front, called "barn doors", for focusing and shaping the light beam.

Above left
This display by Arno Design is backlit by fluorescent tubes concealed within translucent walling.

Above
Open Road Tour, Pentagram, touring exhibition, 2003. Coloured parcans clamped to the central spine of this tensile structure threw coloured light on the exhibits.

Panasonic BlueScape stand, Atelier Brückner, IFA Berlin, Germany, 2003. This photograph shows the use of light projection on a white backdrop to communicate the idea of the "network", a key brand concept for the client.

Trade fairs

For simple lighting set-ups at trade fairs, the exhibition organizer usually offers exhibitors basic clip-on lights, which can be ordered by filling out a form. Anything more complicated usually has to be specially designed and constructed, and connected to the power supply on the stand.

For large shows, designers order cables, usually called "drops", that hang from the roof of the exhibition hall; a bespoke lighting rig is then hung from these. Scaffolding towers or motorized hoists called "genies" are used to mount lamps on the rig and focus them on the exhibits. The power supply for these overhead lights is routed from under the roof structure and, in some cases, is ordered separately by the designer or contracting company. Rigs are sometimes available from local suppliers, which saves time and money, especially in remote locations. Lighting contractors are generally familiar with the installation process and will be able to help the designer when necessary.

If an overhead rig is not available, the designer has to find an alternative means of lighting exhibits. "Sticklights" or spotlights on extended arms are popular and can create a cone of light on a demonstration surface. Storage areas and cloakrooms need illumination, especially if the lighting in a hall is inadequate. The light from fluorescent tubes is generally considered sufficient for areas away from the public gaze.

Professional practice

It is unusual for specialist lighting designers to be employed for small trade fairs, and the exhibition designer generally specifies the lighting. For larger budget shows, specialists work with other team members to produce concept drawings, storyboards, specifications, and lighting plans that show how and where lamps and fittings will be installed. Lighting designers may be responsible for the installation of the lights they specify, but sometimes they simply provide the design and add improvisational tweaks when the lights are in place. Museums and galleries often appoint lighting design specialists

Above
Photograph showing luminaires being installed before exhibits are placed in a gallery.

Left
"Juan Muñoz: A Retrospective", Tate Modern, London, UK, 2008. The spotlights were directed after the exhibits were arranged.

under contract to provide a specified service throughout the year. In many instances, the contract includes provisions about repair and maintenance of existing installations. Particularly in museum work, conservation is a major consideration and the designer is often responsible for ensuring that major works of art are not damaged by overheating or excessive light.

Lighting designers are frequently employed to create theatre-style schemes for one-off events where actors or presenters are on stage; their experience is essential in the production of video recordings and live webcasts. Trade shows often involve product launches or presentations. Lighting design is a key element of these and requires specialist installation crews, audiovisual support and show management staff.

DO...

- Carry out a site survey wherever possible to assess the conditions in which an exhibition will take place, and familiarize yourself with any existing lighting infrastructure and daylight parameters.
- Examine existing electrical installations and determine whether they are adequate to support new lighting. Consider the routing of cables carefully.
- Plan the lighting early on. It is easier to add it at the beginning of the design process than at the end.
- Create a lighting scheme that supports the exhibition structure and helps to convey the show's concept.
- Ensure that all graphical information that is intended to be read is adequately illuminated, and check the readability of the information.
- Consider the amount of heat the lighting will generate. Hot lamps may harm the exhibits and if the heat build-up is too great, additional air-conditioning may be needed.
- Make your collaborators aware of the lighting solutions you intend to provide by circulating your lighting plans to all relevant parties.

DON'T...

- Dazzle visitors with poorly angled spotlights.
- Train powerful spotlights on monitors, display cases or other reflective surfaces at an angle that will cause discomfort to visitors.
- Cover or obscure important exit signs.
- Assume that everyone has perfect vision. Illuminate exhibits so that they are accessible to the wider visiting public (some of whom may have left their glasses at home!).
- Create sudden and dramatic changes in light levels from one area to the next. Eyes don't adjust easily to these.
- Design over-complicated lighting schemes; too many ideas tend to create confusion.
- Leave important circulation spaces, stairways or doorways in darkness.
- Endanger the public through trip hazards or exposed electrical installations.

8.

This chapter describes how interactive techniques, both digital and non-digital, can be used to stimulate visitor involvement in an exhibition. It covers the importance of approachability and feedback, as well as the need for design consistency.

Interactive media

As exhibitions reach out to ever more diverse audiences, and compete with a wide variety of other entertainment channels, interactive media is no longer a novelty for the museum—it is an expectation. Designing for interactivity is a complex subject in its own right, and is often dealt with by specialist media designers and developers. As such, this chapter simply covers some of the factors that might be of concern to the non-specialist.

Interactives offer a unique and often highly memorable way into the subject of an exhibition, particularly for younger audiences. The Launchpad Gallery of the Science Museum in London is an example of an immensely popular, highly interactive gallery that, at peak times, is overflowing with children who are learning and playing.

Interactives should feel integrated into the overall experience of an exhibition—not, as is so often the case, like add-ons. The most successful pieces are firmly rooted in the narrative of an exhibition, contributing a level of content through the type of storytelling made possible by their layered, interactive and sometimes game-like nature. It is therefore crucial, when briefing interactive designers, that any proposed pieces are described within their narrative context, along with desired learning outcomes for the visitors that will use them. It is also critical that interactives convey content suited to their format—or, rather, that content determines the type of interactive experience chosen.

Google Web Lab, Science Museum, 2013, London. Virtual and physical "visitors" could experience and interact with exhibition content simultaneously.

The visitor experience

Interaction should be fun! First and foremost, interactives need to engage visitors through their emotions, before trying to teach or show. Get the visitor's attention with something enjoyable, and the more intellectual content or deeper messaging can follow later. The second most important consideration for interactives is that they are easily navigable and logical. The quicker the visitor understands how to use an interactive, the better; a confusing presentation will result in a rapid loss of attention. Thirty seconds or less is a standard maximum time to "explain" how an interactive works.

Interactives can be created for single users, or for many people at once, and both have their advantages and disadvantages. Single-user interactives create a deep connection between content and person, but only one person can participate at a time. Multiplayer interactives give roles to more people, and when they work they can be enormously rewarding, but they can also be off-putting for some, so designers are wise to consider whether the audiences of the museum in question will be happy to interact with people they do not know. Additionally, if a multiplayer interactive relies on a set number of people to make it work, it will not work on slow days in the museum. Ultimately, the best interactives should not rely on multiple users to convey their message.

It is worth bearing in mind that in museums, visitors look at other visitors, and one person's enjoyment of an interactive can encourage others to have a go. Interactive designers can play on this, and turn single-user interactives into group experiences by allowing others to watch or comment, even though they may not be the ones behind the controls. A "user" need not always be the person with their hand on the button, so to speak.

Queen Victoria Street, Museum of London, London, UK. A smartphone app shows historical events overlaid on contemporary scenes.

Technology

Interactives can make use of the most sophisticated technology, or they can be low-tech—or even no-tech. It all depends on the audience and the aims of the institution, as well as the story that needs to be told. Budget will also play a part in deciding what kind of interactive is most appropriate.

For electronic and digital interaction, an increasing range of devices are now being integrated into the visitor experience: hand-held smartphones, tablets, digital screens and projections. Group interaction usually requires media that is large-scale, while more personal interaction can be encouraged through smartphones and tablets. Increasingly, museums are appropriating existing technologies, such as iPads, and integrating them as a relatively low-cost interactive portal. "The Memory Palace" temporary exhibition at London's V&A, for example, allowed visitors to draw a picture of a memory on to an iPad; this was then uploaded to an online data base and transformed into a poster.

Following the flourishing of hand-held technology over the last twenty years, personal devices are a natural platform for museum interpretation. They have the benefit of being familiar to the user, as well as not costing the museum anything in terms of hardware. However, there is a debate about whether hand-held devices are wholly conducive to the museum environment, as these devices are also used for many other purposes, such as email and social media. On the other hand, making use of phones and tablets in

Below and opposite
London Transport Museum, Ralph Appelbaum Associates, London, UK. The images below show visualizations of an interactive map of transport across London. Visitors choose the type of information they want and the information is instantly relayed through an electronic map with real time camera footage relayed on the screen above. A photograph of the final map in action is shown opposite.

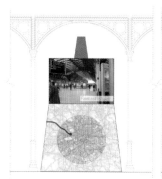
Mainline transport coming in to Paddington Station

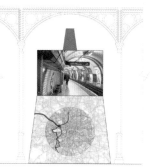
Main connections made from Paddington across London

Further connections made on journeys that started at Paddington

One person's journey across London to work

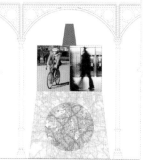
Two people's journey across London to work

Four passenger's journeys across London to work

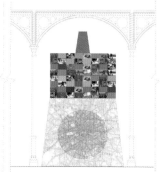
Up to 64 passengers' journeys to work across London

museums creates strong marketing opportunities—visitors can share their experience on social media while in the exhibition, granting the institution a kind of buzz that many find desirable.

Sound is a key component of interactive digital media, and designers can now draw on a range of delivery techniques for audio material—headphones and localized sound are more traditional examples, while bone-conduction technology (placing elbows on a surface to conduct sound through the bones in your arms) offers a more advanced approach.

Digital interactives can be difficult to future-proof as technology changes constantly. Apps and touchscreens can very quickly seem out of date; hardware is superseded, apps need to be upgraded or replaced to meet new expectations, and the way we interact with screens evolves. At the same time, digital interactives can be incredibly effective because of their similarity to the devices we surround ourselves with everyday—people feel comfortable interacting with screens and have more knowledge than ever of how to use them.

Interactive designers may arrange to stay in touch with the museum or institution to roll out an ongoing series of updates, or they may recommend technologies that do not date as easily as others, such as touch tables rather than apps. One strategy is to use technologies that have been in existence for a while, as component and style have been proved to last, at least for a number of years. The most effective interactives often do not seek to use the latest technology, but rather work with existing technological "gestures", such as using fingertips to zoom in, and exploit these.

Given that the only certainty for technology is further change, the success of any interactive is always measured by its usefulness, and its relevance to the exhibition content. The only way to mitigate against obsolescence is the richness of the interpretation—if the story is strong enough, an older technological interface can sometimes cease to matter.

What kind of interactive?

Interactives fall into several different categories, ranging from smaller interactives that allow an individual user to delve further into a topic, to large-scale spectacles that encourage visitors to interact with others.

"Find out more" interactives

These are layered, often single-user interactives that encourage the visitor to go deeper into a particular subject. "Find out more" interactives appeal to visitors of all levels of interest—from those who just want to grasp the big picture to those who wish to dig deeper. In a pre-digital world, this kind of knowledge would have been physical and indexed (like a printed book or portfolio). Now that this information can be presented digitally, the format for these interactives are usually a screen-based interface navigated by touch. They can be delivered through installations within the gallery, such as permanently mounted touchscreens, or through hand-held devices and apps.

"Find out more" interactives are particularly useful for museums that wish to allow visitors to browse online archives. Layered levels of information enable visitors to navigate from broad topics to more detailed information, according to their interests. "Find out more" interactives frequently offer visitors the chance to follow up an area of investigation after visiting, by emailing themselves with links or other pieces of information. Sometimes comment, discussion and feedback spaces are included, to allow visitors the opportunity to ask questions and see what topics are being discussed by others. Each of these actions opens up valuable dialogue between museum and visitor.

Gaming interactives

Gaming interactives use key principles and a non-linear navigation to encourage users to test themselves, compete or complete a challenge. These are active ways of using knowledge and are particularly used by science museums to offer simple explanations of scientific principles. Gaming interactives appeal to those who learn by doing rather than being shown or told (sometimes referred to as kinaesthetic learners). These do not need to be digital—many of the best game-based interactives are mechanical and kinetic. For example, a see-saw interactive mirrors similar game-like experiences users may have outside a museum, but within an exhibition can be used to teach the principles of leverage and balance.

Gaming interactives work by conveying key principles to audiences, then encouraging them to use this knowledge actively. They are often a great way of helping visitors to see how dry content can be applied to more exciting scenarios, which is why they are a popular choice with science museums. Gaming interactives allow users to test out ideas using trial and error. Visitors must engage with the principle quickly, learn how to do it, and in some cases compete or try again and again to achieve the desired outcome. This can be off-putting for some. If the investment of time and effort does not go to plan, it can cause users to fail, which is not conducive to learning. Good interactive designers will be capable of considering these pitfalls, and mitigating them by minimizing the effort needed to understand what is going on, as well as offering a range of ways to interact, which leaves room for those who prefer learning differently.

Environmental interactives

Environmental interactives are immersive interactive experiences, often on a large scale, intended to connect with users in an emotional and awe-inspiring way by carrying a powerful, overarching message. Often, these pieces feel closer to art installations than interactives. One of their primary functions is to bring together many different types of audience in one space, so that they connect with the spectacle as well as with each other. The main outcome of the interactive is often a sensory impression, rather than an intense learning experience.

Environmental interactives can carry a wide range of content, ranging from visitor feedback to a linear story to a complex matrix of content that adds up to a coherent whole. These interactives often take advantage of being able to tell an overarching story through lots of different pieces of information. They are also capable of staying up to the minute through live data feeds. Sometimes the visitor is only expected to look at the spectacle; at other times they may be encouraged to interact. This sub-set of environmental interactives uses visitors' feedback and displays it digitally on a large scale, for the greatest impact. This "digital narcissism" effect allows visitors to input and then see their contribution in a public space—for example, the Science Museum's Who Am I? galleries in London have a digital loop that links different floors of the exhibition with a display of visitor Tweets.

What makes a successful interactive?

Interactives must, above all, be easy, interesting and fun to engage with. Approachability is key. Visitors must feel as if they can easily discover the scope of what is required, and be able to navigate through the framework with a clear idea of what the goals are and how they will achieve them. Building in opportunities for feedback and encouragement are extremely useful, too—such as getting a question right, moving up a stage in the game, or seeing something work in the right way. Consistent interfaces—both within a single interactive and across a set of interactives—will enable visitors to get the most out of the experience.

Writing an interactive brief

Owing to the fact that interactives are likely to be delivered by a specialist consultant, exhibition designers and clients should be able to brief them well to achieve the best results. A good interactive brief should include:

1. The context of the interactive(s) within the story of exhibition.
2. The key content messages.
3. Key learning outcomes—what should the visitor take away from the experience?
4. Details of the assets available—this could be a list of objects, set of reference images, data information or moving film footage.
5. Audience profile—who is the intended audience?
6. Initial specifications of the audiovisual hardware likely to be used.
7. Budget.

Other considerations

When planning interactives in a museum context, there are a number of factors that should be considered.

How will the content for the interactive be developed?

Content development for interactives is a specialist skill, requiring collaboration between curator, content developer and interactive designer. The more complex the interactive, the more rigorous the content development process needs to be, and the greater the need to test the content and its arrangement on users, usually during a prototyping phase.

How will the interactive be written?

Good copywriting is essential for interactives. It needs to balance conveying information with instructions and prompts to encourage users to explore. Often the scriptwriter for the exhibition will be in charge of writing the text, with input from the interactive designers so that the interactive functions as it is meant to.

Expense versus value

Interactives, especially digital ones, can be expensive, so exhibition designers should carefully consider their function in telling the story and the audience they are addressing.

Future-proofing and upkeep

Ensuring the lifetime of interactives, especially digital ones, can be tricky in an age of constant technological change. Any strategy for interactives should include the continued upgrading of hardware solutions (for example, projectors) and, potentially, software upgrades as well. Physical/mechanical interactives should be accompanied by a manual for care and upkeep, to maximize their lifespan.

Sound

Sound can be a highly effective component of an interactive, but too often this is treated as a secondary consideration. Sound should be taken into account when designing and pacing interactives so that it becomes an integral part of the final result. Care must also be taken to avoid sound bleed between spaces. (*See also* Chapter 9.)

Use the professionals

The advice and expertise of professional interactive specialists cannot be underestimated, and will result in a much better product that adds significantly to the visitor experience.

DO...

- Work with the client to get detailed feedback and agreement on the interactive brief.

- Work with client to collect great assets (images, videos, language/quotations, etc.) to include in the brief, and ultimately, in the interactive.

- Ensure that the interactive is fun, easy and rich with ideas.

- Maintain simplicity and accessibility.

DON'T...

- Overcomplicate. Simple interactivity is more successful, and more memorable.

- Force all of your knowledge on the visitor at the expense of their experience.

- Underestimate the cost of good interaction.

- Change the interaction brief once it is agreed, unless absolutely necessary.

UK Pavilion, Expo 2005, Aichi, Japan
Design: Land Design

Intended to be a showcase of British design, the UK pavilion at the Expo 2005 in Aichi, Japan—designed by Land Design in collaboration with 2UP—introduced the visitor to innovative design through a process of interactive exploration. To ensure good visitor flow, the maximum dwell time for each interactive was 45 seconds. The communication of ideas was necessarily concise as well as intuitive.

Each station, some of which are illustrated here, was intended to show how improvements in man-made structures often involve the study of natural phenomena.

Below
A plan shows the overall arrangement of the interactives within the pavilion.

Bottom
This photograph and visualization show the central part of the pavilion lit by ambient projections in which sharks and fish swim up the walls and across the ceiling. Information about the technologies on show was made available on a specially commissioned website to allow visitors to research each topic further.

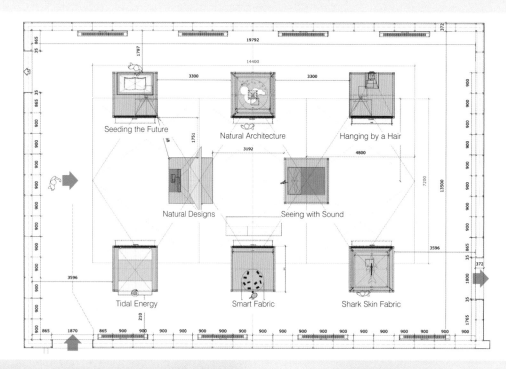

Above

A plan, elevation and section for the "Seeding the Future" interactive show how the height of the interactive table surface is optimized for all users.

Above and right

A drawing and photograph of the "Seeding the Future" interactive table, which provided information on the storing of seeds for future generations to ensure biodiversity.

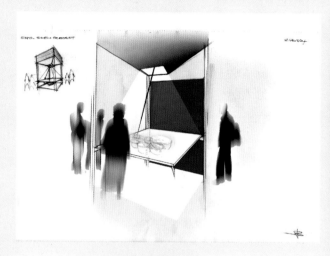

Each station was intended to show how improvements in man-made structures often involve study of natural phenomena. Top row: a visualization and photograph of the "Natural Architecture" table, featuring the Eden Project by Grimshaw. Centre row: "Seeing with Sound" features the bat-inspired technology that allows the sight impaired to sense their distance from obstructions with an electronic cane. Bottom row: "Shark Skin Fabric" explains the fabrics used for swimwear to increase speed.

9.

This chapter explains how sound and film can be used to interpret and support the storyline of an exhibition, and encourage visitors' full engagement. It provides guidelines for writing an audiovisual brief, as well as practical advice relating to the design of an installation.

The benefits of sound and film

Today, audiences are extremely accustomed to ambient sound and moving images. It is no longer surprising to hear a petrol pump speak, or to be addressed by a talking head on a video screen in a shop or post office. The amount of time people devote to watching screens—on their phone, tablet, laptop, television or in the cinema—comprises a major part of their waking hours. Consequently, exhibition visitors now expect to engage with a subject through screen-based media.

Increasingly, our history is captured using sound and film. The way we tell and share stories is intricately linked to audiovisual material, and the way we document our lives has evolved to match this. In exhibitions, film is used not only in museums that tell of the recent past and current events, but also those that go back further into history. Exhibitions about recent events draw from either newly created or pre-existing audiovisual assets, while those that go

Russian Jewish Museum, Ralph Appelbaum Associates, Moscow, Russia, 2012. Due to the destruction of Jewish artefacts during the Communist era, the story of Russian Jewish story is told largely through media (Clockwise) Remembrance Space, Tolerance Centre (an interactive theatre for school groups), Holocaust and Great Patriotic War, Beginnings Theatre.

back into the deeper past can use the creative talents of animators, visualizers and directors, recreating a lost world through film.

Although artefact-based displays are still the staple of most exhibitions and museums, sound and film (now almost exclusively digitally created and stored) are becoming increasingly integral. For designers, the opportunity to use linear media alongside other, more traditional exhibition techniques presents an exciting way to engage with the public. (Linear media refers to multimedia content with a fixed narrative—as with a film—as opposed to non-linear content, where users control the narrative, as with interactive games.)

Film can even solve the issue of an absence of collections by providing the core museum experience. One example of this approach is the Jewish Museum and Tolerance Centre in Moscow. Owing to the fact that very few objects survived the repression of the Soviet state, the story is told through linear media, making use of personal accounts, newsreels and reconstructions. Similarly, in museums that try to reconstruct prehistorical or early human narratives, film is essential—partly because the world they try to present is so distant from today, and partly because the cultures that are the subject of these exhibitions leave behind very few artefacts or structures. Film can be a way to bring lost worlds to life.

"Yves Klein: Corps, Couleur, Immatériel", Katia Lafitte, Centre Pompidou, Paris, France, 2006–2007. Designer Katia Lafitte used a number of life-sized projections of the artist Yves Klein. These projections powerfully communicated how the artist worked by placing him in the same space as the visitor.

The pitfalls of sound and film

Arguably, the use of cinematic technique in exhibitions has brought museums into direct comparison with more immersive film experiences—mainstream cinemas and multiplexes—in both 2-D and 3-D. The prevalence of "trailers" to advertise blockbuster exhibitions is another example of how museums are trying to tap into an existing film industry to drive visitor numbers. Where museums try to mimic the traditional cinema, however, they almost always fail. Appropriate and successful use of film in an exhibition environment is often vastly different from the cinema; it prioritizes different features, such as its capacity to transform space, be played on multiple platforms, and its brevity, compared with a regular feature-length film. These factors all help to give the exhibition environment a more layered, customized feeling, constituting an enhancement of the museum's collections and stories, not a replacement of them.

Types of linear media in exhibitions

Linear media within exhibitions tends to fall into one of four broad categories—short, linear media, environmental media, bespoke cinematic experiences and special effects.

Short linear media

These are short clips that are usually used to deliver concise messages or stories in a short space of time. Most commonly, clips will feature interviews, extracts from archival footage, or short, newly created introductions to the

Oculus: an eye into St Paul's, St Paul's Cathedral, Ralph Appelbaum Associates, London, UK, 2012. This immersive 270 degree environment uses multiple high definition projectors and computer synchronization to deliver an ultra-wide video image.

subject matter in question. They are carefully edited for maximum impact—the aim is to deliver messages simply and clearly in the busy environment of a typical exhibition where there are many other attractions (and distractions).

Short linear media is capable of incorporating a range of voices. This is important because it allows for the provision of differing perspectives on a subject or theme. Depending on the subject matter, these short clips can be very powerful: the Holocaust exhibition at the Imperial War Museum in London uses clips in the form of intensely moving first-person accounts direct to camera to provide a way in to a serious and significant theme.

Environmental media

Environmental media tends to stay in the background. It provides what is known as an "immersive environment", and is often intended to create sensory impressions by summoning a feeling or mood, transporting the visitor to another time and place by providing a necessary context for objects or themes.

The ambient, linear content of environmental media provides a scenographic backdrop, and often works with other exhibition devices such as objects, lighting and text. Frequently large-scale, it can occupy whole walls, ceilings and even floors. Soundscapes can be used to great effect to complement environmental media, too; carefully placed speakers can create "three-dimensional" sound effects that mimic real-world sounds, such as the passing of a very fast vehicle.

The pacing of environmental media is very important—too slow and it fails to engage visitors' attention; too fast or dramatic and it risks disorientating them. Creating this material is often iterative and experimental, requiring constant testing and assessment of sound levels and placement of media within the space.

IBM 100: THINK, Ralph Appelbaum Associates, New York City, USA, 2011. Multiple exterior LED screens show live representations of dynamic data sets.

Bespoke cinematic experiences

Bespoke cinematic experiences are perfect for demonstrating big ideas on a vast scale, and are often used for features such as projection domes or planetariums. For this reason, they are popular in science museums, featuring films about rocket launches, the wonders of flight, space, deep-sea exploration and the like. They are particularly attractive to younger audiences.

These experiences have also begun to incorporate "4-D" effects—such as shaking or moving seats, dry ice, wind or splashes of rain. For example, at the Jewish Museum in Moscow, a 4-D cinema situated at the start of the visitor journey immerses viewers in the story of the Jews, from their exile from Egypt to the present day, accompanied by subtle motion, damp mists and 3-D sound. If combined effectively, and to an appropriate level, these 4-D elements can all add an extra level of realism for the visitor.

Such experiences, though, are usually expensive and complicated to create, owing to the amount of new cinematic material that needs to be created to support them, and the customized camera equipment required to film them. As a result, a small film industry has sprung up, offering ready-made content solutions for such experiences. Individual clients rarely commission one-off projection dome films, and designers should understand that commissioning this kind of feature is more achievable through an agency that holds the rights to dome- or planetarium-specific content.

Special effects

Increasingly, linear media can be projected over a wide range of surfaces, thus transforming a space into an immersive environment enhanced by certain special effects. One notable example is Pepper's Ghost, an illusion technique that make objects (and often people) seem to appear or disappear. These effects are popular with children, and are a staple of so-called "haunted" attractions, like castle dungeons and haunted houses. Pepper's

Ghosts are now also being used in museums and exhibitions to create dramatic scenarios that are sometimes, but not always, used to scare visitors.

The technique works by using a sheet of glass and special lighting effects to reveal or conceal an object in a surprising way, often enhanced by digital developments, such as augmented reality (AR) and sound effects. For museums and exhibitions, this requires the correct lighting, suitable spatial conditions, a substantial budget and enough space to conceal the equipment.

Writing an audiovisual brief

A good audiovisual (AV) brief will break down into a brief for software and a brief for hardware. The software brief describes the media that will play in the exhibition—look and feel, narrative placement, content and tone. AV hardware briefs are a different matter: these may specify equipment, if necessary (for example, if a museum would like to reuse existing projectors), but for new projects, it is best to consult with a hardware consultant for the best possible solution.

The AV software brief

An AV software brief should be as detailed as possible regarding the elements about which the designer and client know the most: design and storyline. Clear information about the positioning of the media within the visitor's journey, the assets that are available and the key visitor outcomes that each piece should achieve will help AV software producers to develop the most successful and appropriate narrative.

AV software briefs should include the following:

- Overall project summary. A quick summary of the key messages and vision for the project, dates for opening and an understanding of the client's objectives.
- Description of the media designer's scope. Typically, this includes the amount of media in the exhibition, and whether or not content development will fall into the media producer's scope.
- Where the media will be situated in the exhibition. This will include an overview of where the media pieces will sit in the exhibition, and will detail what role they will play in telling the story. This should be supplemented by plan and section drawings if possible.
- Overall budget and the required breakdown of costs that tenderers should provide.
- Detailed breakdown of the individual media pieces. This should include:
    Main storyline and key messages.
    How it will complement the exhibition immediately surrounding it.
    Visitor learning outcomes.
- Client assets available (e.g. archival footage, photographic archive).
- Opportunity to film new footage if required/possible.
- Look and feel, and an initial visual treatment. This could describe the type

of pace that is expected, the period in which a film should be set, and any other relevant stylistic features.

- Programme for delivery and details of budget if necessary.

The AV hardware brief

Most designers instinctively try to find out as much as they can about audiovisual displays before speaking to a specialist, and may find themselves writing briefs that suggest particular technologies. However, it is much more effective to try to describe the type of experience you would like to see, feel and hear, without specifying how it should be achieved. This leaves the AV hardware specialist free to explore and recommend the most suitable technologies for the project's aspirations and budget. For example, a brief might specify using a projector, when in fact the desired approach is delivery of film content in a particular space. By leaving the technology open to the AV hardware designer, other possibilities could become available: for example, plasma or LED screens suitable for ambient light levels, picture quality or maintenance criteria.

The same approach should apply to sound. The designer who asks for something like "omnidirectional speakers" is usually entering an area they do not fully understand. It is better to describe the type of sound that is wanted and leave the specification to the specialists able to weigh up complex questions of cost, specification and durability.

All good audiovisual briefs should include scale layouts and/or elevations to show the height of spaces. It is important to mark power supplies on the plans, too, as well as any features that may affect the media.

Acoustic considerations

Though the situation is improving, sound remains an afterthought in most exhibitions, and there are often fundamental obstacles that prevent designers using sound effectively. Before approaching an audiovisual specialist, it is worth thinking about the degree of acoustic separation between spaces. To create discrete areas of sound, it is usually necessary to localize any sound so that visitors are not distracted by noise from other spaces. This can be done through personal devices (e.g. headphones, acoustic sticks) or through directed sound that is controlled enough to affect only a small space. However, this latter approach is rarely completely soundproof from one area to the next.

When considering the acoustic properties of a space, designers should pay attention to the materiality of surfaces. Hard floors and walls are reflective and create messy sound environments as they have no dampening effect. Using foam, acoustic tiles or fabrics on separating walls can minimize this—textiles and heavily textured surfaces tend to break up and dissipate sound waves—but unless the walls are dense it is inevitable that there will be conflict if sound is used at a high volume.

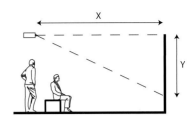

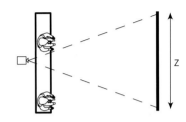

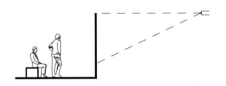

Top and centre
Audio-visual suppliers provide information about the "throw" of light from a projection unit. Using this information, the designer can draw a section detailing the distance of the projector from the screen. Visitors should be seated so that they do not throw a shadow on the screen when taking their seats.

Above
With rear projection, the image is projected onto the back of a translucent cloth. Projecting on the rear of a screen avoids shadows being cast when visitors stand in front of the beam.

ambient sound that will characterize the space. It will be necessary to make a note of when peak times are, to assess the level of noise from crowds, and to find out whether key events take place throughout the day, such as guided tours. Specialist assessment of the space can be useful, too: acoustic engineers can use 3-D models of a space to test reverberation in order to plot any areas that are acoustically difficult. Consulting engineers, such as Arup in London, have sound laboratories that can accurately model the sound qualities of a space and enable a designer to "hear" the acoustic properties of a new building or a refurbished old building during planning stages. This can help to fine-tune a space before construction begins. Acoustic engineers can also recommend the use of sound-dampening materials or design changes that will limit reverberation and uncomfortable sound-spill from one area to the next, and secure a rich tone that works across the frequencies.

How to ensure quality media experiences

The quality of exhibition media, like any feature film or soundtrack, is dependent upon the experience and skill of the director, producers, technicians and sound designers, and the size of the available budget. Choosing experienced AV producers and hardware designers will save a lot of time and money in the long run, and ensure an extraordinary experience that is worthy of the stories it conveys.

The better the media is integrated into the rest of the exhibition experience, the more successful it will be at communicating with visitors. Media should always feel part of the continuing narrative rather than an adjunct. The AV software and hardware suppliers should be able to work seamlessly with the exhibition fit-out contractors so that a high-quality audiovisual installation can be achieved. Early consideration of sound properties and consultation with experienced acoustic engineers can help to guide the choice of surface treatments and appropriate technologies.

Limiting factors

There are a number of limiting factors in audiovisual displays, and the designer's brief should make clear what these are.

Daylight

For any moving picture display, briefs should specify whether there is daylight in the space, how strong it can be, and when it is at its most powerful. This will help avoid washing out many plasmas and projectors, compromising the content of the film. Knowing this early on in the process will help the audiovisual specialist to recommend appropriate technologies to provide reasonable picture quality, even if there is high ambient light. Daylight screens and projections that provide strong images even in outdoor conditions now exist (albeit at a cost). If the designer wishes to use media screens, the brief should include a drawing marking the size and position of any screen on a

should include a drawing marking the size and position of any screen on a plan drawing, and show its proximity to light sources, so that the audiovisual specialist can consider what technologies would be appropriate. A daylight study showing the movement of the sun and its impact on the interior of the space can also be helpful.

Dust and dirt

Mechanical and electrical installations are compromised by airborne dust and dirt, so if this could be a problem the fact must be communicated to the audiovisual specialist. This will ensure that steps can be taken to ventilate machinery properly and prevent dust coming near it. Audiovisual installations are sensitive to any interruption in power supply, and electricians often provide back-up devices that prevent sudden power shutdowns. Video signals through data cables are susceptible to interference from the electromagnetic fields generated by power cables, and audiovisual specialists recommend isolating them. This may necessitate using special trunking for the data cables with built-in insulation to prevent interference.

Placement of hardware

Audiovisual suppliers will provide information about the "throw" of light from a projection unit. Using this information, designers can draw a section detailing the distance of the projector from the screen. This will help to plan the place where visitors will see the projection best, and help avoid the situation where visitors cast shadows on the screen because they stand in the way of the projector. One other option is to rear-project the media: here, the image is projected on to the back of a translucent cloth. Projecting on the rear of a screen avoids any shadows being cast.

Selecting equipment

There is a big difference between equipment for short-term audiovisual installations and long-term solutions for museums or galleries. For temporary exhibitions lasting a few days or weeks, it is possible to use cheap, readily available projectors and sound equipment on hire, especially if budgets are tight. Hire companies provide and install equipment to the designer's specifications and take it away when the exhibition ends; in some cases it may be possible to buy it outright.

Long-term exhibitions require more reliable equipment, which is considerably more expensive than cheap consumer equivalents, often by a factor of five. Bespoke delivery technologies, robust projectors and high-end digital screens will cost more, but will ultimately pay for themselves in terms of maintenance and durability. Moreover, the quality of specialist equipment is much higher and can achieve more: for example, recent developments in the blending of multiple projection images side-by-side has enabled large, high-resolution displays. So too have developments in "warping", also using digital techniques, allowing projection on to contoured surfaces with no loss of sharpness or quality.

players are unsuitable for long-term exhibitions and should not be considered. They are not designed to be used all day for months or years, and will inevitably fail when their components become worn through overuse. In the long run, though more expensive, sturdy specialist equipment is less likely to develop faults and require maintenance.

Specifying equipment and cabling

The sound or film equipment specified by the audiovisual specialist, including any cabling, should be marked on technical drawings. The designer must ensure that cables are hidden, but are accessible for maintenance. In all instances, cabling should be laid before elements such as floors and walls are installed. Typically, good audiovisual hardware consultants offer advice on ongoing maintenance and operability of equipment, and in some instances offer training for staff.

DO...

- Use sound and film to add depth to the theme of an exhibition. Many visitors respond well to audiovisual content, and in some cases, this may be the only bit of the exhibition visitors engage with.

- Integrate sound and film into the overall narrative of the exhibition.

- Develop the content for film and sound at the same time as the exhibition narrative.

- Examine the exhibition environment and make sure that light and acoustic conditions are adequate for audiovisual displays.

- Install acoustic barriers between sound areas where necessary to avoid sound spill.

- Use your imagination to explore how film and sound can be used. Exhibitions offer great potential for the use of film and sound that far exceed how film and media are used in a day-to-day context.

DON'T...

- Put audiovisual equipment in areas where it might be damaged by dust and dirt.

- Use non-specialist equipment for long-term installations.

- Use inexperienced contractors for installations.

- Leave audiovisual cables or trailing leads exposed. The wiring to each electronic unit should be concealed.

- Add sound and film randomly into the experience and assume it will tell the story.

10.

Materials

This chapter discusses the considerations the designer must take into account when deciding on materials, such as their fire rating, durability and whether they are suitable for a specific purpose. It describes how sample boards can be used during the selection process, and emphasizes the increasing importance of using materials that will have a minimum impact on the environment.

Choosing materials

The range of materials available to exhibition designers continues to increase as new suppliers and material databases offer more options than ever before. Not only are there many new manufacturing processes and technologies, but the materials are produced in quantity, and their high quality and reliability have opened up a whole new realm of possibilities to designers. Traditional materials such as timber, aluminium and steel are also undergoing a revolution; the use of lasers and other computer-guided equipment increasingly allows components to be made with extreme accuracy.

Above and opposite
"Region and Harbour", Opera Design, Rotterdam, the Netherlands, 1995. This map, designed by Opera Design, uses a wonderful array of materials including the bristles of assorted brushes to show land use in the port and region of Rotterdam. The show depicted the reconstruction of Rotterdam and the future for the city, and took place in the former arrival and departure hall of the Holland America Line.

In all exhibition environments, the fire rating of materials is very important. Most museums hold extremely valuable collections and the fire performance of everything that is used in their displays must be checked. This also applies to trade fairs. In both cases, appointed fire officers are responsible for making sure individual materials are sufficiently fire retardant. In some cases they test samples, and often ban materials that don't reach the required standard. It is important to understand that the fire rating of a material is determined by how it is used—for example, combined with other materials or in a particular type of construction. Or a thick sample might pass a fire test, while a thin sample of the same material might fail. As fire regulations differ from country to country, it is not easy to make assumptions when working abroad; if in doubt, check materials with local fire officers to avoid mistakes.

In addition to fire retardancy, and a material's aesthetic properties, the designer must check its durability, order times, price, sheet sizes, ease of maintenance and assembly time, and the skills of the contractors involved. Any one of these factors can rule out using the material, so it is worth looking closely at each one. In reality, many designers develop a palette of materials they use consistently, introducing new ones cautiously, and only when they are sure they will perform. It can be embarrassing and expensive if a material starts to peel or disintegrate unexpectedly.

With natural materials, such as timber, it is necessary to consider how they will behave in particular environments. Wood swells when it is wet and shrinks when it dries. In such a case, the designer should ensure that a material can shrink and expand without cracking or warping.

Increasingly, designers are judging materials from an environmental standpoint. For example, those that are high in "embodied energy" are less favoured than ones that are rapidly renewable and low in embodied energy (see chapter 13). Thus locally sourced and renewable timber (where there is no scarcity) would normally be favoured over, say, steel (which has high embodied energy) if a construction could be equally served by both materials. Using composite materials, such as plywood covered with laminates that cannot be removed and prevent reuse, is considered an inefficient use of resources. However, sustainability experts stress that it is often difficult to make decisions based solely on one factor, such as embodied energy, as the overall efficiency of a structure, its fitness for purpose and aesthetic criteria also play a part. On the other hand, good environmentally friendly design has become such a key consideration that the prevailing opinion is that sustainability is now central, rather than peripheral, to the success or failure of a scheme. A green approach to design requires the designer to make judgements about resources and how appropriate materials are for a particular purpose. What were once common practices, such as the use of high-quality materials like marble, granite or steel for temporary exhibition stands, may become things of the past.

A number of sources of information about green products have been collated by industry bodies. For example, in the United Kingdom the Building

Research Establishment has issued a green specification guide that enables designers to source them without laborious investigation. Such guides are instrumental in helping to embed green practices in the industry.

Deciding on suitable materials

A sample board—materials glued to a board—is useful to show the range of materials used for each different aspect of an exhibition, and is often shown to the client as part of a design presentation. It allows the designer to make minute adjustments to colours and finishes to ensure a good result. In many cases, the materials that are chosen will last for the duration of just one exhibition. However, in the light of green design imperatives, materials that can easily be reused for future shows are preferred. Particularly for commercial exhibitors, it is essential that colours and textures are consistent with the visual identity of the company, and that finishes are consistent with its branding material.

For museum displays some materials, particularly those used inside showcases, are tested for conservation purposes. A toxic glue that fixes a laminate, or a painted surface, might be a potential source of pollutants that can accelerate the deterioration of sensitive artefacts. A material may be tested for several weeks, and it is advisable to specify alternatives early in the detailed design phase, and wait for the results of the tests, before ordering it.

Exhibition designers, like architects and interior designers, use swatches to specify paint colours to contractors, based on charts issued by paint suppliers. Swatches are often too small for a considered judgement to be made, and in this case it is often a good idea to obtain samples of the paint and coat a larger area with it. When choosing materials such as those for vinyl graphics, designers use Pantone colour references as these are an accurate match for vinyl colours. Pantone swatches are available from art shops, and are a standard reference system understood by contractors as well as designers. Other paint references include the German RAL system, which is widely used in Europe.

The process of using colour references is simple. Choose a colour, note down its number and write the number on the technical drawing for the contractor or on a specifications sheet. Be clear about the way the colour will be applied—for example, spray or roller finish—the extent of the area to be covered, the undercoats, primers or base coats required, the probable number of paint layers, and any clear lacquer topcoat. Most paints are available in matt, satin or gloss versions.

London Transport Museum, London, UK
Design: Ralph Appelbaum Associates UK

The choice of materials used in the display design for this museum was influenced by the colours, materials and fixtures and fittings used on the London transport network itself.

Above
Picture research by designers at Ralph Appelbaum Associates helped inform fixing methods and the choice of materials for the museum. The eventual design of the graphic walls retained the rugged quality common to buses, trams and trains.

Left
Sample materials were laid out to see how they worked together. In a complex design such as the London Transport Museum, the contractor can provide material samples and constructed details.

SFB (VG) (storyframe backpanel)	n/a	PMS 1817 (colour match, with 66% + 33% shades)	PANTONE® 1817 C	PANTONE® 4985 C	PANTONE® 5025 C
SFB (TT) (storyframe backpanel)	n/a	PMS 229 (colour match, with 66% + 33% shades)	PANTONE® 229 C	PANTONE® 5205 C	PANTONE® 5225 C
SFB (RP) (storyframe backpanel)	n/a	PMS 534 (colour match, with 66% + 33% shades)	PANTONE® 534 C		PANTONE® 5305 C
SFB (MH) (storyframe backpanel)	n/a	PMS 302 (colour match, with 66% + 33% shades)	PANTONE® 3015 C	PANTONE® 5405 C	PANTONE® 5435 C
BIO (biography panel)	RAL 1018	n/a			M (BB 02.05.07)

(handwritten annotations: 5005, 5215, 652, 7458, 3015)

Above
The graphic treatment of the signage was chosen to match the colours of the metalwork construction. A complex colour palette was managed with the use of a guide compiled by the designers with Pantone, paint and material references to aid the build and graphic contractors.

Left
The elements were laid out together on a table in the design studio for a visual check. Graphic sizes and the effectiveness of the junctions were checked at this point before site work began.

DO...

- Examine the durability, fixing methods, cost, sheet size and ease of use of materials.
- Check the fire rating of materials to ensure that they conform to local fire regulations.
- Specify combinations of materials and types of construction accurately, in conformity with local building regulations. Where possible, be specific about the supplier of a material, its surface texture, colours (including the appropriate paint or the surface treatment) and the required fire resistance.
- Ask suppliers to produce prototypes wherever possible.
- Build a library of samples that you can refer to quickly and easily.

DON'T...

- Be vague when you specify a material. If you are not clear about what you want, the contractor will decide for you, and you may not be pleased with the result.
- Ask a contractor to use techniques or materials they are not proficient with.
- Proceed with any construction before consulting a fire officer, structural engineer or health and safety officer if you think any of the materials involved may require their advice.
- Allow a contractor to reinterpret or change your design without your express consent.

11.

This chapter looks at exhibition systems, generally designed for use at trade fairs, that are easily transported to a venue where they are set up on site. The best examples provide for all the needs of a commercial client in a single unit.

Flexible designs

If designers had to build their own exhibitions, there is no doubt that their construction methodology would be very different to what it is. For many of them, the effect of their displays is far more important than the way they are built, and when allowed free rein designers tend to specify higher quality (and heavier) materials that would strain the backs of the hardiest contractors. There is, of course, another way. There are modular, lightweight and portable exhibition systems that are easily transportable, simple to erect and environmentally friendly if they are used frequently. Some are excellent examples of industrial design, and provide flexibility as well as having multiple

Left, bottom left and below
The Burckhardt Leitner Constructiv "Clic" system is so-named because of the subtle click sound made by the tubes as they join together at the nodal points. It is a lightweight system for single-level displays which allows the client to store items within the display, and to attach graphics and integral lighting. The system packs down into separate tubes and nodal blocks that fit neatly into a travel case. The same components are used for walling and storage and can be internally illuminated (left). Aluminium rods are joined at node points to create a framework (below). Lightweight polypropylene panels are attached to the frame to make a surface (below left).

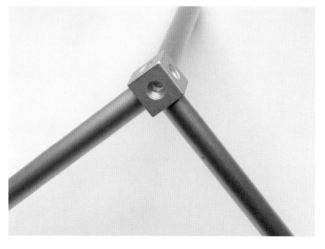

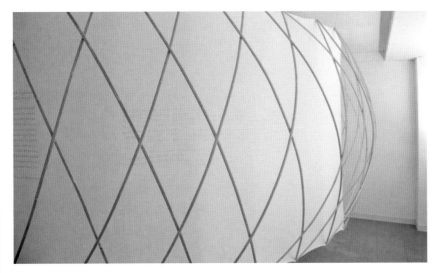

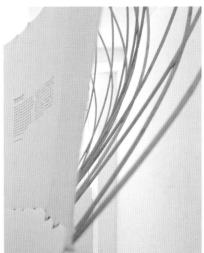

uses. High-quality systems are usually designed with the needs of trade customers in mind, and therefore provide walls, storage, graphic display and lighting within a single integrated unit. The best systems pack down into small cases for easy transport and storage; many can be transported as aeroplane baggage and taken directly to an exhibition venue to be erected on site.

The biggest barrier to using modular and portable displays is that they look too commonplace—which is why they are very rarely seen in museums—and clients who use them complain that too many of their competitors have similar products, and that they are not different enough to give their company a competitive edge. For this reason, many organizations that use these displays attempt to disguise them with graphics and surface finishes. However, for many commercial clients they are an easy and relatively cheap means of maintaining a presence at a particular trade show or conference.

Most systems suitable for trade fairs provide options for mounting computer screens, brochure display and graphic panels. The panels are normally designed by the designer, and the artwork is sent to a printer who outputs the graphics in a format that works with the modular display. Some systems provide for double-storey construction with staircases and upper-storey handrails.

Many designers find exhibition systems an exciting challenge. Designing them requires spatial as well as industrial-design skills. When erected they have to be as engaging and stimulating as any display, but it must be possible to pack them down into a small volume for transport. Because they are used frequently, they must be designed with longevity in mind, with hard-wearing joints and graphic surfaces that are resistant to scratches.

The initial outlay for a portable display is often greater than that for a bespoke exhibition stand, but the ongoing cost of repeat installation is usually lower as transport and labour costs are smaller. The decision to buy a modular system is therefore usually made only if several exhibitions are planned.

Above and above left
Ambassador of Design, Japan, Trans Arts, Nosigner, Tokyo, Japan, 2013. This interpretive screen uses bamboo sticks in tension and a cloth made using the traditional Japanese skill, Shinshibari.

Open Road Tour,
touring exhibition, 2003
Design: Pentagram

For the hundredth anniversary of Harley-Davidson, designers Pentagram devised the Open Road Tour, which travelled to ten cities around the world. Each event was a weekend-long festival with a museum-quality display area housed in a series of tents, with a custom-made circular tent at its core. The event managed to combine the dignity of a gallery exhibition with the atmosphere of a local Harley-Davidson festival.

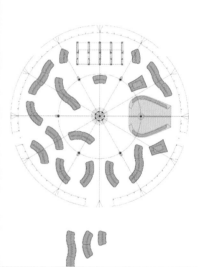

Top
Entrance to the tent.

Above left
Overall view of the interior of the circular tent.

Above
Plan and section of the central display tent.

Left
A display of petrol tanks.

Overall view and details of the "Assembly line" display of Harley-Davidson artefacts.

Image overleaf
Adventure One (1995) was a self-initiated feasibility project undertaken by the design group Imagination. The scheme envisaged a touring brand experience housed within seventy 12 m (39 ft) trailers. At each location, the trailers would be joined together to form a large and flexible environment. All additional equipment would be transported within the same trailers. Structures made using truck trailers with removable sides are commonly used for travelling exhibitions and hospitality units.

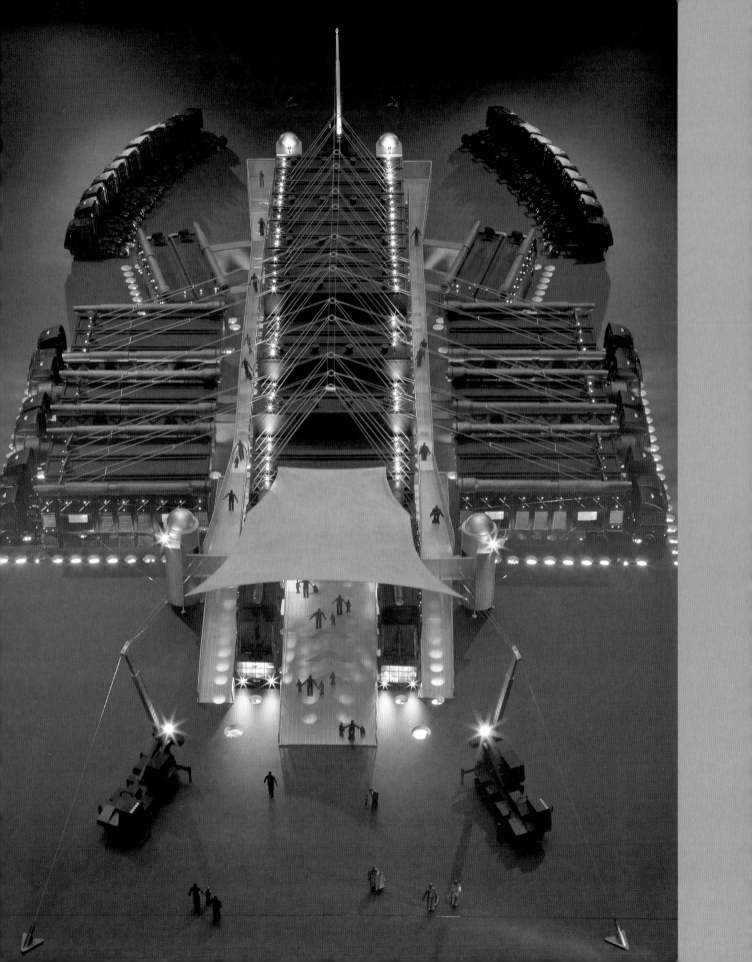

12.

This chapter shows how technical drawings develop and are a visual record of discussions between the designer and client. It describes the importance of accurate labelling and explanatory notes, and the need to produce specific drawings for specialist contractors. It also includes advice about when it is advisable to contact planning or conservation authorities in order to obtain their approval of a design.

The purpose of technical drawings

In most cases, no single individual "owns" an exhibition design and has absolute say over its every aspect. Normally there is a process of negotiation, proposal and counterproposal that involves a number of people with differing perspectives. The sketches, concept models and technical drawings produced by the designer show how the exhibition ideas in the brief could be realized in an eventual design. Many of the parties to the discussion may have very little idea how the content they have provided might appear in the exhibition, so initial sketches and models are able to communicate provisional options. It is important that these are provisional and are not presented as final designs, simply because it is unlikely that the designer will immediately proffer a solution that anticipates all the needs of the client and the exhibition audience as well as health, safety and security requirements. Normally, it is also important for the client to feel as if they have put their stamp on the design in some way, and that the project is a shared vision and not solely the province of the designer.

The provisional drawings are therefore a record of the discussion process and incorporate reasonable input from the client. If the client proposes changes that will make the design ineffective, the designer has to defend his or her proposal. The models, sketches and drawings are an important means of showing how a coherent design strategy will be affected by any proposed changes, and a significant debating tool. At the end of the discussions, the designer has to turn the provisional drawings into technical drawings that can be read by contractors and suppliers, and provide the information for the final built project. As far as possible, the designer must stress that all changes should be made before the drawings are issued. However, it is not unusual for a client to change displays even after the build has started, though there is nearly always a cost implication as contractors charge additional fees for changes to the original design, especially if they involve more work and materials.

Initial technical drawings tend to be schematic, developing levels of detail as the project progresses. Most designers develop their designs through a number of steps, from an initial feasibility study to an intermediate stage of schematic design, ending with a detailed design for construction. The detail required increases with each step until the final drawings are issued. At each stage, the designer produces drawings at different scales starting with the largest, which show the overall site and how the built project will fit within it, and the key elevations and sections. The structure of the project is then broken down into a series of elements, each smaller than the last, finishing with details drawn as near as possible to actual size. These drawings are collated, numbered and given titles, and should show a contractor the entire project, including all the finishes and dimensions, with no ambiguity.

Orthogonal drawings, such as plans and elevations, are the easiest and quickest to draw. However, complex structures may need to be drawn in three dimensions to make details clear to the contractors and avoid misunderstandings. Where very complex structures are envisaged, it may be necessary to use exploded diagrams and perspectives, though most designers try to avoid providing these if flat drawings are sufficient. The focus for many projects is economy of time and effort, and the quantity and type of drawing is carefully considered to avoid unnecessary work but to ensure clarity of communication.

Labels, details and notes

Technical drawings for exhibitions are similar to those produced by architects and interior designers. The sole difference is perhaps the need to label plans carefully and change the labels assiduously when exhibits are moved. Once the initial visuals and sketches have been produced, participants in the project often demand plans to show the positioning of the exhibits and how they relate to each other. This happens quite frequently and the designer has to keep pace with any changes that are made or risk confusion. When a layout has been established, particularly for permanent exhibitions, elevations are often produced to show the vertical relationships. With all exhibition drawings, figures superimposed on section drawings speak very eloquently about the relationship of the exhibits to visitors. Drawings of a range of visitors interacting with displays helps to determine the correct height for display panels, controls, buttons, screens and other interaction points.

Drawings for interactive devices often need to show the exhibit or display in a number of modes to make clear how the user interacts with it, and what changes are triggered by the interaction. This may also be specified in words on the drawings, detailing the stages in an interaction and the intended visitor experience. Notes on technical drawings are always expressed in an odd style that becomes second nature to designers after practice, though it may seem bizarre to non-designers.

The construction of an exhibition always reflects the quality and accuracy of the technical drawings. If the designer creates a drawing that can easily be misinterpreted by a contractor, he or she is unlikely to achieve the desired results. Some contractors help to resolve problems with drawings, but others simply substitute their own solutions. When this happens, there is almost no telling what will be built; certainly, it is unlikely to be what the designer planned. Contractors may produce their own working drawings from those provided by the designer. If so, the designer can ask to see them and make

Levels of drawing

These images by Casson Mann show a
number of levels of drawing for the Churchill
Museum, London, ranging from overall plans
to detail drawings for production.

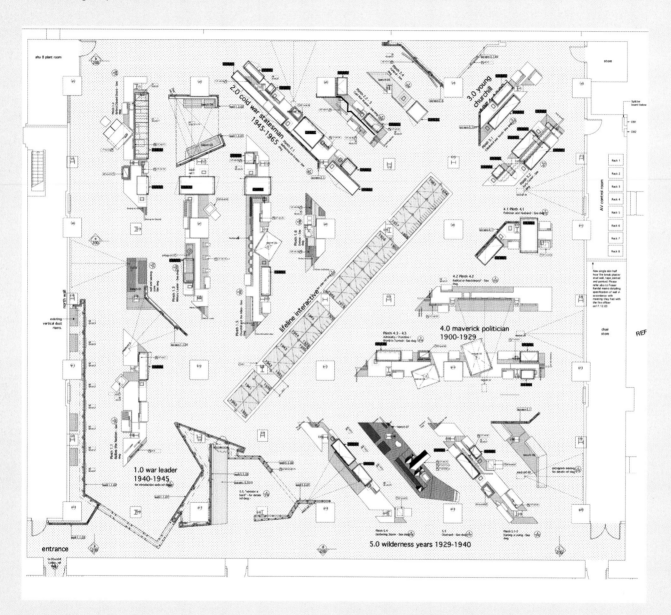

Above
The overall plan shows circulation and the relationship
of the plinths to the room and the other displays.

Opposite top
This drawing shows an individual plinth in plan with both front and
rear elevations. Note that the graphics have been applied to the
drawings and can be used by both construction and graphic
contractors. The overhead structure and pillars are also shown.

Opposite bottom
These drawings of the leather cladding for a display plinth show
the exact details required, including the stitching, cut and placement
of the leather over the plinth.

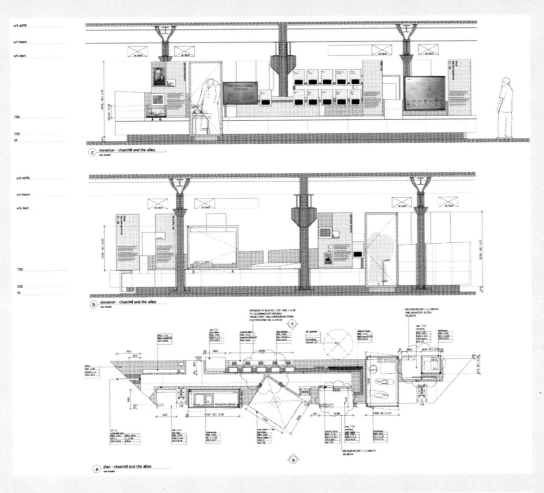

u/s soffit

u/s beam

u/s duct

700

200
ff

ⓒ elevation - churchill and the allies

u/s soffit

u/s beam

u/s duct

700

200
ff

ⓑ elevation - churchill and the allies

ⓐ plan - churchill and the allies

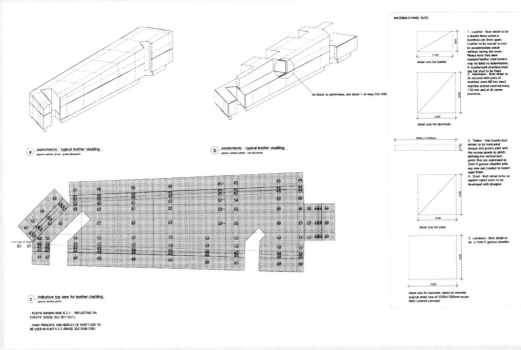

ⓐ axonometric - typical leather cladding

ⓑ axonometric - typical leather cladding

for block to plinth-base, see detail 1 on dwg 202-400.

ⓒ indicative top view for leather cladding

- PLINTH SHOWN HERE IS 2.1 - 'REFLECTING ON
EVENTS' (DWGS 202-307/357).

- SAME PRINCIPLE AND MODULE OF SHEET SIZE TO
BE USED IN PLINTH 2.2 (DWGS 202-308/358).

MATERIALS PANEL SIZES

sheet size for leather

sheet size for aluminium

sheet size for steel

sheet size for laminate, based on material
original sheet size of 5050x1300mm as per
Abet Limited Laminate

1. Leather - Butt detail to be
a double 8mm stitch in
brainless set 8mm apart.
Leather to be routed to rear
to accommodate stitch
without raising the seam.
Please note that were
exposed leather clad corners
may be liable to delamination.
A countersunk stainless steel
top hat stud to be fixed.
2. Aluminium - Butt detail to
be secured with pairs of
stainless steel M6 box head
machine screws centred every
150 mm and at all corner
junctions.

3. Timber - Oak boards butt
details to be horizontal
tongue and groove joint with
the excess panels to plinth
defining the vertical butt
joints that are expressed as
1mm V groove chamfer with
any new oak treated to match
aged finish.
4. Steel - Butt detail to be an
applied raised seam to be
developed with designer.

5. Laminate - Butt detail to
be a 1mm V groove chamfer.

small amendments if he or she feels that they deviate from the original design. Drawings change throughout a project and, where the client needs a quick answer, initial prices are often estimated before they have been finalized. If the client agrees the price, the designer can continue to develop the design but must be mindful that additional details may take the project outside the contractor's initial estimate.

Technical drawings always have explanatory notes and include specifications for materials. Good, accurate notation helps contractors to build quickly and efficiently, and reduces the need to constantly question the designer about his or her intentions. The more information the drawings include, the easier it is to achieve high-quality construction that achieves the designer's objectives. All the details required to specify a material should be available through literature from suppliers—information about, say, timber flooring should include the length and width of strips, available finishes, timber types and laying methods. This information should be noted on the relevant drawing to help the contractor read the designer's intentions.

Specific technical drawings are produced for specialists such as electricians, and flooring and lighting contractors. It is important that their activities are centrally coordinated by the designer or project manager—

Left
Royal Albert Memorial Museum, Ralph Appelbaum Associates, Exeter, UK, 2011.

Opposite (from top)
Sketch layout shows arrangement of content across the floorplan; Graphic elevation shows layout of graphic screens; Section through gallery; Plan drawing of displays (bottom).

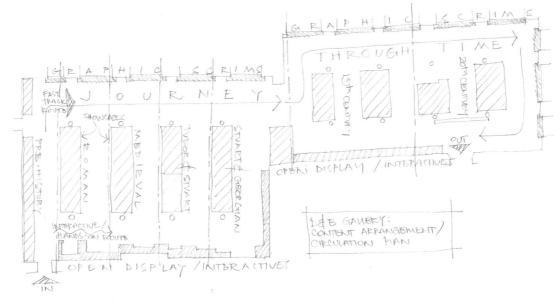

Sketch plan

Section A-A Window graphic scrims

Section B-B Open display interactives

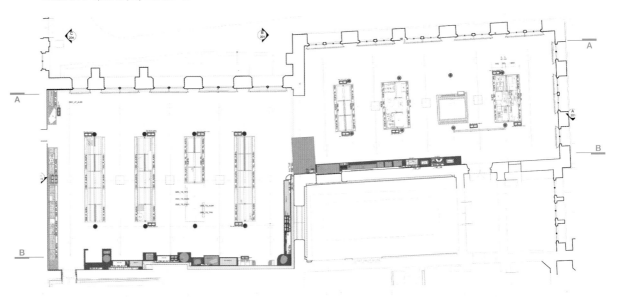

Plan

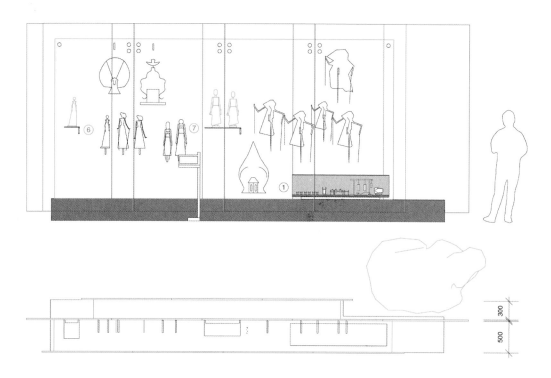

Above and below
National Museum of Ethnology, Leiden, the Netherlands. These elevation and plan drawings specify in detail the placement of small artefacts in a glass cabinet.

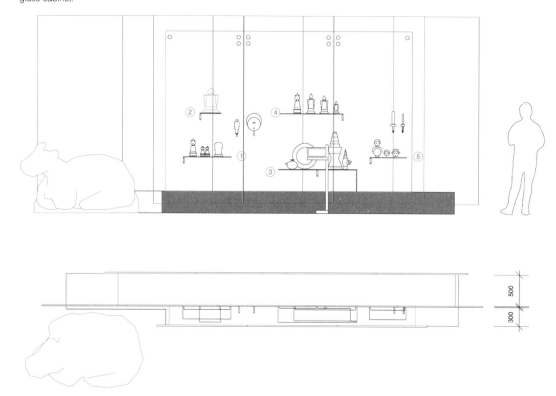

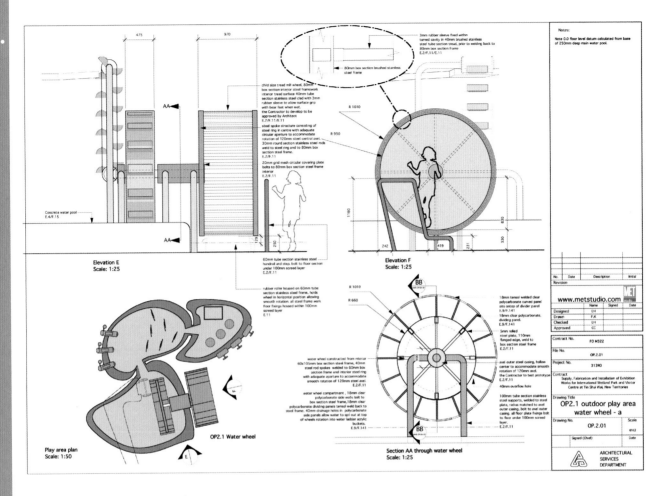

Play area plan
Scale: 1:50

OP2.1 Water wheel

Elevation E
Scale: 1:25

Elevation F
Scale: 1:25

Section AA through water wheel
Scale: 1:25

Official approvals

A number of factors that may have a significant impact on the development of an exhibition design should be considered early in the design process. If any changes to a structure are envisaged, it is advisable to talk to planning or conservation authorities. Similarly, fire precautions and health and safety issues require official approval. Any constraints imposed by the authorities can then be factored into the design.

Tenders

Contractors quote on the basis of a package of drawings and documentation. The drawings must show:

- The relationship of the exhibition space to the overall site (a site plan)
- A plan of the exhibition space with all the exhibit areas
- Elevations and sections that demonstrate the vertical height of the exhibition
- Detailed drawings that show surface finishes and important junctions between materials and surfaces

Hong Kong Wetland Park, Hong Kong. These detail drawings explain a water wheel that can be powered by children. Note that the scale figure of a child is helpful in explaining the function of the device. The drawings include a plan of the completed device in the context of the pool in which it turns (bottom left).

- Details of finishes and materials with exact references and, if necessary, where they can be obtained
- In rare cases, the designer may mock up a detail in card or another modelling material
- For small exhibitions, electrical information is super-imposed on the site plan; larger ones require a separate drawing for the sole use of an electrician
- Ask suppliers to produce prototypes and create samples wherever possible, so that you can check the quality of the construction and what the final outcome will look like
- Build a library of samples that you can refer to quickly and easily

Amending drawings

All too often changes are made after the technical drawings have been issued. These have to be noted on all relevant drawings, and the drawings must be reissued to any contractor to whom a previous set has been sent. The date of the amendment must be marked on the drawing and noted. Often, it is important to telephone the contractor to inform them about the amendments. The contractor will usually keep the original set of drawings but mark them as superseded.

DO...

- Record discussions and ideas on scale drawings.
- Increase the detail and accuracy of the drawings as you come towards the construction phase of the project.
- Ensure that the project can be easily understood through a series of drawings, from large-scale plans of the site and the overall layout through to detailed construction drawings that show details of material finishes.
- Provide as much detail as possible when specifying. Show exactly how materials will be used, on drawings as well as specification sheets and through labels on the drawings.

DON'T...

- Leave anything to chance. If something can be misinterpreted it will be.
- Change drawings without telling parties who will be affected, such as lighting designers, contractors, subcontractors and clients.
- Invent symbols or drawing elements if well-understood conventions already exist.
- Specify constructions that are impossible to make, or materials that are impossible to obtain. When possible, check the sources of materials with contractors or suppliers.

13.

This chapter describes the factors involved in the construction of an exhibition or display, including the transport of exhibits and structural elements, collaboration with contractors and how green design can be implemented. It looks at additional services that the designer may provide, and gives practical advice on trade practices and project management.

Construction

Although construction in the exhibition sector is in many ways similar to construction in the retail sector, it involves a number of unique practices. Speed is often vital and most exhibition specialists are used to the rhythm of careful preparation and planning, and short intensive periods of build-up before the opening of a show. Most venues try to minimize the length of time for which they are closed, and squeeze the installation and dismantling of displays into a short period. Construction, graphics, and electrical, multimedia and lighting installations have to be strictly timetabled, which often means working late into the night to meet strict deadlines.

First of all, the designer should consider how the elements of an exhibition or display will be transported and installed. Large constructions have to be broken into smaller segments for transport and access into the exhibition space. Many venues, particularly museums, have restricted access and it may be necessary to consider how to disassemble individual elements in order to take them through restrictive doors or corridors before they are reassembled on site. For travelling displays, constant assembly and disassembly can be inconvenient and expensive, and the designer has to consider this from the outset. Weight also has a considerable impact when displays are transported over long distances as freight charges are often calculated on this as well as volume.

Most displays are designed to be only as durable as they need to be, given the length of time for which they will be installed. Short-term installations are relatively crude in construction while permanent ones are often designed with higher specifications. This applies particularly to how displays are finished. Non-durable paints that can be easily painted over when they get dirty are often used for short-term installations. Longer term displays have durable finishes that will withstand the public handling them over a period of years without the need for maintenance. Children's displays are particularly vulnerable to rough handling, and even temporary ones must be robust. The designer needs to estimate the effects of use and specify materials accordingly. Like a stage set, exhibition structures often look rough behind the scenes, with unfinished walls and large unpainted areas. Although this would not be appropriate for an interior design scheme, in exhibitions most clients are keen to spend their money where it can be seen and appreciated, to give visitors a high-quality experience, and are less concerned about anything that is not visible the public.

The cost of construction is influenced by a variety of factors, including transport, materials and the labour required to make and install each item. Most designers add as much sophistication to their design as their budget allows, and often overspecify in the first instance. If the prices quoted by contractors mean that particular details cannot be achieved, the designer meets the contractors to discuss what can be done for the money available, and amends the details to achieve the highest standards that are possible and the necessary budget savings. It is preferable to have all elements constructed off site. As time is always limited, it is easier and faster to reassemble them at the exhibition venue than start from scratch on site.

Many staples of exhibition design, such as glass cabinets and light boxes, are available from specialist suppliers, who are often able to achieve high-quality details and engineer specialist features such as fire and security precautions, and environmental controls for humidity and temperature. These are complicated to manufacture and generally time consuming to build, so the client and designer should look carefully at their schedules to ensure that they can be constructed in the time available. Generally, the longer the designer has to prepare for an exhibition, the more he or she is able to use high-quality specialist suppliers and achieve high-quality details. Poor detailing and finish often reflect inadequate preparation time.

Working with contractors

As in any industry, there is a range of contractors with a range of specialities. Very often, the designer employs specialists in lighting, graphic production, construction, model-making, sound, interaction and projection/moving images. Different jobs require different skills and it is necessary to examine the credentials of each contractor—the type of work they have done in the

Opposite top and bottom
PlayStation Exhibit, E-3 Expo, Mauk Design, Los Angeles, USA, 2005. This exhibit for PlayStation included a two-storey steel frame with a glass balustrade and an illuminated glass floor. Panels were used above the first-floor deck to partially block the view of the exhibition venue ceiling. Two-storey or "double-deck" constructions are common at fairs where space is limited or expensive.

Above left and above
Tridonic.Atco stand, Arno Design, Light + Building Fair, Frankfurt, Germany, 2008. Most exhibitions are built off-site and assembled at the exhibition venue. This display for a lighting manufacturer comprises a number of pre-constructed components rapidly assembled during the short exhibition build-up. Above left is a computer rendering of the final design while the photograph above shows construction in progress.

past, its quality and what it costs. As with a house builder, before taking on a contractor it is useful to find out as much as possible about them and see work they have done. Contractors vary from one-man bands to huge global conglomerates, and designers normally try to find one that is the appropriate size for a particular job. Large-scale work demands large contractors, but the construction for smaller exhibitions can often be handled very adequately and more cheaply by a small firm as long as it has sufficient manpower and experience. Each case requires careful judgement, balancing the cost of hiring an expensive heavily resourced contractor against the risk involved in using an inexpensive but under-resourced firm that may be too small to do the job successfully.

It is necessary to develop a relationship of trust with contractors because the consequences of poor performance, not finishing a job by the time an exhibition opens, or poor workmanship reflect badly on the designer as well as the client. Contractors need good organizational skills to avoid difficulties and the best installations are carefully orchestrated. However, even the most organized contractors can be defeated by a job that is too big for them, or outside their area of expertise, and designers should use those who are most appropriate, not just the ones they know. If a designer is working in a venue for the first time, and especially if it is abroad, it may be wise to choose a contractor who has worked there before. Some venues are problematic and are governed by complicated rules. In these circumstances, someone with prior experience of the venue can be a vital asset.

Contractors' workloads change during the course of a year. If they are already working at over their normal capacity, they will increase their charges if they take on additional projects. By asking several contractors to tender for the same job, the designer is more likely to identify a specialist with a slim workload who is willing to charge a reasonable price. However, as with all construction, the cheapest is not always the best and tenders should only be sent to contractors who are competent to work on the project.

Above and opposite
Antarctic Dome, Inflate/Land Design Studio, "Ice Station Antarctica", Natural History Museum, London, UK, 2007. This pneumatic structure was created to give the impression of an ice station at the Antarctic. Inflatable structures can be erected very quickly on-site and make very effective temporary exhibits. The drawings opposite give measurements for contractors.

Sustainable construction

A commitment to sustainability will change how many designers decide on construction methods. Adherence to the green principles of "reduce, reuse and recycle" means a less flippant and unthinking use of resources, and a great deal more consideration given to thoughtful construction methods that allow for dismantling and reuse. In most cases the exhibition industry (see chapter 14) is not geared to deal with the intelligent use of resources and, for the most part, supply chains that will help designers to promote green methods of construction do not exist. There is considerable scope for new practices to emerge in the future, arrived at through agreement between exhibition builders and legally enforceable through construction contracts.

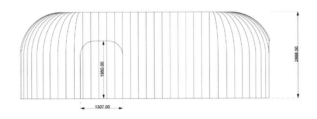

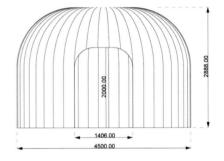

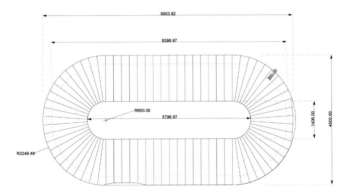

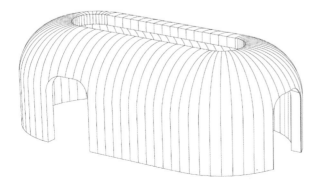

Trade fairs

Shipping is often a vital part of the design management of trade fairs stands. There are a number of firms that specialize in exhibition shipping, taking large containers of display equipment and exhibits to foreign venues. They offer bespoke services for transporting delicate or valuable exhibits, with additional security personnel where necessary. Reputable shipping agents often have representatives in almost every country, enabling them to organize shipping and delivery at a local level and to avoid some of the worst bureaucratic delays. Containers are ordered from the shipping firm and sent to contractors to be filled. They are then sent by sea to the venue, where the contractors unpack them. In other instances, when shipping isn't involved, for example, a main contractor may hire lorries and organize the transport of the exhibits and display equipment.

The services provided at a trade fair, and the relevant order forms, are available from the organizers of the show, with key dates and milestones in the build-up to the fair. The maximum height of construction is published in the exhibition manual, with information about any columns or features that may obstruct a display. The organizers will, on request, send the contractor a detailed floor plan that shows the exact measurements of any obstructions.

Below left, below and opposite
Saloni display, Francesc Rifé, Valencia, Spain, 2005. This display of ceramic wall tiles for the Spanish manufacturer Saloni is divided into a series of pavilions. The designer, Francesc Rife, used a carefully chosen palette of materials including timber, ceramics, and glass clad with graphics and laminate to create a number of distinct yet complementary areas. The central circular desk lit from below is clad with a tiled graphic.

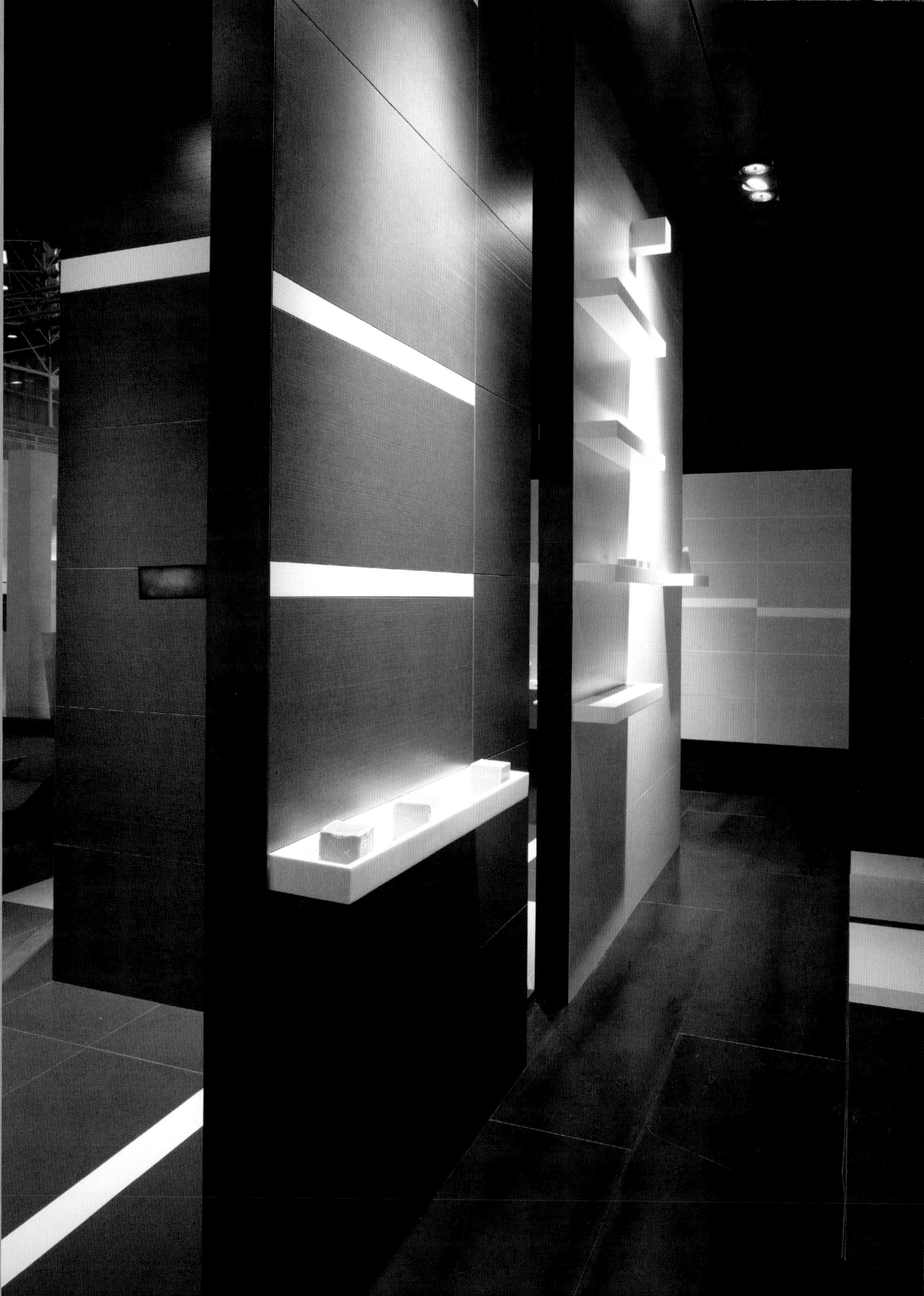

Electrical requirements have to be submitted a few weeks before a show and any later requests are usually subject to a surcharge. Where large constructions are envisaged, structural calculations based on the designer's drawings must be made by an experienced structural engineer, and submitted to the venue's structural engineers for inspection. All these stipulations are in the exhibition manual, which should be read in detail to avoid later problems. Trade fairs are subject to the same building and safety codes as other forms of construction, such as house building. These regulations are frequently explained in a distilled form in the manual but, like any legislation, they are often exactingly applied. Exhibitors try to skirt around them at their peril, and designers must comply with them. In the worst cases, a construction may be condemned and roped off from the public until remedial work is carried out.

At most trade fair venues the floor is made from rough concrete that is too unfinished to be used in a display area. This space is often carpeted or, for most bespoke displays, overlaid with a timber platform on which the displays will be placed. All electrical wiring is laid under the platform, and holes are drilled through it to bring the wires up in the right place. Many venues allow constructions to be hung from cables, called "drops", which are suspended from the ceiling to allow exhibitors to hang signage, for example, above the exhibition stands.

In any trade-fair venue, most exhibitors compete with each other to create displays that outdo those of their neighbours, so most clients have a vested interest in building as high as they can within the rules. This involves using ladders, lifting equipment and scaffolding towers. Construction supervision legislation often requires designers and design companies to consider these issues before the start of a project to avoid unsafe practices and accidents. Short installation periods encourage haste, and there is therefore an element of danger for contractors if safe practices are not considered. Safety should be paramount at all times. Mechanisms such as "risk assessments" and "method statements" maximize the care and forethought given to construction practices.

The green agenda

Currently, the emission of harmful greenhouse gases into the atmosphere has risen to the top of the green agenda, driven by climate change. Other issues of concern to the green exhibition designer are: scarce resources (especially natural ones), toxic materials (for example, paints and other coatings with harmful components), toxic processes used in the extraction, production and refining of raw materials, destruction of environments and biodiversity, waste produced during production, and the pollution of water supplies or the overuse of water where it is scarce. It is difficult for designers to act on the basis of these broad categories. This is why industry bodies such as the Building Research Establishment in the United Kingdom have issued guidelines for green specification. Where no data is available, designers often have to do their own research or work from first principles. However, some common sense is required. Locally sourced and rapidly renewable resources are more likely to be environmentally sustainable than scarce materials transported over long distances, though each case must be judged on its merits. Sustainability consultants can be called in to advise on these issues.

There are a number of important concepts that are helpful in understanding green design, and "embodied energy" is particularly useful. It is all the energy required to extract and produce a material to a specified point. Materials that are low in embodied energy are preferred as less energy is required to extract, refine and process them into a usable state. Timber, for example, is low in embodied energy as it requires relatively little energy to cut down a tree, saw it into planks and process the planks for use. Materials such as steel, which requires very hot furnaces and high energy consumption to be

Natural History Museum of Utah, Ralph Appelbaum Associates, Salt Lake City, Utah, USA,2011. This museum attained a LEED Gold standard award for sustainability and incorporates important sustainable features such as rainwater collection, solar energy use, local sourcing of materials and recycling of construction waste.

processed and rolled, are much higher in embodied energy, though in many cases the performance of steel may justify its use in preference to timber. Surprisingly, rather than large construction elements, it is the finish materials such as carpets, stone and wall finishes that are principally responsible for the embodied energy contained within a building, and can often account for up to 50 per cent of the total.

Green dos and don'ts

DO...

- Try to use materials that are low in embodied energy, and which can be found locally and fashioned into building materials as simply as possible without using energy-intensive extraction procedures. Rapidly renewable materials are preferred.
- Use materials certified by reputable industry bodies. For example, the Forest Stewardship Council provides certificates for timber that assure users that it is produced in well-managed forests and according to green principles.
- Consider how you can follow the hierarchical green principles of "reduce, reuse and recycle". First, by reducing the scale of a construction or increasing the efficiency of the design; second, by incorporating reused materials; and third, by considering how materials that cannot be reused can be recycled.
- Ask questions about the environmental impact of your actions, deal proactively with green issues and draw sustainability issues to the attention of your clients, contractors and colleagues to encourage them to cooperate with you.

DON'T...

- Use materials that have proven toxic impacts on the soil, air and water.
- Use composite materials unless they are really necessary. It is difficult to reuse or recycle sheet materials clad with laminates.
- Use scarce materials unnecessarily; consider the impact on the areas where those materials are sourced.
- Transport materials and labour to distant exhibition sites unnecessarily if you can reduce the environmental impact this would involve by using local resources.

The designer's responsibilities

The responsibilities of an exhibition designer vary considerably throughout the industry and may change from project to project. In some cases, often in trade-fair design, the designer is responsible for the construction as well as the design. This is called a "turn key" service, and the designer takes charge of every aspect of the process of exhibiting from hiring contractors to delivering the exhibits to the site. This type of service requires more project management from the designer, but the advantage from a client's point of view is that they can hold the designer responsible for all aspects of the exhibition, and avoid the complicated chain of command that often causes confusion when a number of specialist agencies work alongside each other. The designer is responsible for any fault with the design but also for the quality and safety of the display construction.

In other cases, the designer and contractors are employed separately by the client, all of them being answerable for their own areas of expertise. This means the designer is not responsible for the quality of manufacture; however, he or she has to manage a potentially tricky relationship with the contractors, whose interests lie in minimizing their scope of work. In these circumstances, the designer's specification drawings for contractors must be unambiguous, to avoid argument or litigation. The designer has to make clear whether or not he or she is responsible for supervising the site.

In many countries, designers are responsible for ensuring that what they design will be safe and structurally sound, and hire structural engineers to give advice on construction details. Increasingly, exhibition designers and contractors have additional responsibilities for maintaining safe practices on site and assessing health and safety risks. Governments around the world continue to legislate in this area, and designers who work internationally have to conform to new rulings wherever they are practising. In any venue, there are usually officers responsible for health, safety, fire precautions and accessibility for the disabled—in the event of any doubt, it is a good idea to show proposals to them before building starts, to avoid later problems and questions. Designers also take on the responsibility of ensuring that their proposals satisfy environmental criteria, with advice from environmental consultants.

Trade practices

Trade practices vary enormously across the world, and it is best to research contracts and common industry standards before working abroad. In the United States, most trade-fair activity is unionized and all the work at an exhibition venue must be done by union members. The unions responsible for carrying out exhibition work are often affiliated to those of the delivery drivers and shippers, whose members decide on the fees that should be paid to them for the work they perform; they have sole responsibility for moving or freighting, which is known as "drayage". If a client or a designer even picks up a box in contravention of union rules, the union may decide to deny them vital services such as power or lighting.

In Europe there are very few union practices, thus allowing designers more freedom to design their exhibitions in the way that best suits them. Nevertheless, they often find that large contractors have common ways of achieving particular aims—for example, building walls—and to save the budget it can be necessary to hire their stock material rather than create new display equipment. Asian exhibition firms have their own construction techniques and labour practices. It is often up to designers to investigate local construction methods and see how they can work with existing systems; and, if they can't, decide how to produce suitable alternatives. Labour practices affect the way exhibitions are designed and detailed. If contractors are not familiar with a construction method, they will inevitably increase the price because the job will take them longer. If, as sometimes happens, a few complicated details consume a disproportionate part of the budget, discussing the problem with the people concerned often results in finding good solutions that are within the scope of the contractor's expertise.

Children's exhibits

As children tend to wear down materials and mechanisms very quickly, their exhibits are usually made to a very high specification, suitable for heavy industrial components. In nearly all displays where there is interactivity, technical back-up is required to repair broken exhibits. Small children like to poke their fingers into any holes or gaps in an exhibit, so the designer must take care to avoid traps that might catch their fingers.

Project management

Once the technical drawings have been issued the project manager, if there is one, takes over and is responsible for the contractors and suppliers. The client deals on a day-to-day basis with the project manager, who will share with the designer the responsibility for delivering on time, within budget and to a high standard. The project manager should also be responsible to the designer for maintaining the quality of the design and must take care to preserve its essential qualities, especially if there are budget constraints. He or she must ensure that specifications are met or, in some cases, that reasonable substitutions are made. Careful project management is required for the implementation of green design, along with good communication with contractors and a thorough wide-ranging approach to all aspects of construction, transport and resource management.

Ancillary services

Some exhibition-design companies offer additional services, connected with the delivery of the design, to their clients. Many provide the "turn key" service described on page 211, and take responsibility for nearly all aspects of delivery. Other services are at the request of the client who, if a company does not have the necessary resources, may ask the exhibition designers to take on extra responsibilities. Large organizations are often keen to outsource

services to suppliers because this means they do not have to employ personnel in-house. If design companies provide additional resources, such as a marketing strategy and help with the management of the stand during the show, they must ensure that the income from their clients is sufficient to pay the wages of the individuals they hire. To some degree, big trade-fair design companies are as busy dealing with logistics as they are with design, and a large part of their effort is often concentrated on delivering the design.

For museum and gallery designers, gathering the information relevant to the design process is half the task. Although many clients are adept at doing this and handing the results on to the designers, many are not. If there is nothing for designers to work on, the design team will be idle. Some design companies offer their clients a "content management" service to help manage the flow of information to the designers. Content managers tell the client what is needed to ensure a successful show, help with the task of carrying out research and cajole the providers of content.

Gardens By The Bay, Land Design Studio, Singapore, China, 2012. This huge greenhouse was conceived in conjunction with landscape designers, architects and environmental and structural engineers. Narrative interpretation is ingeniously integrated into an engineered garden ecosystem.

Handover

Before a completed design is handed over, the designer produces a checklist, called a "snagging" list (or a "punch list" in the US), which highlights "snags" or construction defects. The client often adds their own "snags". The list is helpful to contractors as it helps them to focus on outstanding tasks. When all the construction tasks are complete, the designer must ensure that the client has a complete understanding of the workings of any sound, projection or computer equipment, and is aware of any maintenance requirements.

DO...

- Consider how constructions or exhibits will be taken into the exhibition building and whether doors are wide enough to accommodate them.
- Design structures that can be broken down or dismantled for transport where necessary—especially for temporary exhibitions.
- Make clear decisions about how contractors will work together and organize detailed contractual arrangements.
- Manage your projects so that they are within cost, health and safety, and environmental constraints.

DON'T...

- Use suppliers whose work is faulty or inconsistent. Wherever possible try to use suppliers or contractors whose work is proven, without being over-reliant on any single provider.
- Agree to arrangements where there are open-ended responsibilities for the designer or contractors.
- Leave your client to identify and deal with faults in construction. All quality issues should be addressed by the project manager and the designer before handover.
- Design or specify constructions that have structural problems. Where safety is at stake, you should take all reasonable steps to identify potential problems and get competent advice to solve any potential issues.

14.

This chapter explores how exhibition design is evolving with many commercial clients perceiving it as a major factor in communicating their brand. It discusses the increasing importance of green issues, and describes how museums, galleries and other attractions contribute to the economies of countries throughout the world. It also emphasizes that designers have a responsibility to use their skills with integrity.

An evolving discipline

Exhibition innovation has been driven by a new generation of exhibition professionals with a deep commitment to understanding how best to serve the needs of visitors. This has led to a more purposeful approach to engaging the public in activities that respond to differing learning styles and levels of understanding. It has also helped to inject a measure of fun into exhibitions, which visitors might have previously attended out of a sense of duty but which provided little entertainment. Nevertheless, the best exhibitions continue to convey ideas but are imaginative in how they are conveyed.

Alongside the newer aspects of exhibition practice, designers need many of the traditional skills of planning spaces that serve the needs of visitors and respond to developed exhibition strategies. Site analysis and the physical linking of spaces to create satisfying visitor journeys remain central to exhibition design. Museums that have evolved piecemeal over many decades, by extending galleries, storage and cafés to serve immediate needs, are often no longer fit to provide what visitors require, and in many cases need a thorough overhaul. The reworking of spaces to ensure logical visitor journeys continues to be a major aspect of modern museum practice.

Many clients, particularly in the commercial sector, see exhibiting as a major element in brand communication. While visitors frequently pay only passing attention to two-dimensional branding in the form of brochures, catalogues and promotional material, by creating "brand environments" exhibitors are able to attract the attention of their audiences and create deeper responses to what they offer. The brand environment has thus become a major tool in promoting products and services, and the powerful "total" and "immersive" exhibition environment, pioneered by the commercial sector, has become an important influence on museum practice.

Although there is much that is new and innovative in exhibition design, there are many aspects of the discipline that will be wholly familiar to many design practitioners and are an application of common sense. As with product design, interior design and architecture, the exhibition designer is constrained to think about the ergonomics of the visitor experience. He or she has to devise displays that the wider visiting public, including disabled visitors, can see and experience comfortably. The provision of interactive displays in particular, that are shaped to respond to human dimensions and

Above
The Connect Home, Kengo Kuma Associates, Milan Furniture Fair, 2007. This conceptual representation of a house demonstrates how the inside and the outside of a house can be connected though the use of sustainable materials such as bamboo. Sliding bamboo partitions (sumushiko) create soft divisions between the spaces with the intention of decreasing the sense of rigid boundaries.

capabilities, is a central part of the exhibition designer's job. In addition, it is necessary to meet the needs of large groups and the flow of visitors comfortably, respecting fire and other safety regulations.

For graphic designers, the three-dimensional environment provides a fascinating opportunity to collaborate with specialists in other fields and direct interaction and multimedia design. The combination of these powerful elements has become the springboard for innovation, and a key reason for the resurgence of interest within exhibitions. In addition, graphic, interaction and multimedia designers play an essential role in determining the "voice" of an exhibition, alongside their responsibility to ensure engagement with its content.

Green design

Green design is an increasingly important issue. Though few countries rigidly enforce green legislation at the time of writing, a number have set ambitious targets. The green issue has been discussed fitfully since the 1970s, and though there is a sense that exhibition practices will change there have been few dramatic developments. Inevitably there will be stricter regulation in the near future, and governments will begin scrutinizing exhibitions and their design more closely in order to reduce energy use, greenhouse gases and environmentally harmful practices. A stricter legislative regime is coupled with a growing preparedness by institutions and business to tackle green issues, motivated partly by a change in public attitudes.

"Market Values—Smithfield: Past Present and Future", London, UK, 2007. Thomas Matthews is a design agency with a commitment to a green approach to exhibition design. This image shows the use of fully recyclable cardboard exhibition panels for an exhibition about the Smithfield meat market in London. Local printers were used to minimize the financial and environmental cost of transport. Vegetable-based inks were used instead of more common solvent-based inks. In some cases, Thomas Matthews salvages old exhibition installations and refashions them to produce new displays. This approach minimizes the environmental impact caused by the dumping of obsolete exhibition materials.

This remarkable design by Zaha Hadid Architects for the proposed Guggenheim Hermitage Museum in Vilnius, Lithuania, fulfills the clients' desire for a landmark building. However, like many iconic museum structures, it threatens to overwhelm the exhibits.

Green issues encourage a holistic approach to activities and construction. Thus, the building and design of exhibitions is seen as just part of their overall impact on the environment. For example, the millions of visitor journeys to and from shows weigh heavily in environmental terms, especially when they involve flights and long-distance car journeys. For this reason, organizations such as the Cape Town International Convention Centre in South Africa, while making a business case for expansion, have addressed the carbon cost of staging larger events that would draw foreign delegates and therefore significantly more flights to the city. By negating the carbon impact of these flights through carbon offset, they aim to make a business case that is environmentally, as well as economically, viable.

At present, many large companies produce corporate social responsibility reports and have made public commitments to do their business in a sustainable way. They are asking their suppliers to prove their green credentials, and any designer making a proposal to one of them would do well to check its websites or ask to see any policy documents. This would provide a good reference for making a green pitch. However, despite public commitments to new targets, in practice the industry is wasteful and has grown accustomed to a cycle of speedy fabrication and dumping of exhibition materials, often after only a single use. For trade fair stands, bespoke materials are routinely discarded after just three or four days' use. Public exhibitions usually have a longer run, but materials or building practices are rarely considered from a green standpoint. Most travelling exhibitions involve long-distance haulage with its attendant costs to the environment. Inevitably, these practices will come under review as environmental legislation is imposed. However, new legislative measures—for example, a tax on materials dumped in landfill sites—are not the only answer. The better solution is a readiness by designers, clients and contractors to work in a sustainable way to reduce harm to the environment.

In many cases, poor practices are caused not purely by poor design or uncaring attitudes, but by a competitive system of rapid production and response that leaves little time for intelligent planning of services, sustainable construction methods and the sourcing of green alternatives. High-quality green design takes time and a great deal of careful consideration from project managers, designers, clients and contractors, in order to reduce the use of resources, increase reuse, reduce transport and increase the percentage of materials that can be recycled from any given construction. Clients need to add the necessary time to their schedules and be willing to pay for thoughtful design and planning that is more environmentally sustainable. This is an unwelcome message for many clients who are under pressure to attract more visitors to their exhibitions or generate more sales. What is the incentive to promote green design when their jobs, their promotion prospects and their prestige are governed purely by the number of visitors they can attract to their events? Why spend their precious budgets on sustainable construction when wasteful (and cheaper) design works equally well? The answer is to ensure that all the individuals who manage projects are sufficiently incentivized by their institutions to implement green initiatives. Design awards that recognize good green practice, whether by contractors, subcontractors, designers, project managers or clients, sponsored by industry bodies in both the commercial and museum sectors, might help to drive this agenda.

The future

Museums, galleries and other visitor attractions make a major contribution to tourism and therefore the economic well-being of any country. People often return to a place they first visited for pleasure in order to exploit its business opportunities, so the income generated by ticket sales to exhibitions is often only a proportion of the wealth created by staging them. So-called "invisible" earnings, through hotel accommodation, restaurants and other related journey costs are a further addition to the economic benefits stimulated by exhibitions. This lesson has not been lost on some of the world's newly wealthy countries, which have sought to invest in public museums to display and interpret art, science and history not only for their own populations but also for new generations of visitors from overseas.

For many countries and their governments, museums, archives and visitor attractions that explain and interpret the past are of great significance. The opportunity an exhibition provides to create narratives, supported by artefacts that evidence the past and help a community to understand its history and the histories of others, is precious. As communities develop, the need for such exhibitions becomes part of an economic and political evolution, where narratives are constructed with the participation of the community and evidenced through the selective use of an archive. These narratives can be the cornerstone of an emerging awareness of political and social history.

It is worth mentioning that all interpretations of exhibition themes are by their nature selective and partial. Those that are historical will be rooted in current preoccupations and narratives, and will doubtless seem quaint to future historians. In most cases, interpretations are innocuous—expressions of opinion based on sifted evidence—and are accepted as such by normally sceptical exhibition audiences. However, some interpretations are morally repugnant: history has a number of examples of dishonest exhibitions mounted in support of odious regimes. Exhibition designers have powerful tools at their disposal; they must always take care how they use them.

In recent years, exhibits concerning national or cultural identity have sought to introduce a content development practice termed "co-development". Exhibitors around the world have and continue to create exhibitions that represent cultures and identities other than their own. For example, a national institution in, say, the United States or Germany might create a display on the subject of Pacific Islanders from Samoa. In such cases, the display is often supervised by a curator with knowledge of the Samoan community but without the consent of that community or local participation. This can, and has in the past, led to inadequate and patronising displays that paint a skewed image that causes offence and can lead to allegations of racism. A co-development approach brings members of a community into the process of developing the content and design of a display. The consultation process needs to be well designed and rigorous. Necessarily, co-development will require choosing representatives of a community with the authority to speak on behalf of that community and trusting relationship between the parties. It is certain that any portrayal of a community will arouse some controversy and criticism, but a well-designed co-development process is a necessary beginning for such projects.

The opportunities for exhibition designers and professionals have never been greater. Countries around the globe are discovering that exhibitions are a sophisticated and significant medium of expression and, judging by the furious activity in the world's most prestigious design agencies, we stand on the cusp of a new era. Centres in countries that have no tradition of exhibiting will reach out to millions of visitors, many of whom will learn about themselves, their countries, their history and their traditions for the first time, through the medium of interpretative design.

Accessibility guidelines—excerpts from guidelines prepared by the Victoria & Albert Museum, London (courtesy of Barry Ginley/Victoria & Albert Museum)

Entrances/exits

- Access to be level at entrances and exits. Thresholds should be flush (flat).
- Provide a clear circulation space either side of doors or entrance spaces and elevators.
- Keep doors open or use automatic doors if possible.
- Entrances to be clearly visible (for example by using a colour that contrasts with nearby gallery space).
- Provide a visibility strip between 1400–1600 mm (55–63 in) AFFL (above finished floor level) on glazed doors or walls.
- Provide clear operating instructions (for example "push/pull") and push plates for doors.
- Provide contrasting door furniture.

Stairs/ramps

- Changes in level should be avoided where possible.
- Ramps (accompanied by stairs if necessary) to be used if a change in level is required. Ramps to be at a 1:20 incline, if possible, with frequent flat rest areas.
- Clear circulation spaces required with tactile or differently coloured warning surfaces at the top and bottom of raised areas.
- Mark the edge of each stair step with a strip of contrasting colour.

General seating and rest areas

- Provide plentiful seating with adjacent wheelchair spaces.
- Seating should consist of a firm, fairly upright static seat.
- Provide some seating with arm rests or supports either side at 580 mm (23 in) above the floor.
- Seating should have a heel space underneath of at least 100 mm (4 in) to make rising easier.
- Ensure that seating contrasts with the surroundings.

Through routes

- No change in floor level is preferred.
- Primary circulation and escape routes should be a minimum of 1500 mm (59 in) wide, or 1500 x 1800 mm (59 x 70 in) at turning points.
- Straight routes, avoiding cul-de-sacs, are best for visitors with mobility difficulties.
- Provide a visibility strip between 1400 and 1600 mm (55 and 63 in) AFFL on glazed doors or walls.
- Provide a high colour contrast between floor and walls.
- Provide a consistent choice of colours to help locate items such as entrances, doors, furniture and display stands.
- Use matt floor finishes to avoid visual confusion caused by reflections and glare.

Displays

- Circulation areas around individual displays that are not main circulation routes to be 1200 mm (47 in), preferably 1500 mm (59 in).
- Objects ideally to be displayed between 750 and 2000 mm (30 and 79 in) from the floor for ease of viewing.
- Desk cases to be 800 mm (32 in) from the floor with an overhang, and with a 750 mm (30 in) wide clear space underneath for wheelchair parking.
- The preference is for wheelchair users to be able to see displays face on. This can be achieved by providing a toe space around constructed walls, cases and large plinths to allow wheelchair access, or space for a wheelchair to draw alongside the case.
- Case background should be in a contrasting colour to the object exhibited inside, with at least 70% contrast between foreground and background.
- Position wall-mounted display cases so that the lower edges are less than 685 mm (27 in) high.

- Keep projections to a minimum and provide visual and tactile warnings as well as a guard rail when the overhang projects more than 100 mm (4 in) at a height of between 300 and 2100 mm (12 and 83 in).
- Plinths should be a colour that contrasts with the floor to increase visibility.

Interpretative devices and audio-visual displays

- Seating should be removable to enable wheelchair access.
- Dedicated AV areas to have two wheelchair spaces, with adjacent standard seating.
- Activity surfaces or computer stations to be no higher than 800 mm (32 in) AFFL and fully accessible for a parked wheelchair, with no solid fronts or obstructions.
- Surfaces, screens and user controls should be adjustable in height and angle.
- Controls should be fully operable with one hand, require no tight grasping, or turning of the wrist, and be at least 75 mm (3 in) in their smallest dimension, and colour contrasting. Provide a place to rest the hand while using the controls.
- Controls needing precise hand movement should be 750–1000 mm (30–39 in) high. The maximum height for simple push button controls is 1200 mm (47 in).
- Provide induction loops for interpretative devices that use sound, marked with the standard symbol. Provide all audio information in an alternative format (for example print).
- All screen programmes should have clear stationary text. If subtitling is not possible then a typescript should be made available. Indicate the length of the programme, and if on auto-timer, when the next show will start. State if there is no soundtrack.

- Telephone headsets or other exclusively aural information should have a script. Provide inductive couplers for handsets, marked with a standard symbol. Mount on a desk-height terminal or wall mount between 750 and 1000 mm (30 and 39 in) above the floor.

- Provide power points around the galleries in places where it is likely that portable induction loop systems will be used.

- Specify fluorescent lights carefully as they can create interference with hearing aids and induction loops.

- Touch screens are useful for visually impaired visitors and those with limited manual dexterity. Roller ball devices are preferred to mouse controls for similar reasons.

- Consider providing the ability to zoom in on text and images in computer interactives. The ability to alter the contrast of images could be a useful feature.

- Menu options could be given for speech output or large print. Sign language images could also be included as a menu option.

- Consider providing visual information in an audio format. This could be an audio version of text panels/labels or audio description of visuals.

- Consider providing space for a guide dog to lie down at an interpretative device.

Tactile displays and visual aids

- Where possible integrate tactile displays—such as museum objects, replicas and models—into object displays, preferably in quiet places. These could be identified and visually linked through design, colour and lighting to the objects.

- It may be necessary to provide supplementary information (for example audio programmes) at tactile displays.

- Place tactile displays at a height between 710 mm (28 in) and 800 mm (32 in) AFFL, to allow for children and adults to touch, with a clearance of 700 mm (28 in) to allow wheelchair access.

Graphic information

- Display graphics should be considered as an integral and essential element of the overall design.

- Sizes of labels and panels should be consistent throughout the exhibition—it is confusing for the visitor when labels and panels change in format and size from one theme to the next. The hierarchy of graphic elements should be clear and easy for the visitor to understand.

- Labels should be as close to the objects they describe as possible and section or theme panels should be prominently positioned at the beginning of each section or theme.

- Main panel texts should fall within 1200–1600 mm (47–63 in) above the floor when vertically mounted, and 600 mm (24 in) from floor to base of an angled graphics panel.

- All graphics should be prototyped/ tested in actual conditions for legibility by user groups prior to production to ensure clarity, legibility, position, height, colour and contrast. All graphics to be lit adequately.

- Typefaces should be selected for clarity and legibility as well as style and propriety to the 3D design.

- Make all printed matter non-reflective with good contrast between paper colour, ink colour and type style.

- Use dark inks and pale backgrounds; never use yellow for text, and avoid pale colours on coloured backgrounds (for example grey on blue) or colours indistinguishable by people with colour-blindness (especially red on green).

- Do not mount lettering directly onto glass.

- Graphics/panels/labels should also have good contrast against the background wall or case interior. They should not be in the shadow of the viewer.

- Try to avoid the complexity caused by running text across photographs or around irregularly shaped illustrations. Avoid running text across images, as this can make the text illegible to many visually impaired visitors.

Where possible avoid busy, confusing images, and consider enlarging the important part of an image.

- Avoid difficult/indistinct typefaces, and excessive use of italics or block capitals.

- Avoid complex mixes of typefaces.

- Use an appropriate, legible text case—generally lower-case for the main text—in medium to bold.

- A minimum type size of 18–36pt is suitable for most panels/labels. Main texts on introductory panels/labels should be considerably larger— around 48pt. In-situ mock-ups are essential before final approval.

- Provide information (such as panels, labels and instructions for interpretative devices) in an alternative form (for example audio or on large-print bats).

- Provide Braille labels for all tactile displays and for objects that have high contrast, clear detail. Place Braille labels flat as they are read with the fingertips, at a minimum height of 700 mm (28 in) AFFL. They should be located in a similar position outside each case, and must be easy to find by visually impaired visitors. Braille labels should have a printed text label nearby, to be read by escorts.

Signs and orientation

- Information graphics, such as explanations for low light levels and "please do not touch" signs, are to be designed as part of the package and not added in as an afterthought.

- Make signs at entrances/exits and throughout galleries and displays simple, short and consistent in design and layout.

- Use good contrast (70% minimum) on a matt surface on signs, with clear, legible typography, and use recognized symbols where appropriate.

- Large signs to be viewed from 3 m (9 ft 9 in) away, letter heights should be between 100 and 170 mm (4 and 6¾ in). Smaller signs should have text at least 70 mm (2¾ in) high.

- Use lower-case letters predominantly as these are more easily distinguished by people with dyslexia and a visual impairment. If it is necessary to give a sign a border (e.g. for increased contrast) then this should be 10% of the width of the sign.

- Signs to be well lit and be fixed at a consistent location and a consistent height between 1400 and 1700 mm (55 and 67 in) above the floor.

- Visitors should be able to stand/sit 500 mm (20 in) away from tactile signs, so that they can be touched easily. Tactile signs should be embossed, not engraved, with a 15 mm (⅝ in) minimum character height.

Lighting and visual contrast

- Avoid extreme contrasts in lighting, though some contrast is needed to give form to 3D objects.

- On main circulation routes gradual changes are helpful, including a lighting transition zone between the external environment and lower light levels in the galleries.

- Ensure all entrances, exits, stairs, ramps or obstacles are well lit.

- Avoid unexpected shadows, glare or reflections as these create visual confusion.

- Provide at least 100 lux of light on objects, unless conservation requirements demand lower levels.

- When conservation requirements demand low light levels, position objects to allow visitors to approach them as closely as possible. Ensure that the accompanying texts are well lit, and consider temporary illumination of objects (for example by timed push button).

- Cases or areas that are low-lit should have a notice explaining that this is to protect sensitive artefacts.

- Use non-reflecting glass on cases, displays, paintings, signs and interactives.

- Ensure that lights (or daylight from windows) do not dazzle the viewer and that the viewer does not cast shadows on the objects. Check this at the height of a wheelchair user as well as at standing height.

- Ensure lighting on all interpretive devices does not cause glare, especially on interactive computer screens. Allow individual adjustment by the visitor where possible.

Smithsonian Guidelines for Accessible Exhibition Design

This comprehensive document, written by Janice Majewski, is in part based on legislation including the Americans with Disabilities Act of 1990. It covers such issues as content, label and text design, language usage, audiovisuals and interactives, lighting, circulation, emergency egress and access symbols, with methods for achieving required standards. The document can be downloaded as a PDF at http://accessible.si.edu/pdf/Smithsonian%20 Guidelines%20for%20accessible%20design.pdf

Sample storyline

Written by Stephen Bury of the British Library, London, the text below is a model of a brief storyline that gives an introduction to a topic, outlines the curatorial approach and provides chapter headings to help show natural breaks in the narrative.

Breaking the Rules: the Printed Face of the Avant-garde 1900–1937

The first four decades of the twentieth century saw a remarkable efflorescence of European culture associated with the avant-garde. This was characterized by a rejection of the traditional hierarchies of society and by a challenge to an aesthetic based purely on nature or on art for art's sake: the role of art and the artist in society was made problematic.

The avant-garde manifested itself in a variety of artistic styles—Expressionism, Cubism, Futurism, Dadaism, Constructivism and Surrealism. Traditionally, these 'isms' have been seen as discrete movements. This exhibition will show that they shared many characteristics—for example interest in the "primitive" and children's art (in Expressionism, Cubism, Futurism, Dadaism and Surrealism) and permeation of most art forms (theatre, performance, poetry, the novel, photography, cinema and music as well as painting)—as well as many common participants (such as Apollinaire, Breton, Duchamp, Tzara and Malevich), who were active in more than one "ism". Another deep characteristic was the permeation of the media by the avant-garde. For example, Marinetti and Breton courted the press and manipulated their print appearances, creating their own media images. Breton (in Paris) and Stefan Themerson (in Warsaw) kept meticulous collections of press cuttings about themselves.

Indeed, the printed format was of great significance to the avant-garde. They published manifestos in newspapers and little magazines and separately as pamphlets or flyers. They edited and published their own little magazines, and created a cross-European network of distribution by cross-advertising other little magazines in their own. They made *livres d'artistes* (a direct result of the capitalization of the gallery system), and inexpensive artists' books made from wallpaper, collage, rubber stamps, stencils—even gingerbread. Cubist painting and printmaking took fragments—physical or pictorial—of the newspaper or the ephemeral printed bottle label back into the surface of the painting, while Schwitters's Dadaist paintings recycled tram tickets and other ephemera from ordinary life.

The avant-garde is traditionally associated with Paris or Berlin. This exhibition will look at its presence in many European cities—London, Brussels, Amsterdam, Groningen, Hanover, Munich, Weimar, Zurich, Vienna, Milan, Rome, Barcelona, Madrid, Lisbon, Copenhagen, Warsaw, Kraków, Prague, Riga, St Petersburg, Moscow, Vitebsk, Tbilisi, Bucharest, Budapest. Many participants and publications moved between cities, taking advantage of improved railway, shipping and airline routes. Ideas moved more rapidly than ever before.

The rise of Nazism (with its "Degenerate Art" and "Degenerate Music" exhibitions) and Stalinism initially sped up the dissemination of avant-garde ideas as its participants were proscribed and forced into exile. Finally, the cross-Europe European avant-garde ceased to function, although its ideas survived in Bauhaus-influenced art education, modernist graphic design and performance art, all of which are profoundly influential on current creative players.

Structure of the exhibition

1   Enter through a non avant-garde environment/room.

2   The manifesto: origins, characteristics and functions for the avant-garde. Its different manifestations—in newspapers, little magazines, posters and pamphlets, and even books (Surrealism). "Rose/merde" and "bless/blast" dichotomous lists, championing of the new and attacking the old. Influences on the avant-garde—primitive art, children's art, speed, noise, Jarry, Lautréamont, Freud, Charlie Chaplin. The "Degenerate Art" and "Degenerate Music" catalogues, with their prioritization of the kitsch and neo-classical, represent the end of the European avant-garde.

3   Impact of the 1914–18 war: casualty list of the avant-garde—Boccioni, Gaudier-Brzeska, Apollinaire, Marc, Macke, etc. Dadaist anti-war stance. Revolutions in Russia and (post-war) Germany and Hungary.

4   Theme of the city. Individual cities: printed avant-garde materials, sound (poetry, music), avant-garde film and photography in and of the city. Important events—exhibitions, plays, film, performances—in that city (for example *Victory over the Sun*, St Petersburg).

5   Impresarios of the avant-garde: Marinetti, Apollinaire, Breton, Tzara, Rodchenko.

6   Legacy of the European avant-garde: photomontage in advertising, the new typography, modern music (for example Michael Nyman's opera *Man and Boy: Dada*), collage novels, graphic novels, artists' books, concrete poetry, face painting, Brechtian theatre, method acting, stand-up comedians, the "hates and loves" T-shirt of Rhodes and McLaren (Sex Pistols) compared with the manifesto. [This section may possibly be distributed throughout the exhibition rather than at the end or the beginning.]

Glossary

Artworking The preparation of a computer graphic for print and screen use.

Assets The "stuff" of the exhibition, and the resources clients can draw on to tell their story. This general term can refer to objects, images, film, a particular building or location, or even opportunities, such as partnerships with universities.

Brand environment An immersive commercial environment where all the elements of the exhibition are inspired by a company's brand.

Business-to-business (B2B) Exhibitions or events in which the exhibitor shows their products to other businesses rather than consumers.

Circulation The movement of visitors through a three-dimensional space. Good circulation allows visitors to move comfortably around an exhibition without undue crowding. Circulation is said to be poor if visitor movement is restricted or fire escape routes or other exits are blocked.

Content developers/managers Professionals, usually on the staff of a design company, who aid clients with the development of exhibition themes and the selection and cataloguing of artefacts and specimens for exhibition.

Contractors Workers appointed by the design company or the client to carry out fabrication and installation of an exhibition.

Delivery technique The strategy by which a story will be communicated in the exhibition.

Dwell time The average time taken by visitors at individual exhibits.

Elevation A drawing or design that describes a vertical object or structure. For example, a "wall elevation" is a drawing that shows the features of a wall surface with doors and windows.

Engagement The process of gaining a visitor's attention and encouraging him to bring his faculties to bear on a topic.

Exhibitors' manual A compendium of useful information compiled by a trade show organizer for the benefit of the exhibitor.

Formative and summative evaluation Research carried out on audiences (existing and/or potential). Formative evaluation takes place before a project begins, and can help shape the design. Summative evaluation is done after the exhibition has been delivered and is used to measure the success of the project and understand audience feedback.

Futureproofing The process of considering and planning for the future life of an exhibition or exhibition component, such as media.

Immersive environment/experience Highly controlled environments with sophisticated multi-media effects and lighting where the visitors are "immersed" in the themes and content of the exhibition.

Inclusive design A general approach to designing in which designers ensure that their products and services address the needs of the widest possible audience, irrespective of age or ability (source: UK Design Council website www.designcouncil.org.uk). (Also known as **Universal design** in the US.)

Induction loop A device used to assist the hearing impaired by transmitting sound from a sound system, microphone or other source, directly to a hearing aid.

Interactives Interpretive devices that deliver feedback to the user. Software or electronic interactives use computer systems to deliver feedback. Mechanical interactives react to user inputs by the use of mechanical elements.

Interpretation The explanation and dissemination of concepts and facts about exhibits to an audience through media such as text panels, video, interactives and others.

Key performance indicator (KPI) A type of performance measurement, usually in the form of written statements. An organization may use KPIs to evaluate its success, or to evaluate the success of a particular activity in which it is engaged. Success can be defined as making progress toward strategic goals, but it can also be the repeated, periodic achievement of a goal (e.g. visitor satisfaction).

Key message An overarching statement for the museum or exhibition that summarizes the main understanding that all visitors should gain. It is not a vision statement for the museum, but a short description of the key content/storyline contained in the exhibition.

Layering The process of using a variety of media to communicate ideas to diverse audiences.

Learning outcome Knowledge skills and abilities attained by visitors as a result of a visit to a museum or visitor attraction.

Modular exhibition system A manufactured flexible temporary exhibit structure made up of a kit of parts that can be quickly assembled, installed and dismantled.

Moodboards Boards on which images are mounted to help clients to understand the "mood" or type of experience the designers are trying to evoke.

Narrative visitor journey A description of how a visitor or set of visitors will experience the exhibition. Often written and supported by images, sketches and visuals, narrative journeys feature in stage-end reports and pitches as a way for the designer to sum up their design and communicate it in the way it will ultimately be experienced: through the eyes of the visitor. It is sometimes helpful to think up different journeys for different visitor types, such as a school group or a family, to understand what they may each get out of the experience.

Plan A drawing showing a design scheme from above.

Plinth A raised surface within the exhibition environment onto which objects and graphics can be placed. Generally plinths support the showcases that contain objects.

Precedents Reference material that shows relevant inspirational and/or influential examples of built design schemes.

Primary, secondary and tertiary information Layered information is described in terms of whether it is of primary, secondary or tertiary importance. This can be a useful tool in helping clients prioritize their information and stories. In a traditional exhibition context, this translates to primary panels (large graphic introductory panels), secondary panels (to tell a mid-level story), and tertiary panels (more detailed stories and object labels).

Prototype An early mock-up of a design that will be constructed to decide whether a particular feature fulfills its function. Prototypes of interactive devices, for example, are tested by users before final modifications are made, after which either an improved prototype or the final designed piece is made.

Risk assessment An assessment of the personal risks that fabricators and installers are exposed to during the course of constructing or dismantling an exhibition (a legal obligation in many countries).

Section A drawn representation showing a design as if it has been sliced through along a single line.

Shop drawings Precise drawings of a design produced by an exhibition contractor to show their tradespeople how they have interpreted the designer's drawings. These drawings are used by the fabricators during construction and assembly.

Site The location of the exhibition.

Site plan A plan showing the entirety of the building and the area around it, with the exhibition shown within it.

Specification Detailed instruction about installation or construction methods, materials or finishes issued to contractors.

Stakeholder(s) A person or group of people who will be involved in the exhibition and design process, but who is not directly on the client team. Stakeholder engagement and management are often important considerations for exhibition designers and may affect how presentations are structured and to whom they are presented.

Storyline The content of an exhibition expressed as a story. Usually a document that outlines the premise for an exhibition, the context, how the exhibition content should be organized and any thesis the exhibition is intended to prove.

Technical drawings Formal drawings, now usually created on a computer, which are issued to building contractors and graphic production facilities to produce and install elements of the exhibition.

Theme Usually a short sentence describing a key idea that visitors should understand: for example, train travel was invented in the nineteenth century. Often many themes are grouped in logical arrangements to make an overall narrative.

Topic A subject area of the exhibition: for example, nineteenth-century train travel.

Touch tour A guided tour of a museum for visually impaired visitors where exhibits can be touched by hand.

Turn key A service in which companies provide all design, fabrication and installation services for a completed exhibition.

Visitor attraction This term describes a wide range of leisure facilities intended to appeal to the visiting public. In some instances, exhibiting bodies that emphasize visitor experience over the acquisition of collections prefer to be known as visitor attractions to distinguish themselves from traditional museum displays.

Visual identity The "look" of a company evidenced through a logo, corporate images, prescribed fonts and other visual indicators.

Visitor profile/visitor demographic The types of visitors who will come to an exhibition are often described in terms of their profile or demographic. This can indicate a great deal of information, such as where they come from, what languages they speak, what they enjoy doing, what their motivations are, how much money they earn, or what kind of work they do.

Voices Especially for historical subjects, museum curators and designers report events through the eyes of a variety of observers or participants in the story. These varied perspectives are often known as "voices".

Further reading

Staniszewski, Mary Anne, *The Power of Display: A History of Exhibition Installations at the Museum of Modern Art*, MIT Press, Cambridge, MA, 1998

Black, Graham, *The Engaging Museum*, Routledge, Abingdon & New York, 2005

Brooks, Peter, *Reading for the Plot*, Harvard University Press, 1992

Brückner, Atelier, *Scenography: Making Spaces Talk*, avedition, 2010

Dernie, David, *Exhibition Design*, Laurence King Publishing, London, 2005

Ehmann, Sven, Robert Klanten, and Shonquis Moreno, *Play All Day: Design for Children*, Die Gestalten Verlag, 2009

Neuhart, John, Marilyn Neuhart and Ray Eames, *Eames Design: The Work of the Office of Charles and Ray Eames*, Harry N. Abrams, Inc., New York, 1994

Marincola, Paula, (ed.), *What Makes a Great Exhibition?*, Philadelphia Center for Arts and Heritage, Philadelphia, 2006

Reinhardt, Uwe, and Philipp Teufel, *New Exhibition Design 01 and 02*, avedition, 2008 and 2010

Simon, Nina, *The Participatory Museum*, Museum 2.0, 2010

Stall, Gert, Martijn de Rijk and Terence Riley, *IN side OUT ON site IN: Redesigning the National Museum of Ethnology*, BIS Publishers, Amsterdam, 2003

Hooper-Greenhill, Eilean, *The Educational Role of the Museum*, Routledge, Abingdon & New York, 1999

Hall, Margaret C., *On Display: A Design Grammar of Museum Exhibitions*, Lund Humphries, London, 1987 (out of print)

Parker, Lauren, *Interplay: Interactive Design* (V & A Contemporary series), V & A Publications, London, 2004

Moggridge, Bill, *Designing Interactions*, MIT Press, Cambridge, MA, 2006 (with an introduction by Gillian Crampton)

Useful websites

Exhibition designers

Ralph Appelbaum Associates
www.raany.com

Nick Bell Design
www.nickbelldesign.co.uk

Atelier Brückner
www.atelier-brueckner.de

Casson Mann
www.cassonmann.co.uk

Imagination
www.imagination.com

Kossmann DeJong
www.kossmanndejong.nl

Land Design Studio
www.landdesignstudio.co.uk

Metaphor
www.mphor.co.uk

Opera Design
www.operadesign.nl

Interaction designers

Action Time Vision
www.actiontimevision.co.uk

AllofUs
www.allofus.com

Ars Electronica
www.aec.at

Jason Bruges Studio
www.jasonbruges.com

Christian Moeller
www.christian-moeller.com

Random International
www.random-international.com

Small Design Firm
www.davidsmall.com

Thoughtden
www.thoughtden.co.uk

United Visual Artists
www.uva.co.uk

Lighting designers

Cowi
www.cowi.dk

DHA Designs
www.dhadesigns.co.uk

Erco
www.erco.com

Index

Page numbers in *italics* refer to picture captions

Picture credits

1 © Peter Mauss/Esto

7 © Photos Thijs Wolzak; Kossmann.dejong

8 Deutsche Messe

9 Museum of London

11l Martin Charles

11r Marc C. Johnson

12l © The Natural History Museum, London

12r © 2003 Photo Scala Florence/HIP

14 © Pitt Rivers Museum, University of Oxford

15l © 2008. Digital Image, The Museum of Modern Art, New York/Scala, Florence © 2003. Photo Scala Florence/HIP

15r Wurts Brothers; IN34.2 © 2008. Digital image, The Museum of Modern Art, New York/Scala, Florence

16 © Photos Philippe Migeat, Georges Méguerditchian/Centre Pompidou

17l + r © Exploratorium, www.exploratorium.edu

18 Thought Den Ltd and National Museums Scotland © 2013

21 Stefan Brentfuehrer

25 Andrew Kellard Associates

28 Ralph Appelbaum Associates

37 © Albert Vecerka

39 © Photo Nick Wood; Land Design Studio Ltd

40-41 © Chuck Choi

43 John MacLean/View

44 Lee Mawdsley/Robin Clark

45-46 Imagination Ltd.

47 Carlo Valsecchi

47bl + br Migliore + Servetto Architetti Associati

48-50 Opera Design/Reinout van den Bergh

51 Cultural Innovations

52-54 Jump Studios

58 Holmes Wood

59 Opera Amsterdam bv/V&A Images

60-61 Imagination Ltd.

62tl Ralph Appelbaum Associates

62tr Peter Mauss/Esto

62bl + br Ralph Appelbaum Associates

63 Imagination Ltd.

65 Ralph Appelbaum Associates

66-67 Ralph Appelbaum Associates

68 Ralph Appelbaum Associates

69tl + tr Ralph Appelbaum Associates

69c MFP

69bl + br Peter Mauss/Esto

70 © Chuck Choi

72-73 Philip Hughes

75-79 Philip Hughes

82 makato yokomizo Architects Inc.

85 Imagination Ltd.

86-87 Metaphor Limited (www.metaphor.eu)

88-89 Casson Mann; photograph John Mclean

90 Land Design Studio

91tl Stefan Brentfuehrer

91tr, bl, br Prof. Uwe Brückner

91 Andrew Kellard Associates

92-93 © Peter Mauss/Esto

94 Casson Mann

95t + br Casson Mann

95bl © John MacLean/View

96 Metaphor Limited (www.metaphor.eu)

97 Casson Mann

98 © John MacLean/View

99 Metaphor Limited (www.metaphor.eu)

100-101 Pentagram Design

104 Thomas Manss & Co.

105tl + tr Thomas Manss & Co.

105b Opera Design/Reinout van den Bergh

106 ACME Studios: art director Andrea Chappel, designers Malcolm Clarke & Caroline Claisse

107 Thomas Manss & Co.

108 Ralph Appelbaum Associates

109 after Herbert Bayer

110-113 Ralph Appelbaum Associates

114-115 Nick Bell Design

116t Thomas Manss & Co.

116b Atelier Brückner/Dominik Hegemann

118t Andreas Schmidt

118c + b Nick Bell Design

122-123 Andrew Kellard Associates

126tl © Hufton + Crow

127 Thomas Matthews

129 Tristan Dellaway

133 Casson Mann; Lighting design by DHA

134-135 DHA Designs

137 © Photo Andrew Lee; Ralph Appelbaum Associates

139-140 © www.erco.com

141 Sarah Morris, installation 'Los Angeles', © the artist; photo: Stephen White, courtesy Jay Jopling/White Cube (London)

142 Seth Taras

143 centre right © www.erco.com

144-145 Met Studio

146 © www.erco.com

148-149 DHA Designs

150t Martin Professional

150b Ralph Appelbaum Associates

151l Arno Design

151r Pentagram Design, photo: Timothy Hursley

152 Atelier Brückner/Markus Mahle

153 © www.erco.com

156 © Science Museum/Science & Society Picture Library all rights reserved

157 Museum of London

158-159 Ralph Appelbaum Associates

164t + br Land Design Studio

164bl Lee Mawdsley & Robin Clark

165t + bl Land Design Studio

165br Lee Mawdsley & Robin Clark

166 left column Land Design Studio

166 right column Lee Mawdsley & Robin Clark

168 © ACCIONA Producciones y Diseño

169 © Centre Pompidou–Bibliothèque Kandinsky

170 © Peter Mauss/Esto

171 © Albert Vecerka

173 Philip Hughes

182-183 Ralph Appelbaum Associates

186 Burckhardt Leitner

187 Design by Eisuke Tachikawa, Nosigner; Graphic Design by Shun Kawakami (Artless); Client: AODJ

188-189 Pentagram Design, photo: Timothy Hursley

190 Imagination Ltd.

194-195 Casson Mann

196 © Photo Andrew Lee; Ralph Appelbaum Associates

197 Ralph Appelbaum Associates

198 Opera Design/Reinout van den Bergh

199 Met Studio

202 Mauk Design

203 Arno Design

204-205 Inflate

206-207 Francesc Rifé

209 © Chuck Choi

213 Land Design Studio

216 Kengo Kuma & Associates

217 Thomas Matthews, photo: Amy Scaife

218 Zaha Hadid Architects

Acknowledgements

I am very grateful for the insights provided by a number of individuals and companies whose ideas and comments informed my understanding of this subject. I have received very generous assistance from a number of outstanding designers: Ulla Winkler at Action Time Vision; Ralph Appelbaum, Nick Appelbaum, Phillip Tefft and Vicci Ward at Ralph Appelbaum Associates; Dinah Casson and Roger Mann of Casson Mann; Douglas Broadley at Imagination; Marcus Nonn at Jump Studios; Peter Higgins at Land Design; David Prior at Liminal; Thomas Manss of Thomas Manss & Company; Lloyd Hicks at MET Studios; Stephen Greenberg at Metaphor; Nick Bell of Nick Bell Design; Frans Bevers and Jo Pike at Opera Design and Lorenzo Apicella at Pentagram. Special thanks are due to Adam Grater of DHA Designs for providing the fine examples of DHA's work. His patient explanation of the principles of lighting helped steer the chapter on that subject, though I should add that any errors or omissions are my own. Thanks also to talented lighting designers Dan Heap and Andy Grant for their insight and assistance. The late Simon Beer of Integrated Circles generously gave time to help me understand the world of audio-visual design and implementation, and I have tried to relay his words in the relevant chapters without pretending to have his expertise. Particular thanks to Charlotte Kingston for her timely and well-judged support with re-drafting chapters for the 2nd Edition, most notably Sound and Film and Interactive Design and to Lydia Hughes for her thoughtful and dedicated assistance with image research for the second edition.

I am indebted to a number of individuals at major institutions for sharing their knowledge of the preparation and planning essential to good exhibition installation. My thanks to Barry Ginley and Linda Lloyd-Jones at the Victoria & Albert Museum; Jane Samuels at the British Museum; Jo Quinton-Tulloch, Anthony Richards and Alex Burch at the Science Museum, London; Katia Lafitte at the Centre Pompidou; Suzanne Bardgett at the Imperial War Museum and Martyn Myrone at Tate Britain. Martyn Best at Cultural Innovations provided many insights into the increasingly global world of international exhibition planning and design. I am indebted to Stephen Bury at the British Library for allowing me to use his wonderful storyline from the exhibition "Breaking the Rules".

I would like to acknowledge the patient assistance of the many individuals who have provided images for this book: Casey Lynn and Jenni Bell (RAA); Tristan Dellaway, John Pickford and Madeleine Cooke (Casson Mann); Dieter Kursietis (Metaphor); Tara Hanrahan (Thomas Matthews); Martin Krauter (Erco); Roddy Macintyre (Inflate) and Joana Niemeyer (Thomas Manss & Co.).

The encouragement and inspiration of friends (Simona Sideri, Joseph O'Neill, Fran Van Dijk, Adrian Campbell, Ed Carpenter, Helen Eger) and colleagues (Belinda Mitchell, Hans Bromwich and Lorraine Farrelly of Portsmouth University and Peter Waters of the University of the Creative Arts) have sustained me through the writing of this book. Above all, the emotional support of my wife Vanessa Hogge and Casper, Lydia, Kay, Cliff and Shirlee Hughes have been instrumental to its completion.

I would like to thank the Editorial Director at Laurence King, Philip Cooper, for his enthusiasm for this project. Finally, profound thanks to Liz Faber for her patience and expertise, particularly for the first edition. For this second edition, deep gratitude to Gaynor Sermon for her tremendous attention to detail and professionalism. Again, thanks to Draught Associates for their tireless work with the design.